THE POLITICAL TRIAL OF
BENJAMIN FRANKLIN

THE POLITICAL TRIAL OF BENJAMIN FRANKLIN

A PRELUDE TO THE AMERICAN REVOLUTION

KENNETH LAWING PENEGAR

Algora Publishing
New York

Library of Congress Cataloging-in-Publication Data —

Penegar, Kenneth Lawing.
    The political trial of Benjamin Franklin: a prelude to the American Revolution /
Kenneth Lawing Penegar.
      p. cm.
    Includes bibliographical references and index.
    ISBN 978-0-87586-849-3 (soft cover: alk. paper) — ISBN 978-0-87586-850-9 (hard
cover: alk. paper) — ISBN 978-0-87586-851-6 (ebook) 1. Franklin, Benjamin, 1706-1790. 2.
Franklin, Benjamin, 1706-1790—Homes and haunts—England—London. 3. Statesmen—
United States—Biography. 4. United States—History—Revolution, 1775-1783—
Diplomatic history. 5. United States—History—Revolution, 1775-1783—Causes. I. Title.
    E302.6.F8P36 2011
    973.3092—dc22
    [B]
                              2011004000

Front cover: Franklin Appearing Before the Privy Council" — painting by Christian
Schussele. Courtesy of the Huntington Art Collections, San Marino, California.

Printed in the United States

Dedicated to the memory of my parents
Ethel Lawing and Oscar Penegar
(1899–1974)   (1898–1997)

TABLE OF CONTENTS

Author's Preface

We are all historians, to one degree or another. We tell stories, weave narratives to and about ourselves or others, and recast experience. And we do it all our lives. Some of us of course write and talk professionally. Others because we want to, have to.

My need or desire to tell this story comes from the "discovery" (mine, not history's) that one of America's truly iconic figures experienced a searing public humiliation in the prime of his life. And we scarcely mention the fact in our continuous appreciation of the Founders.

Yet we do know and appreciate a great deal about Franklin. Pick a topic or aspect or time of his life, and everyone will have something to add by way of fact, myth, opinion or impression.

He was a self-made man; he ran away from home and found a good trade and made it into something. He was a civic innovator, starting lending libraries and street lighting and volunteer fire departments, self-help clubs. He became a publisher as well as a printer. He was a charmer, clever in politics and journalism. He added to our lore of epigrams in a very profitable venture: Poor Richard's Almanac. He helped our country with its independence through his diplomacy with the French. He discovered that lightning is a form of electricity. He invented things, the freestanding stove, the lightning rod, a musical instrument, and a new alphabet for the English language.

For the benefit of workmen's schooling Franklin left a considerable monetary legacy that didn't pay out for two hundred years. He was not a religious man in conventional terms. He liked the company of women but probably was intimate with only a very few. He maintained a prodigious correspondence throughout his life. He built an extensive personal library, started an academy that became a great university. He was honored abroad for his scientific work, no less than he has been revered in his own country as exemplary, intriguing if not heroic, perhaps the very embodiment of what it has meant to be American.

Amid so much accomplishment, why concern ourselves with the shadows in such a life? Call it the pull of tragedy, perhaps, or the renewed recognition that even great men's lives have, in common with the rest of us, moments of genuine defeat and loss. To share that sense of loss, whatever its weight in the totality of Franklin's life, is to know the man more fully. To see into those moments more sharply is to try to re-live that life—vicariously—from their origins forward instead of only in hindsight.

The reader is invited into what Daniel Boorstin has called "a willing suspension of knowledge" about how Franklin's life ended with the triumphs of independence and a new constitution shared with the other Founders. What the reward for that effort might be is, in Boorstin's words, "a new access to surprise" not only of "how and why and when and who" but also of "connections and unexpected consequences."

The difficulty of reliving or at least re-creating such a life cannot be overestimated. Not only must we try to see what he saw, think what he must have thought, and connect with those whose letters allow us now to do that. But we must also try to account for the experience, understandings and attitudes of so many others who were Franklin's contemporaries. These include his friends, associates and correspondents of course but also his adversaries and any number of others of significance with whom he shared the age, both in the colonies and in Great Britain. This broadening force of context is what may reassure the reader that the account is not meant to be one sided. The judgments Franklin made, along with all the trimmings of his life in those years, are on display and opened to critique just as much as the other events and personalities that intersected or paralleled them.

The work of researching and composing this narrative of Franklin's life, small as it is as a fraction of that life as a whole, has had this splendid dividend. It has permitted, no, necessitated a re-examination of the origins, causes or contributing factors leading to one of the world's great modern epochs. Nearly every high school graduate in America, it might be supposed, has a dash of understanding of these things. Yet the common understanding rests more in abstract ideas, celebrated events of memorable particularity and feelings of satisfaction and gratitude than in an appreciation of the complexity and contingent nature of this history.

Working one's way through that time albeit always with one eye always on Benjamin Franklin, and with the help of historians of first rank in both Britain and the United States and combining their sweep and insights with the details of this singular man's life through his correspondence, principally, has afforded a much more nuanced grasp of what lay behind 1776.

If there were one man through whose life we could see in microcosm the whole of the crosshatched picture of the separation of Britain from its thirteen contiguous colonies in America, that man would very likely be Franklin. At critical times he had one foot on each side of the Atlantic. He had numerous and important connections, varied responsibilities and family in America and in Britain. More than most of his contemporaries, Franklin was in a position to see the strengths of each society and to understand how their differences might be bridged. Whether Franklin used that unique advantage wisely is one of the questions worth considering in what is written here.

It is also worth pondering, in the light of so complex a life as Franklin had created for himself by the 1770s, whether his ultimate tilt to the cause of his native country's independence should be seen as the product of deliberate choice or whether it was simply the end of a path that began with seemingly neutral or ambiguous steps at various points up to the time when this story begins. The very contingent nature of such steps is nowhere better illustrated for Franklin than in the improbable effect of an old fashioned, spontaneous duel in London in late 1773.

The way forward is rarely if ever as clear to the contemporaries who inhabit the past, even of great and influential men, as it is made to appear in history.

We can perhaps see in the swirl of events around Franklin during the 1770s a reflection of the contradictions, uncertainties and anxieties of a great many in his homeland of the same era. That would be reason enough to consider afresh what happened, where, with whom—"off stage" and on.

Introduction and Overview

On the eve of America's lurch toward independence Benjamin Franklin, the most famous of his countrymen in the world at large, was in London. The prospects for peace and the avoidance of civil war within the British Empire declined precipitously in the last two years of his stay. Franklin's part in that dramatic shift is the story of this book. It explores the various decisions and choices Franklin made. He was then serving among other roles as agent for the Massachusetts House of Representatives. Both the consequences and assumptions of those decisions are examined, as well as their avowed purposes. Other facets, too, of Franklin's life in that critical period, 1773–1775, are collected and focused to shed light on those decisions and their impact. The purpose of this Introduction is to reconstruct important elements of that wider context of related circumstances.

Franklin's Situation in the 1770s

First, there were his many roles and interests.

Several circumstances stand out from those several years of Franklin's last stay in London. Perhaps the most notable of them is that Franklin wore so many hats that it is difficult to see how he kept them straight. He was there, from the start of this eleven-year stint, to finish the business of the Pennsylvania House in challenging the Penns' hold on the charter and lands of the province. He acquired shortly two other agencies, one for New Jersey where his son was the governor and another for Georgia.

Added to these, moreover, Franklin was still serving as head of the royal mail system for the colonies. To be sure, he had several assistants in place back in the colonies to keep the institution working smoothly. It is not possible to say how much time was devoted to each of these various tasks, but one must assume that the time and energy required were not insignificant. Franklin's correspondence about them certainly reflects that estimate.

Beyond these more or less routine responsibilities were those from which Franklin evidently derived far greater personal satisfaction. His calling as essayist and commentator on a considerable range of topics, none closer to his heart than the subject of America and all things American, provides an expansive view of the man. And there are also those interests that were scientific or technical. If Franklin was not much engaged during this time in fresh experiments, he was nonetheless occasionally engaged in correspondence with others about his prior work and that of others, both in Europe, Britain and the colonies. Thomas Priestly, for example, in writing his history of electricity had eagerly sought Franklin's contributions about his own work. His design of a freestanding stove and another for the lightning rod were of continuing interest to people at great distance from him. He even found time to devise a new English alphabet and began to write his autobiography.

It was probably as true in the eighteenth century as it is now that "if you want something done, [you'd better] ask a busy person to do it." Franklin was certainly that, and he must have had extraordinary powers of concentration and organization. He did not have the benefit of an administrative assistant or, for most of this time, even a secretary, though his friend and landlady Mrs. Margaret Stevenson certainly aided him in many ordinary chores. But the principal point about his many roles and interests is not merely to wonder in amazement but to raise a serious question about how these various roles could sometimes become entangled and blunt the effectiveness of those of a more politically sensitive sort.

There were several times when the various strands of responsibility or vocation became twisted around one another. In his role as publicist for helping Britons better understand America and Americans, his published work conceivably undercut efforts he was making for one colony or another. In the case of Georgia, for example, Franklin in 1772 was commenting publicly on an important English court case dealing with the status of slaves in England when that colony's assembly was asking him to present to the Privy Council a new legal code for Georgia's slave population. Probably the most celebrated of such instances involves the deeply satirical essays he wrote and published in the autumn of 1773, these at a time when the affairs of one his agencies, the last one to be added to his array, Massachusetts, had reached a point of acute crisis.

The Massachusetts agency provides the most extreme example of the complexity of Franklin's life in London. This involvement led directly to his showdown with British authority and sensibilities before the Privy Council of King George III in 1774. But for his representation of the Massachusetts House of Representative and his own initiatives for it, Franklin might indeed have served a more ameliorative or conciliatory role in London during the slide toward war with the colonies. That estimate is conjectural of course, but what is relatively free from doubt is that his undertaking midway in this last decade of his London presence to represent the Massachusetts House led him deeper into the swirls of emerging conflict than anything else he was doing, including his writings in the press.

The House elected Franklin in October of 1770, and we have the letter of appointment sent to him by Speaker Thomas Cushing dated October 31st. Although Cushing's letter does not mention the fact, the election came on a divided vote between himself and Arthur Lee, Reverend Cooper supporting Franklin and Sam Adams behind Lee. And it was Lee who would become his designated successor upon his resignation in March 1775. Why he accepted it is itself uncertain, if not puzzling. Franklin actually seems to have sought the appointment, although in his letter of acceptance he describes it as all the more of an honor since he did not solicit the post. It could not have been the money, but Franklin would not have known for certain that the House's determination to pay him (£600, voted at a later time) would be blocked by Governor Hutchinson's refusal to confirm his appointment. The governor later said his refusal to confirm the appointment was responsible for Franklin's enmity toward him.

Perhaps Franklin was drawn to the sheer drama of the colony presenting, as it did, positions at odds with British rule earlier and more assertively than any of the other colonies. Perhaps he could see in this activity the wave of the future, and he wanted to be on the winning side. If he could succeed, however, and for even a short interval of time, at helping to fashion a better relation between that colony and London, well, the rest would be little trouble at all. No one can fully know Franklin's mind about these possible explanations.

The agency for Massachusetts was not only uncompensated for all the time he held it, but the very limited nature of the appointment was also itself a problem for him from the start. When he tried to present his letter of appointment to Lord Hillsborough in a courtesy call, the colonial secretary refused even to look at it. The question worth pondering is, why did Franklin want this assignment? It seems plausible, looking at Franklin's other commitments and undertakings, that he was in 1770 casting about for reasons beyond the existing agency appointments to stay in London. The work for the Pennsylvania House had concluded, however unsuccessfully. And the work for the other two had problems of their own. If indeed he needed further justifications to his wife Debbie, long suffering and constantly asking him to return, or to his friends and associates in Philadelphia, the new position would have its convenience. An active agency, even one of controversy, would extend his stay like nothing else could. Or so he might have thought in 1770.

Second, there was the speed of events.

It is difficult to sort out now just how much Franklin was aware of or fully understood at any given time in the last five years of this final London residency, either on the western side of the Atlantic or there in Britain. Necessarily all his information from Boston was delayed and frequently news of one thing crossed with his dispatch of another, thus complicating a real-time feel for events. A sample of the letters, for example, exchanged with his chief correspondents, Cushing and Cooper, reveals how each side was struggling to keep clear what the reference was: to this or that letter or event in the recent past.

Franklin had been absent from the colonies continuously for six years when he took up the Boston agency. He was nominally informed of major happenings but tardily. His absence meant that he was deprived of the sensory experience of things and the collateral conversations with others beyond his correspondents. He did not actually witness the Stamp Act riots of 1765, occurring in his own city of Philadelphia as well in and around Boston. He was absent, too, from discussions with merchants and others who would enter into the compact of non-importation of British goods following passage of the Townshend Acts in 1767. Nor did he experience the arrival of

British troops landing in the port of Boston in 1768 nor observe the "massacre" of 1770 and the locals' provocation of the soldiers.

By 1772 and the adoption of the Boston Town Meeting Declaration, Franklin was being overwhelmed by events. They tumbled out upon him with increasing frequency and sharpness of tone and implication. He seemed startled by the pamphlet that came to him that year from Boston and was apparently reluctant to have it published. He delayed for two months after its arrival and printed it with his own preface that addressed the economics of the relationship, not the constitutional claims of the impassioned Bostonians. As agent he had of course to see to its printing and circulation, but he did not have to, or chose not to, endorse its provocative content. Governor Hutchinson had characterized the Boston "resolves" as a virtual declaration of independence. In the end it did not matter, for news of the Declaration had made its own way into the London papers by that time.

OUT OF THE LOOP AND FRUSTRATED

During these five years, 1770 to 1775, Franklin seemed to have considerably less information of current saliency, compared to earlier times, to pass on to his sponsors in the colonies. His letters to the Speaker of the Pennsylvania House Joseph Galloway all during the 1760s were numerous and filled frequently with details of ministerial and parliamentary thinking from an array of contacts. The reports of Franklin to Speaker Thomas Cushing of the Massachusetts House, by contrast, from after his appointment in the fall of 1770 through the rest of his agency for that colony, were relatively spare in terms of specific contacts with officials or members of parliament. The letters to Cushing tended to be weighted more with his own opinion on likely measures and speculation about possible outcomes.

To some extent this could have been due to the estrangement or enmity between Lord Hillsborough and himself or attributable to the generally tighter organization of the ministry and its loyal supporters in parliament than that of previous governments. When the Earl of Dartmouth replaced the irascible Irish earl in 1772 as the officer principally responsible for colonial affairs, the mood changed for Franklin to be sure. But there was not much of an increase in reported contacts or volume of information.

At one point Franklin missed an act of parliament that affected the dockyard at Boston, and Speaker Cushing criticized him for that lapse. This was in addition to the censure he received about his handling of the ministry's move to pay the salaries of royal governors and judges directly. In response Franklin was appropriately apologetic but he was also clearly miffed at the remonstrance.

> I have submitted to reproof without reply in my public letter out of pure respect. It is not decent to dispute a father's admonition.... But to you in private permit to observe... I did not know, but perhaps I should have known that [the dockyard clause] was [in the bill]. And yet in a parliament that during that whole session refused admission to strangers, wherein near 200 acts were passed, it is not so easy a matter to [have] knowledge of ... every clause ... especially when it is not uncommon to smuggle clauses into a bill whose title shall give no suspicion...[1]

A year earlier the agent from Massachusetts had observed to Cushing that colonial agents seemed then to be of little use in London. But this time his lament has a more personal tone to it. "This censure," he writes further in his letter of July 7, 1773, "though grievous does not so much surprise me, as I apprehended from the beginning that between friends of an old agent, my predecessor, who thought himself hardly used ... and those of a young one impatient for the succession [referring to Arthur Lee], my situation was not likely to be a very comfortable one, as my faults could scarce pass unobserved." Franklin went on to add that he was thinking about leaving England in September of that year, 1773.

Who could blame him? By that time Franklin had endured the first two years of his appointment singularly out of favor with the leading official on colonial affairs of the time, Lord Hillsborough. He was in trouble with his bosses in Boston. And they were continually pestering him with new petitions and intemperate resolutions. For his part he could urge restraint, apologize for his errors, and temporize with the new colonial secretary, Dartmouth, whose favor he thought he was winning.

Franklin did not resign his post as agent for Massachusetts until the early spring of 1775 on the eve of his departure for America. It seems remarkable that he did not step aside before then. He tried to do so right after his trial, but the alternate agent, Mr. Arthur Lee, was out of the country on his way to Italy. He stayed on as a very lame duck for a full year after his humiliation in the Privy Council. He was persuaded by one or another of his

---

1 BF to Cushing, July 7, 1773. *Papers of Benjamin Franklin*, Vol. 20, pages 27176.

remaining contacts in London to wait for one more development, one more opportunity for reason to take hold in the ministry or in Parliament.

It seems clear enough that Franklin was reluctant to let go. It was very probably the hardest thing he ever had to do. Compounding his frustrations was the fact that Arthur Lee, his foreordained successor, was of no help to the agent at all, offering neither counsel nor even his presence at critical times.

A third major element of Franklin's London situation involves influences of style and personality. Franklin was no ordinary diplomat, if by that we mean a representative who is present but little seen or heard, one who gathers information widely and has influence only very subtly and indirectly. Indeed, until his time in Paris for the last and most important mission of his career, he probably did not think of himself as a diplomat at all. Objectively we would have to call him an operator verging on lobbyist. Interested in many subjects, concerned about some and focused on a few at any given time, Franklin rarely failed to engage what interested him. Yet his engagement took different forms and outlets. Collectively these interests have produced an enormous record of writings, letters and memoranda. His stature as scientist, or "natural philosopher" in the parlance of his day, certainly brought him fame and recognition in Europe and Britain. What brought him notoriety, however, and not a little criticism or resentment, were his published essays and opinions.

Writing was his principal outlet and his instrument of choice, in London as it had been in Philadelphia. Franklin trusted the efficacy of what he wrote to inform at least but probably more often to provoke or challenge the conventional wisdom of London. While he was an accomplished conversationalist as well as a practiced writer and had a variety of contacts, it is not clear that he really expected these to have concrete objectives. People came to see him all the time, often other colonials asking for introductions or the like and sometimes Brits who were headed to the colonies for the first time, like Thomas Paine. His "network"—if a heterogeneous collection of people from science, religion, publishing, business and political life can be called that—was not something he "worked" to any over-all desired effect, certainly not on a sustained basis. He did of course use these contacts for one tactical end or another, such as the person or persons who told him about and brought him the collection of Hutchinson letters in 1772. And he became affiliated in potentially profitable initiatives, like the Walpole

Company for a land grant in the Ohio Valley, through such contacts. It was through another such contact, a fellow member of the Royal Society, that he had the opening to enter into some last minute "secret negotiations" of his final winter in London.

Franklin often conferred with his publisher and long time confidant William Strahan about many of the numerous essays and pamphlets he would publish in London. That he sometimes published these pieces under a pseudonym indicates that he was aware that his name could be a negative factor in their reception or for other initiatives. It is not that Franklin was a self-effacing man, although he did appear modest or taciturn in personal encounters. Rather he was sure enough of what he wanted to say and how, but he would leave to chance how the results played out. There seemed to be a certain pride in this published work that is comparable to the evident satisfaction he had with two other major facets of his long life, scientific experimentation (notably but not exclusively on electricity) and the postal system in the American colonies of which while he was not the founder, he certainly was the most successful leader and innovator for the longest time.

It seems that the writer in Franklin cared as much about the quality and cast, even beauty, of an essay as he did its impact on events. His very clever set of essays in the autumn of 1773 stirred some to laughter for the moment but angered just as many others in important places with their "impudence," this at a time when the Hutchinson letters scandal had emerged and the petition for the governor's removal was being delivered to the king. And as a writer on contemporary affairs Franklin appreciated that he had to be aware of timing. These same essays, had they been initially published in an anthology of the author's work, would be far less compelling than they were at those moments. Their very timing made them compelling.

Perhaps in some such way, though he certainly did not compose them nor did he alter their appearance, the Hutchinson letters in his hands seemed to appeal to Franklin's sense of drama in the contemporary events of Boston. This was their time, if ever, to be of interest, certainly, and of import—good or not so good perhaps, he may have thought. There is always a risk that one's efforts, be they writings or something else, will be unappreciated or even troublesome. Thus, even though he did not compose or edit any of those Hutchinson letters, he became effectively the author of the crises that followed from their publication.

Being an author or publicist and being a diplomat are not often compatible roles, at least when pursued simultaneously. If Franklin did not think of himself, primarily, as diplomat, as we have suggested he did not (although at one point he wrote in a letter to son William that he was often sought out by ambassadors posted in London), how did he think of himself when he had to think about his representational activity? And we know he had to think about his work for Massachusetts rather a lot in these few short years. We have also suggested that the work he did for the other colonies probably would not have seriously conflicted with his publishing, but the case of agent for the House of Representatives in Massachusetts was something entirely different. It is that role that brought him to his trial and to limbo afterward. Without it Franklin might have lived on in England for some time and pursued his other many interests; he might have become a real conciliator, as some wanted him to be even after the calamity of the Cockpit. None of that was realistically possible after January 29, 1774.

He likely thought of himself as he is now perceived: a polymath and almost omni-competent, always willing to try to make a difference in the world. Not in those very terms, of course, but he did appreciate that his array of interests was very wide, and he was certainly aware that he often undertook to do a lot of things almost at once. Often, these multiple undertakings had good outcomes; sometimes they did not. And this was the biggest of them all that did not turn out so well. Or so it might have seemed in the winter of 1774 and much of that spring when Parliament was on its tear, closing the port of Boston and passing the other "coercive acts."

To some of his contemporaries it must have seemed that Franklin tried to be "all things to all men" or causes. The initial support of the Stamp Act in 1765 followed by his brilliant efforts a year later to have it repealed lend credence to that impression. His sensitivity to Lord Dartmouth, newly appointed as secretary of state for colonial affairs, by giving him time to settle into his office before presenting him with the petition from Massachusetts over royal payment of the governor's salary in 1772, also contributed to this reputation for duplicity or at least ambivalence. Sam Adams mistrusted Franklin from the start of the agent's service for the House of that colony as being too much enamored of Britain or the British to be an effective agent for that body. Arthur Lee, nominally Franklin's assistant agent, wrote to Adams a letter very critical of Franklin, claiming he was either Hillsborough's agent or duped by the secretary of state for the colonies, a claim that reveals more about Lee than Franklin, given the otherwise known facts of the relationship.

Franklin was neither ambivalent about the various roles he filled nor unable to choose which was primary; rather, he was unapologetically confident that he could attend properly to all of them. So, yes, he would appear to some at times to be trying to please too many with expectations of him that might clash. If others appeared to see a problem with his multiplicity of roles before he did, it is part of the strength of the man that Franklin did not lose confidence in his own abilities. Nor did he regret the efforts he had made. Seeing the devastation to his own career in London after the trial did not lead him to re-examine his tactics, let alone question his earlier decision to accept the agency for Massachusetts. Rather he regretted, he said, only that the bearer of petitions for royal favor from the people of that place had to be so badly abused.

It is easy to dismiss the comment as bravado or face-saving rationalization. But it may well be more than those things. If not, Franklin might be forgiven some self-indulgence after the humiliation of his trial. What this notion of supreme self-confidence bespeaks of Franklin is that he really did believe he was serving the interests of both colony and mother country, the common interests of both. What he could not at the moment fully appreciate, largely because of his long absence from the colonies and the inadequacies of communication in a time of rapid change, was how these interests were being defined or spelled out in fundamentally divergent ways. Commonalities became harder and harder to find.

AGENT, PUBLICIST OR LIGHTNING ROD?

Ironically Franklin "managed" finally to serve the interests, if not all concerned, then quite a few on both sides of the Atlantic. For his brethren in Boston, principally the movers and shakers in the House, his service helped them, even if unwittingly, to precipitate the crisis some among them were said to have wanted. For hardliners in the ministry and Parliament the agent became the personification of so many of the things disturbing about the colonies, especially Massachusetts: the clandestine and frequently violent reaction to British authority, the double-talking ("we're loyal subjects of the Crown but do not recognize the authority of Parliament to govern us"), self-righteous ("we know our rights even if you corrupt British politicians do not!"), and selfish ingrates ("we will gladly vote our assistance for mutual defense when asked but will not be taxed for it!").

Whether anyone in those circumstances could have done more to ame-liorate anger and frustration is very doubtful. Yet, as things turned out, Franklin's London maneuvers in those few years served as catalyst to, not a brake upon, the dynamics of dissolution. The acceleration of that process was pronounced in the months immediately following his trial before thir-ty-five lords of the Privy Council. According to one well-known Member of Parliament, Charles Jenkinson who held office in Lord Bute's ministry of the 1760s, the letters affair "had finally convinced the ministry to act against the colonial rebellion."

A major legacy of Franklin's public career is his reputation for pragma-tism, his cool reason in the face of passion, conviction or mere ignorance. His bigger challenge in the London political scene of the 1770s was indif-ference or apathy born of tradition, self-satisfaction and smugness. Against that kind of challenge, it is difficult to imagine what efforts to conciliate could have been effective. But there was little about Franklin's use of the Hutchinson letters viewed from our distance and through the record that history has left us that bespeaks conciliation.

By the time our story begins, in the winter of 1773–74, any apathy re-maining in the North ministry and Parliament had given way to alarm and strong suspicions of conspiracy to unsettle the empire of Great Britain. Pur-suing another course Franklin might have abated such attitudes marginally, but by that time the fat was in the fire. His hand in the letters affair revealed, there is little surprise in what happened next. Excruciating though the trial and his firing from the Post Office were, he might have fared worse. It is little short of amazing that he and a few others still imagined that negotia-tion might proceed to some common good.

Even men of great calm and practiced in the exercise of cool reason can, on occasion, be lost to the pull of those qualities. Our estimate of such men of course depends on more than one or series of events or judgments. The wise old printer of Philadelphia lived an extraordinary life, found fame in his experiments, stirred controversy with his writings, yet exercised a consid-erable capacity for reasoned compromise in the affairs of his time. Moreover he survived to surface again, in Philadelphia to assist Jefferson in drafting the Declaration of Independence and in Paris as his country's first emissary, when those qualities would serve him and his country very well indeed. At one critical time, however, Franklin's reach exceeded his grasp, that time in London just before the American colonies made their final break from Great Britain.

Time Line for and during Franklin's Time in London

Major events on both sides of the Atlantic

1724: Franklin, aged 18, goes to London to purchase a printing press on behalf of his Philadelphia sponsor, goes home in two years empty-handed but resumes pursuit of his trade with others.

1737: Secures appointment as Postmaster at Philadelphia.

1752: Elected member of the Pennsylvania Assembly.

1754: French and Indian War begins. Franklin co-authors draft of colonial union, the Albany Plan, never adopted.

1755: Organizes transport and other services for British Army heading into wilderness against French. Named colonel in the militia of Pennsylvania.

1757–62: Goes to London as agent for Pennsylvania Assembly, accompanied by son William who will study law in London.

1760: Wins concessions on taxing of Penn's lands in the colony from Privy Council.

1761: Attends coronation of King George III.

1762: William marries in London and takes up governorship of New Jersey; Franklin returns to Philadelphia with hopes of returning to London.

1763: Peace Treaty between Britain and France; France cedes Quebec and interior of the continent of North America to Britain.

1764–1775: Second London residency representing several colonies: 1764–1775. Once again stays in the boarding house of Mrs. Stevenson in Craven Street.

1764: Passage of the Sugar Act, actually lowering import duties on molasses from foreign colonies in the Caribbean into the mainland British colonies of North America.

March 1765: Stamp Act passed in Parliament to raise revenue directly from the colonies; requires official stamps on legal papers and commercial documents of all kinds.

August 1765: Riots in Boston (& other cities) in protest of the Stamp Act. Significant damage to homes and offices of officials.

1766: Franklin speaks in Commons on repeal of the Stamp Act. The Act is repealed.

1767: Townshend Revenue Act passed in Parliament placing tariffs on certain products imported to the colonies from Britain.

October 1767: Non-import compact among traders and merchants in the colonies begins.

May 1768: London crowd of supporters of imprisoned John Wilkes turned into a mob; army troops called out, their shooting results in deaths of several civilians at St. George's Field.

October 1768: Four regiments British troops sent to Boston from New York in wake of riot over customs' seizure of ship belonging to John Hancock.

February 1770: George III finds a leader to his liking: Lord North becomes First Lord of the Treasury.

March 1770: Confrontation between a crowd of civilians and British troops leads to "Boston massacre."

March 1770: Partial repeal of Townshend duties passes in Parliament. But tax on tea remains.

October 1770: Franklin elected agent for Massachusetts House over Arthur Lee. Later Hillsborough rebuffs him on presenting his letter of appointment.

1771: Against Hillsborough's recommendation, the Privy Council votes to grant the Grand Ohio Company an expanse of land west of the mountains; Hillsborough resigns in protest.

1772: Dartmouth replaces Hillsborough as colonial secretary; Franklin is encouraged.

November 20, 1772: Resolution of Boston Town Meeting adopted and given wide circulation. Published months later in London with preface by Franklin.

December 1772: Boston Committee of Correspondence established.

December 2, 1772: Franklin sends batch of three- and four-year-old Hutchinson letters originally written to Thomas Whately in London to House Speaker Thomas Cushing for limited circulation among Boston leaders. Does not disclose his source.

January 6, 1773: Governor Hutchinson gives speech to Council and House of Representatives of Massachusetts outlining his views on the charter of the province and its relation to the authority of Crown and parliament. He calls Boston Resolution a virtual "declaration of independence."

June 1773: The Hutchinson letters are published in Boston. There are riotous protests against the governor.

June 1773: Massachusetts House adopts a resolution and petition to the Crown for removal of Governor Thomas Hutchinson and Lt. Governor Andrew Oliver.

Autumn of 1773: News of the letters' publication creates scandal in London amid speculation over the identity of the person responsible for obtaining and sending them.

Autumn of 1773: Petition from Massachusetts House to remove Governor Hutchinson presented to Dartmouth by Franklin.

December 11, 1773: Temple–Whately duel in Hyde Park fought to stalemate; one man is injured, the other's honor remains unsatisfied.

December 25, 1773: Franklin's letter of revelation is printed in the London Advertiser.

January 7, 1774: Chancery Court proceeding filed against Franklin by William Whately for accountability in the taking and misuse of letters belonging to his late brother Thomas.

January 9, 1774: Petition for removal of royal governor first heard in Privy Council. Postponement gives time to the agent to secure counsel.

January 27, 1774: News of Boston Tea Party reaches London.

January 29, 1774: Final hearing on the petition held in the Privy Council among a throng of dignitaries. Solicitor General Wedderburn condemns the radicals in Boston for inflaming the colony against Britain and excoriates the agent for leading conspiracy.

January 30, 1774: Franklin fired from position of Deputy Postmaster for the colonies.

March to June 1774: Parliament passes series of punitive bills, the "Coercive Acts," against Massachusetts.

Spring and summer 1774: Effigies of Wedderburn and Hutchinson burned in Boston and elsewhere.

Summer of 1774: Thomas Hutchinson with most of his family arrive in England, having turned his post as royal governor of Massachusetts Bay Colony over to General Thomas Cage.

September 1774: First Continental Congress held in Philadelphia.

October 1774: Parliamentary elections in England called on short notice by the North ministry; alignments unchanged.

December 1774: Deborah Franklin dies of a stroke in Philadelphia.

December 1774–February 1775: "Secret negotiations" between Franklin and would-be conciliators take place quietly in London ending without agreement.

January 29, 1775: William Pitt (the elder), by then Earl of Chatham, on the first anniversary of the Privy Council humiliation calls on Franklin for help in his attempts for conciliation. Proposal in Lords subsequently voted down decisively.

March 1775: Parliament adopts declaration to the King that Massachusetts was "in rebellion."

March 20, 1775: Franklin with limited notice to friends of his departure from London takes grandson Temple out of school and sails for Philadelphia from Portsmouth. He writes a memoir of the "secret negotiations" on the long voyage. Also conducts studies of the Gulf Stream's strength and plots its course.

April 1775: British regulars and militiamen exchange rifle fire at Lexington green and Concord bridge.

May 7, 1775: Franklin arrives in Philadelphia on the eve of Second Continental Congress.

CHAPTER 1. A DUEL IN HYDE PARK

In the afternoon of December 11th, 1773, two men who barely knew each other arrived, somewhat earlier than the agreed upon hour, at the place chosen to settle a score. It was a spot near the Serpentine of the great public park on the western edge of London, between the Borough of Westminster and the village of Kensington. The duelers commenced their exchange before the seconds for Temple arrived. Whately had elected to have none, so eager were they, or at least so eager was the challenger, to assuage his anger. And the other man, the one who had insulted the challenger by publicly accusing him of theft, was also impulsive in accepting the challenge of the duel for the same day it was issued. And it was a rainy day, at least by the time the two men met.

The challenger was a man named John Temple, formerly a mid-level customs officer in New England. His adversary was a London banker named William Whately. Temple apparently had some familiarity with weapons, and he brought along both a pair of pistols for the duelers and two swords. Whether by lot or by whim, the engagement started with a single round of pistol shots, both of them missing their mark.

From all appearances, it was a clumsy, almost comical affair. Whately had not handled a sword before at all. Although he was overweight and not particularly fit, the banker tried to overcome these deficiencies with sheer vigor of effort. He thrashed the air with wide strokes while struggling to keep his footing in the rain sodden ground. The pair slipped, stumbled and flailed at each other for almost an hour before coachmen passing in a nearby road heard the fray and intervened and ended the encounter. Not, however, before one the duelers was seriously wounded.

It could have been worse. Temple's hearing was impaired, and he claimed later that he did not hear Whately exclaim: "Truce!" when Whately realized that he had taken a cut in his side. But for the timely third party intervention, the banker might well have been killed. Had his sword done its worst that day, Temple could well have faced criminal charges for homicide. To commence a duel with diminished hearing and without a second present would seem at least imprudent, if not reckless.

As duels go, this had to be one of the least memorable, even in an age when planned resort to armed settlement of personal affronts was infrequent. London society in the eighteenth century was more accustomed to lawsuits for libel and sharply worded exchanges in the newspapers. Indeed these two men had already published letters of accusation and denial. Temple's urge for more immediate and personal satisfaction would not be assuaged through a resort to the prolonged processes of a trial for defamation. Thus the pair took their grievance to the relative seclusion of Hyde Park—historic preserve of trees, long grasses, ponds and gravel pathways—not far at all from the tidy Georgian squares of Mayfair.

What makes this semi-pathetic spectacle important is the part it played in the forced departure of London's best-known resident American, Benjamin Franklin, in just a matter of fifteen months. Unwittingly these two men, one an English banker and the other a career-seeking colonial with family ties to the establishment, began a cascade of events that led in a few weeks to Franklin's public humiliation in the Privy Council of King George III. Their quarrel led ultimately to Franklin's leaving both the country and the sympathies he had nourished there for much of his adult life.

How could that be? How could this angry and almost spur-of-the-moment encounter have much, if anything, to do with the most severe crisis in the life of Benjamin Franklin? That is the story of this chapter. It is of course merely a story-within-a-story—the larger one of Franklin and his dreadful encounter with high British contempt just over a month later. To be sure there were other contributing causes that led to Franklin's downfall in January. And many of these will take their place as the larger landscape unfolds. In the shortening days of 1773, however, this inconclusive but nearly tragic contest over personal honor was the most proximate of the causes of the great man's trouble to follow.

Who exactly were these men? Why were they so indignant? The banker William Whately led a quiet London life, cultivating interests in literature and gardening. His tenuous connection with the other man in the duel came about this way. Whately was surviving brother of Thomas Whately and had been since the latter's death executor of Thomas' estate. It was Thomas' political significance in London that brings the substance of the dispute by the duelers to the start of this whole story. Among other things, Thomas Whately had been principal assistant to George Grenville when the latter was, as head of the treasury, principal minister in his majesty's government. It was Thomas, too, who had been Grenville's steward for drafting and orchestrating adoption by Parliament of the notorious Stamp Act of 1765. Whately received a stream of letters from colonial officers in America and cultivated a continuing correspondence with a variety of sources.

Even after Grenville left office, Whately continued to have correspondence with one or another person of significance in the colonies, including a number in Massachusetts. They provided information and opinions of interest either to those still in the ministry or even for those, like Grenville, out of it with prospect of returning to it.

Among the letters from Massachusetts that remained in Whately's files at the time of his death, 1772, or that had been in his possession for some time prior to that, were letters from two men who would later become governor and lieutenant governor of that colony. They were Thomas Hutchinson and Andrew Oliver. Copies of some these letters found their way into print in Boston, which fact became scandalous news in London by the summer of 1773. Among those wondering how the letters got there was William Whately, who was responsible, as executor, for the safekeeping of his late brother's papers and effects.

John Temple had lived in his native New England up to the recent time when he came to London in search of new prospects. Back home he had been employed as a royal customs officer but fell out of favor. Temple was apparently handsome and married well, to the daughter of James Bowdoin, an influential person in his own time and in whose memory the private college in Maine was founded. Apart from these advantages, Temple's greatest political asset was certainly his own family's tie with the Grenvilles, brothers Richard (better known as the first Earl Temple, a title taken from their mother's heritage) and George, the more enduring as a public figure.

At the time of the duel, John Temple held the position of surveyor of the royal customs in Britain, a position of significantly greater status than the one he held in New England. Temple counted Benjamin Franklin a friend, although they do not appear to have been often in contact. The two had met when they sailed on the same ship from America to Britain in 1757, during an earlier visit.

When London papers reported the news that letters written to the late Thomas Whately had been published in Boston, it was at first rumored that the executor brother, William, was responsible since he had possession of Thomas' papers from 1772 when Thomas died.

Under the pressure of these accusations, the executor remembered that John Temple had asked to see some of the correspondence of the decedent. Permission was given on the basis that a letter of his own, of John Temple, had been sent to Thomas while Temple was still residing in America—not an implausible connection given that both men had political careers. Perhaps to have them copied for his own files, Temple was allowed by the executor to take those letters away with him. It seemed to the executor now, in 1773, in the wake of the loss and misuse of his late brother's correspondence, that Temple must have also taken other letters from the deceased's files. He must be the party, Whately concluded, who took those additional letters without permission and sent them to Boston.

Temple vigorously denied the charge, repeated by Whately in the papers. And Temple issued the challenge for a duel. In point of fact, Whately's last letter in the papers seemed to accept Temple's explanation that he had taken only those that he himself had penned. But it was a half-hearted acceptance. Temple's anger persisted. One man's reputation was sullied, and he a banker, by the suggestion, widely circulated, that he might have sold or given the letters to nefarious people. Another was understandably affronted at being called a thief.

Yet these accusations alone cannot account for the notoriety surrounding the disappearance and publication of the letters. Of course men might demand an apology and even fight each other when it is not forthcoming. But what was it that gave these letters such importance that the reputations of these two men would be prominently tested in the London press? What was so significant about the missing letters that someone in Boston would want to publish them? And why would publication make news in London?

The reading of other people's mail was not unusual in the eighteenth century, and sharing some of what one has read with friends and associates was but an expected corollary of the practice. Nonetheless, when someone goes to the expense of printing and circulating such correspondence, it could well be supposed that the letters have some powerful public dimension or sensational character. The very fact of their being printed was itself the great sensation in London in that season of 1773. There would yet be other startling surprises in the days to follow. Did their content reveal some hidden personal scandal of men in high places? Or did the content have more to do with issues of statecraft in which the writers had been engaged? If so, what? And who were the authors and what had they done?

Portrait of Thomas Hutchinson as a young man.
Artist unknown.

CHAPTER 2. PRIVATE LETTERS, PUBLIC CAUSES

Of the collection of approximately twenty letters[2] that influential men in New England wrote between 1767–69 and sent to Thomas Whately in London, most were from the then chief justice of the colony, Thomas Hutchinson, and the secretary of the colonial administration, Andrew Oliver, Hutchinson's brother-in-law. Hutchinson and Oliver subsequently became governor and lieutenant governor, respectively, in 1771, after the previous governor, Francis Bernard, resigned and returned to England.

---

2   The exact number of individual writings considered part of the "Hutchinson letters" has been a matter of interpretation. There were six from Hutchinson himself, four from Oliver, one each from Charles Paxton, Nathanial Rogers and G. Rome plus four from Thomas Moffat. The letters were first printed in Boston in pamphlet form. And there were multiple printings of the pamphlet. The ones used here were published in Boston in 1773. Another printing of them occurred in London in 1774 following the Privy Council proceedings of that January. The first such pamphlet had slightly fewer letters than subsequent printings. The editors of the Franklin papers have adopted the convention of using the largest grouping of these letters and that is the version of them reprinted here as *Verbatim B*. The difference in numbers is small, and those excluded from the earliest version were from marginal figures in the story or ones only forwarded by the major writers like Oliver and Hutchinson. See *The Papers of Benjamin Franklin*, Vol. 20, pages 549–580, Appendix: The Hutchinson Letters.

THE WRITERS

Hutchinson, by whose name the whole collection of these errant letters has come to be known, was a native of Massachusetts.[3] A notable political figure, he was also a close student of the colony's history. He and his family were active in the trans-Atlantic trade through the port of Boston. When he became royal governor, Hutchinson was clearly identified with the status quo in colonial affairs, a principled spokesman for maintenance of traditional ties to Crown and parliament. Moreover, he had taken on himself public discussion of some very contentious issues, clearly marking himself as conservative. It is fair to say that, at the time of the duel in London, Hutchinson and the leadership of the popularly elected assembly of Massachusetts including notable figures like Sam Adams, as well as James Otis, Jr. and John Adams had become not merely unfriendly but uncompromising adversaries in nearly every aspect of governance of the colony. The antipathy of quite a few was based as much on Hutchinson's aggregating powers as it was on ideological differences. Hutchinson offended John Adams and other lawyers, for example, when he accepted the post of Chief Justice without himself being trained in the legal profession.

When these letters were passed around in Boston and then published, it is not entirely clear how or by whom, the position of Hutchinson's detractors had already hardened. Anger was added to defiance when Bostonians believed they saw in the letters the prospect of yet more repression. The sentiments expressed in these letters to an old London associate, Thomas Whately, may not have told his readers in Boston anything new about Hutchinson's constitutional views. That he expressed them in writing, however, and in terms of obvious anxiety, to a politically significant London figure, added considerable fuel to the fire of resentment already burning among the dissidents and the disaffected of Boston and, in short order, beyond.

In the wake of the publication of the letters in June 1773, another development occurred that made waves both in Boston and in London. In the

---

3   The letters could just as logically be called "The Whately letters" since it was to Thomas that all of them were initially sent in London, but convention has it otherwise. Nevertheless, Thomas Whately has his own kind of memorial in having a town in Massachusetts named for him whereas Hutchinson, the native son, has none. The 2009 website for the town declares that Whately was Hutchinson's "mentor" and hence the name was given by a grateful governor in 1771 soon after taking office.

same month the House of Representatives adopted a resolution declaring their new governor completely lacking popular support in the colony and petitioned the Crown for his removal. Scarcely two years had passed since his predecessor, Francis Bernard, had asked to be relieved in the face of civil disobedience, and now Governor Hutchinson, too, faced that challenge. The petition for his removal had been sent to London by the time of the duel and was then awaiting official attention. Prophetically, both Bernard and Hutchinson had feared that their letters were being clandestinely read and misused. It was uniquely Hutchinson's fate, in a bewildering extension of his fears, to see them printed and immediately and roundly condemned in the press.

The storm that broke over Boston with the publication of the letters was full of anger and a sense of betrayal. A riotous crowd burned effigies of Hutchinson and Oliver on the Boston common. By contrast the reaction over the news about the letters in London was uncomprehending: how could these private letters be taken and so badly exploited and by whom?

Explanations would be called for in London, certainly, but in Boston nothing more was necessary than the names of the authors to make sense of the paralysis that had gripped the colony for years. So it seemed to those who had the initiative there. Readers in the twenty-first century, however, likely require some review of the context of those times.

CRISIS IN LAW AND ORDER

What the writers of these letters describe and complain about, in to-day's terms, is nothing less than a chronic break down of law and order. Customs officers were being abused and threatened with such frequency in Boston that several of these Crown officers took their families, left their homes and moved aboard the man-of-war HMS *Romney* as she was lying at anchor in Boston Harbor, protected by a contingent of Royal Marines. The letters also contained complaints of interference with the grand jury that Hutchinson, as chief justice, had appointed to determine whether a criminal libel had been published against Governor Bernard. In one of the letters, Hutchinson included a personal letter sent by a local lawyer to him, then serving as chief justice, concerned for the personal safety of the jurist. "This is most certainly a crisis," Hutchinson wrote in a letter of January 1769. "I really wish that there may not have been the least degree of severity beyond what is absolutely necessary to maintain . . . the dependence which a colony ought to have upon the parent state. . ."[4]

By that time London had already dispatched two regiments of regular British troops, whose presence had had some at least temporary "calming" effect on the colony. Abuses and threats to the good of the colony contin- ued all the same. Notable among these was the avoidance of the customs imposed in the Townshend duties, the principal resistance to which was effected by the "combination of the merchants" to boycott importation of British goods. In his letter of October 1769, Hutchinson claimed that, "pen- alties adequate to the offence" should be exacted. The ministry and Parlia- ment should not simply lay on more taxes or crippling regulation for that would hurt the innocent as well as those individuals directly responsible for the disobedience.

"An Abridgment of English Liberties"

His letter of January contains Hutchinson's most poignant expressions of fear and the most extreme of his political sentiments. "If no measures shall have been taken to secure [the colony's] dependence, or nothing more than some declaratory acts or resolves, *it is all over with us.* [Emphasis in the original.] The friends of government will be utterly disheartened, and the friends of anarchy will be afraid of nothing . . ."[5] Later in this same letter Hutchinson wrote the lines that saw their most notorious quotation in the subsequent resolution to unseat him as governor:

> There must be an abridgment of what are called English liberties. . . . . I doubt whether it is possible to project a system of government in which a colony 3000 miles distant from the parent state shall enjoy all the liberty of the parent state. . . . I wish for the good of the colony when I wish to see some future restraint of liberty rather than the connexion [sic] with the parent state should be broken; for I am sure such a breach must prove the ruin of the colony.[6]

Was Hutchinson saying that he feared that the people of Massachusetts could not manage on their own? Whatever it takes to maintain the impe- rial ties must be done? A different system of government might have to be put in place to do that, different from what we have now and different, too, from that of Great Britain itself. Highly symbolic language it is and perhaps

---

4 *Papers* vol. 20, pages 549–50.
5 Ibid.
6 Ibid.

also the words of someone at his wit's end. Yet it is not easy for the modern reader to make out what exactly the soon-to-be royal governor and long time public servant of his colony had in mind, if he knew himself. Was it more than a simple *crie de coeur* coupled with a desperate plea for imaginative leadership and encouragement?

Hutchinson does not explicitly ask for more troops or other forces, although such a request might be read into the letters between the lines. It is entirely possible that Hutchinson had in mind limiting the role of the House of Representatives and the town councils' increasing activity and boldness while he wrote these letters; but he does not spell out such thoughts in these letters.[7] In any case, when Hutchinson wrote these letters to London in the late 1760s he was not yet governor. Nor does the resolution adopted by the Massachusetts House allege specific wrongs or over-reaching while he was in that position later, from 1771.

> Their [Hutchinson and Oliver's] conduct thereafter was irrelevant to the petition [for removal], which charged them solely with having written letters, in 1767–69, that "tended" to deter the King from hearing the grievances of his colony and to exacerbate friction between it and the mother country.[8]

Andrew Oliver (married to a sister of Hutchinson's wife) and Hutchinson were long-time friends and associates in many aspects of colonial administration. His appointment as Secretary to the Massachusetts Bay Colony had assured him contact with the records and other papers and correspondence of the colony and, equally significant, the personnel and personages of any consequence in and around Boston. Evidently, authorities in London trusted him for other missions as well. He served as a member of a commission appointed by the Crown to mediate the boundary dispute between New York and New Jersey in 1769.

---

7 Ironically there were in fact other letters that Hutchinson had written, unbeknownst to Franklin or his associates in Boston, just a year or so later. These letters were not only more extreme in sentiment but they were also addressed to public officials. For example, in April 1771, the governor wrote to John Pownall, under secretary for colonial affairs, suggesting that Parliament enact a statute making it "high treason" to write or print that an act of Parliament was of no validity. Copies of these later letters were not discovered in Boston until 1775, a year after the governor had taken leave and moved with his family to England. See Knollenberg, Bernard, Growth of the American Revolution, 1766–1775 (2003), pages 127–129 and sources cited there. Hutchinson also advocated changes in the structure of Massachusetts's colonial governance as well as prosecutions of those in the colony who were leading the non-importation agreements.

8 Editors, *Papers*, Vol. 20, pages 540–41.

Oliver's letters to Thomas Whately in London in these years closing out the decade of the 1760s are similar to those of Hutchinson's in tone. They describe a deteriorating condition in terms of respect for British authority, and Oliver almost despairs of any prospect for "authority of government... [to be] restored" (letter of August 12th, 1769, from New York on the boundary dispute commission). And he deprecates what look to be half-way measures coming from London at that time: "Government at home [London] will deceive itself, if it imagines that the taking off the duty on glass, paper and painter's colors will work a reconciliation.... It is the principle that is now disputed; the combination against importation of tea, although it comes cheaper than ever...." (letter of August 12, 1769). (Here Oliver was referring to changes that London approved in the revenue measure that replaced the Stamp Act, namely the Townshend Duties Act of 1767.

Unlike Hutchinson, however, Oliver was willing to suggest some specific changes in the existing arrangements to effectuate a return to normalcy. For instance, he thought that election of members of the upper house in Massachusetts, the Council of the colony, might be changed from popular election in the House to direct appointment by the Crown, perhaps through the creation of a pool of well qualified men of talent and ability, if not property, similar to the House of Lords or the Privy Council (letters of May 7, 1767; and February 13, 1769).

Other messages in the collection of the "Hutchinson letters" included several from a customs official based in Rhode Island named Thomas Moffat who reported on conditions in that colony after the disturbances over the Stamp Act. They contained vain attempts to have the colonial legislature compensate those (including himself) whose property was damaged by a mob.

Moffat also sent along the letter of another commissioner, named George Rome, who complains that the local courts in Rhode Island are so thoroughly controlled by local politicians that claims by "Europeans" resident here are thwarted by one means or another. "We have appealed to his Majesty In Council for redress, got their verdicts reversed, and obtained the King's decrees for our money, but that is all [Letter of G. Rome at Narragansett, December 22nd, 1767]." "We have...in vain waited with great impatience for years past, in hopes his Majesty would have nominated his judges and other executive officers in every colony in America, which would in a great measure remove the cause of our complaint."[9]

---

9 Ibid.

"POWER IN THE POPULACE"

What are we to make of this anguish and the insistent calls "to do something"? They seem both real and deeply troubling for those closely connected with traditional institutions and practices. It is helpful to keep in mind that no British colony in North America was organized as fully as a modern state. There was no municipal police force, no state police nor any of the other related instruments of executive enforcement of the criminal law. Such peace officers as there were consisted of popularly elected sheriffs who depended in the main on community assistance where any resistance to or evasion of arrest was expected. The courts, too, depended on these officers for execution of their judgments. The only apparatus independent of this very loose and decentralized collection were the royal customs officers who could and did often call on the governor (especially in Massachusetts) for assistance which, in these strained times, was rarely forthcoming, for there was little the governor alone could do. The civilian militia, subject in theory to the call of the governor, depended on the voluntary service of its members. It is no wonder that customs officers eventually, as the reins of the customs service were tightened in London, called upon the Crown's military and naval forces for enforcement of the law. Until the time of these crises of the 1760s, no such units were closely available, nor were army troops or warships, before this time, ever thought to be necessary or desirable to have a presence in the colonies of America.

The concerns expressed were not only of those born in Britain. Thomas Hutchinson was a life-long resident of the colony and educated in Harvard College. And so was Andrew Oliver. Their attitudes, as expressed in their own letters, were not noticeably divergent from those of Thomas Moffat, the Crown's Customs Officer in Rhode Island, a transplant from England. All of them were troubled by the breakdown of observance of the law and were also deeply dismayed by the apparent indifference in London. A temporary return to quiet occurred with the landing of two regiments of British troops, backed up by royal navy ships of the line. But the pattern that emerged around the time of the Stamp Act's enactment was not so easily erased. As one of the writers observed, so much power had been relinquished to, or seized by "the populace," there would great difficulty in reclaiming it.

If the views expressed in these letters seem all too understandable to us, why would they have been so provocative and inflammatory for Thomas Cushing, speaker of the House, to whom their London custodian had sent them? Why would they not appear as totally predictable, if not agreeable, to those like Sam Adams or others with whom Cushing shared them in 1772?

NOTORIETY IN LONDON

This, then, is the scene in late December of 1773. All London knew of the Hutchinson letters affair. And literate London knew also that William Whately and John Temple had fought an unsatisfactory duel over the letters' disappearance and publication. It looked as if a second duel would be called for.

On Christmas Day, in a letter published in the London, in *The Public Advertiser*, Benjamin Franklin, agent for the Massachusetts House, declared that he was personally responsible for obtaining and transmitting the Hutchinson letters to Boston. (Franklin's Christmas Day letter is reprinted in full as the first of several documents in the appendices.) Both William Whately and John Temple were innocent, Franklin revealed, because the one never had possession of them and the other, Temple, could therefore not have taken them from Whately, the executor of his late brother's estate. Franklin wrote that he took the step of disclosing his own personal role in order to prevent "further mischief."

Apparently Franklin believed that this published explanation would be as effective as contacting the antagonists individually and privately. Given the personal stake that he had in the matter, he might well have attempted a more discreet means of communication first. The consequences for Franklin could not have been graver. He had publicly declared himself guilty of, or complicit in, the theft or misuse of correspondence without the knowledge or consent of either the writer(s) or the recipient Thomas Whately. Franklin's humanitarian impulse is understandable, certainly, perhaps even commendable. Probably the published letter did serve to prevent a second duel and thereby perhaps save one or two lives.

FRANKLIN'S EXPLANATION

Assuming that it did prevent a second duel, his letter in the press achieved Franklin's immediate and practical objective merely by taking

Whately and Temple out of the picture. The greater part of Franklin's Christmas Day surprise focused on why he had used the Hutchinson letters as he had. The letter amounted to an informal defense for his action. Franklin characterized the letters as public and not private in that they were "written by public officers" to other public persons. Plus, their purpose was to influence public "measures." Their "tendency," Franklin argued, was "to incense the mother country against her colonies." Under these conditions a colonial agent would feel it his "duty to transmit them to his constituents."

What Franklin's published letter did not attempt to explain was whether the Deputy Postmaster for the royal mail in America had abandoned a duty to safeguard the security of postal correspondence. How, in other words, could Franklin choose to let one duty override another? He might have considered that the letters had lost their character as items subject to postal protection by the time he got them, given that they were, presumably, in the hands of persons for whom the information was intended. In other words the letters were no longer in transit but had reached their destination and taken on a different character altogether.

Something of that understanding seems implicit in his later reflection on the events. In a letter to Thomas Cushing dated April 16, 1774, Franklin wrote that "as [the letters] had been handed about here to prejudice [the people of Massachusetts], why not use them for their advantage?" This was hardly a direct or complete answer to the question over conflicting duties, to be sure. His rhetorical question may, however, suggest that Franklin felt his larger or higher duty lay with the colonists who had engaged him as their agent in London. To be completely fair to his recorded thoughts about the matter, though, Franklin believed that the larger or longer term interests of both colonists and the British Empire were overlapping if not the same. In short, while he knew he and others might suffer in the meantime, if his efforts could eventually succeed in composing those interests peacefully, all else would be worth the price.

Were the Letters Influential?

Evidently, Franklin believed that, before he received them, the letters were in the hands of cabinet ministers or their close associates. Whatever their initial character when written, dispatched and first received, these letters, he seemed convinced, were being seen or had already been seen by one or more ministers, possibly by Hillsborough or Dartmouth, those directly responsible for colonial policy.

This was not the last flourish Franklin would make about the status of the letters and his treatment of them. In a set of incomplete and unpublished notes he began probably in February of 1774, he offered one more justification for his actions. "Copies of [my letters] too had been returned here by officers of government, why then should theirs be exempt from the same treatment?"[10] It is very likely true that much of Franklin's mail was being read, copied or returned for official perusal. Still, so far as we know, none of it found its way into the newspapers. Further, in fairness to Franklin, he wrote his additional flourishes soon after his brutal experience in the Privy Council. The Christmas Day letter with its simple distinction of public versus private letters was made in the relative calm of his own timely humanitarian intervention to prevent a second duel. He could be expected to be more summary, abrupt and even frankly angry in the after-thoughts. Perhaps they express, at bottom, what he felt all along: the matters addressed in the letters were indeed matters of grave public concern. It is the quality or spirit of the letters that ultimately persuaded Franklin of the legitimacy of his actions. And on that score, his later notes and the Christmas Day letter to the paper agree. The letters' purpose, he concluded, was to drive a wedge between the mother country and the colonies by inviting measures of repression inconsistent with previous relations of the two. The other contention was technical and perhaps overly formal. It is, however, the point of defense over which historians have poured heaviest criticism.

It is in these after-notes (the "Tract") that Franklin gives us a fuller picture of the underpinnings of his concern for the estrangement he feared was worsening.

> It has long appeared to me that the only true British politicks were those which aimed at the good of the whole ... empire, not those which sought the advantage of one part to the disadvantage of the others.....

> From a thorough enquiry [on the occasion of the Stamp Act controversy] into the nature of the connection between Britain and the Colonies, I became convinced that the bond of their union is not the Parliament but the King. ...

---

10 "Tract Relative to the Affair of Hutchinson's Letters," two copies in Library of Congress, reprinted in *The Papers of Benjamin Franklin*, Volume 21, at pages 415–435.

[The puritans] took with them ... by compact their allegiance to the King, and a legislative power for the making of a new body of laws, with his assent, by which they were to be governed. Hence, they became distinct states, under the same Prince, as Scotland and England before the Union....[11]

Historians have most frequently treated two elements of Franklin's rationale or explanation critically. One concerns the "public vs. private" distinction he drew over the character of the letters. A second targets Franklin's claim that the Hutchinson letters were designed to bring about a tough or tougher policy toward the colonies, or at least toward Massachusetts in particular.

Crucial to any considered understanding of Franklin's motives about the Hutchinson letters is his belief that Thomas Cushing and other elected leaders would in reading those letters realize the repression they had witnessed was not the product of a vengeful or tyrannical British King and Parliament. Rather the design of the colonists' own misguided native-born, royally appointed leaders in the colony itself was to blame.[12]

Whether Franklin was reasonable in that belief is debatable. Most of his biographers brush past the question and at least assume that it was a belief held in good faith. Whether the activists in Boston would distinguish between motives driving the local authorities like Hutchinson and Oliver, on the one hand, and those in London who actually imposed the objectionable measures, on the other, seems at best questionable, if not a very naïve supposition. Why should the colonists believe one group less tainted than the other if both were in fact cooperating?

---

11 "Tract," *Papers* vol.21, at page 417.

12 Franklin certainly wanted to appear, in London at least, as a conciliator between the colonies and Britain at most times in this period of several years. Various shadings of that posture, as seen through his correspondence, will be explored in later chapters. Until the Hutchinson letters affair the agent's efforts along these lines had been more conceptually oriented, as in constitutional issues or particular laws and practices. In this episode he can be seen as introducing, whether consciously or not, a shift in focus to particular actors and their influence as another means by which the two sides might be drawn closer. The "blame game" surely is one of the oldest political tactics. In this instance, however, the agent was slow to adopt it in the context of Massachusetts politics already used to the practice.

COLONIAL ANGER TOWARD HUTCHINSON HEIGHTENED

Franklin's efforts over the letters did have the effect of renewing and intensifying anger toward Governor Hutchinson in Boston. That much was achieved. The House of Representatives adopted a petition calling for the King to remove him and Lt. Governor Oliver from their posts. It is not known how seriously anyone expected that this request would in fact be granted. What was clear is that the dissident leaders in Massachusetts Bay were unhappy with and opposed to their colonial administration. That much, however, had already been abundantly clear for some time, at least since the Stamp Act crisis of 1765. What the activists in the House now had was an occasion, one marked by vigorous public clamor, with which to assert themselves more formally and decisively. It was also an occasion for the House to appear responsive to local opinion, expression of which was frequently induced, either visibly or behind the scenes, by more than a few of the House's members.

Yes, the subjects the Hutchinson letters dealt with were political in nature. They were political in the most fundamental sense: an extended failure in civil observance of law and order. Yet what the letters expressed, although dealing largely with public matters, were merely the opinions of persons not then (1767–69) occupying positions of executive authority. What probably tilted the analysis for Franklin was that the letters were treated in London as if they were in the public domain and were being copied (one biographer maintains) by third persons who indeed could have influence on imperial policy. This aspect of the Hutchinson letters affair draws the most puzzlement and mystery. Who exactly had them just prior to Franklin's possession? And the question, why does it matter who had them, follows closely behind the first.

WHO WAS FRANKLIN'S SOURCE?

There are almost as many answers to that question as there are historians writing about it. Suffice it to note here that there is no definitive answer. It is one of the secrets that Franklin never revealed, although the major candidates are rather few.[13]

---

13 The question of the identity of Franklin's source is explored fully in the *After-Word* of this book.

What is more useful to pursue here in the main current of the story of Franklin's trial is why the identity of is important at all.

For one thing, if we knew the identity of the person or persons who brought the letters to Franklin or told him about them, we might discover distinctive motives or purposes of these other participants. Accounts of the Hutchinson letters affair have largely assumed that the significance that Franklin attached to the letters was shared by these unknown third persons. If their purposes diverged in some way, that divergence could itself tell much about the character of the trial that Franklin was shortly to endure. Such divergence could also illuminate more fully any connection between the trial and other perils Franklin faced, such as a private lawsuit over the disappearance of the letters.

At the very least, a surer answer to the question of the identity of Franklin's source would help provide a fuller picture of his circle of associates in London, their sympathies, ties and expectations.

Such significant questions take on greater intensity in the light of the very clear fact that Franklin himself was determined not to reveal his source. Whatever his other duties and loyalties were, he would honor this pledge throughout the rest of his long life. For a man who liked to write so much and about so many things, it seems remarkable that Franklin did not ever, so far as we know, write about this singularly interesting detail.

HANDLING OF THE LETTERS IN BOSTON

The agent sent the Hutchinson letters to Boston as enclosures to a cover letter to Thomas Cushing, Speaker of the House. In that letter Franklin set out certain conditions on their use and exposure. Notably, the letters were not to be printed or published. They could be seen by a few persons whom Franklin named and such few others of like status to whom the Speaker would see fit to show them. In the end, neither of these conditions was honored. The letters were passed around rather widely and then eventually read, in "closed session," to the whole membership of the House. Very shortly after that, only days later, they were printed, first in pamphlet form and then in newspaper serialization.

Whether Franklin, himself a journalist, genuinely expected that the letters would only be circulated among a few people must be questioned. At least initially, however, he did register chagrin over the fact that they were printed and published. Speaker Cushing explained that the House came to believe that other copies of the letters had arrived in Boston and were being shown about, a condition Cushing evidently thought relieved him and his colleagues from their agent's restriction.[14] Franklin did not believe that copies from other sources were circulating in Massachusetts.

Unauthorized publication is not the most remarkable part of the handling of this collection of letters in Boston. Whoever arranged their printing took some pains to "doctor" the letters so that in their printed form they took on a more sinister cast than they could have had as separate, unconnected documents. In particular, the letters from several different persons over a period of two years were printed together as if to suggest that all of them were in collaboration with each other, so that the most extreme position taken by one person or another would be made to appear the view of all. Guilt by association was clearly part of the design of the pamphlet. The very title of that first printed pamphlet (several other editions were printed in a few months) of the letters was calculated to bias the reader: *Copy of Letters Sent to Great Britain by His Excellency Thomas Hutchinson and the Hon. Andrew Oliver in which the Judicious Reader Will Discover the Fatal Source of the Confusion and Bloodshed in which This Province Has Been Involved and Which Threatens Total Destruction of the Liberties of All America.*[15] Moreover, punctuation was altered and italics added to highlight certain words and phrases.[16]

---

14 Contemporaneous circumstances suggest that the reported arrival of other copies was merely a ruse concocted probably by the House's clerk, Sam Adams, to avoid Franklin's restriction. The Journal for the House reflects that it was Adams who made the claim. See Bailyn's *The Ordeal of Thomas Hutchinson* at page 240, note 32. Adams was not only pushing for early publication and notoriety but also he had little sympathy for the House's agent whom he had opposed for the job two years earlier. Adams had lingering doubts as to Franklin's devotion to the cause of liberty, believing him to be too cozy with British authority. It would not be beneath Adams to embarrass Franklin by ignoring his plea for a ban on publication, particularly if his own demonstrable political purposes were served. Caution is warranted in conclusively assigning to Sam Adams the role identified here in view of the fact that in a letter to Franklin from House Speaker Thomas Cushing, John Hancock is given that distinction. Ltr. of June 14, 1773, TC to BF, *Papers*, Vol. 20, page 235.

15 Originally printed in Boston by Edes and Gill, 1773. Reprinted in *The Papers of Benjamin Franklin*, Volume 20, Appendix, pages 539 through 572.

16 Perhaps the most effective of such editorial devices was the subtle one of innuendo by abstracting the letters from the context in which they were written. All of these points were exposed and thoroughly explored in a series of essays to the press at the time, written by the province's attorney general and friend of the governor, Jonathan Sewell, using the pseudonym Philalethes. They were also

---

By the time his own hand in the letters affair was revealed, Franklin could not long be preoccupied with any of these details, for he would short-ly be engaged in his own confrontation with outrage. He might have time later to reflect on certain aspects of the episode.

the subjects of Hutchinson's own reflections on the letters affair later, writing in exile in England. See Bailyn, *Ordeal* pages 245–52 and sources cited there.

George Grenville. Courtesy of National Portrait Gallery, London. ©National Portrait Gallery, London

Chapter 3. Imperial Over-Reach: The Political Context of the Letters

In the years when Hutchinson, Oliver and the others wrote their letters, the political scene in the Massachusetts Bay Colony was one of recurring tension nearing crisis proportions. Almost every move of royal authority to enforce its new will was met with verbal challenge, administrative avoidance, or, sometimes, physical sabotage or open destruction by rioters.

Two considerations lay behind this new imperial will of George III and his serial ministries of 1763 to 1770. The first was that the older arrangements, those implemented through a set of Navigation Acts (1651 through 1696), were being undone by a combination of factors including active smuggling and avoidance (such as direct colonial trade with the Dutch in their nearby colonies in the Americas or later the French, especially for sugar or its companion product molasses) as well as the benign neglect of Whig leaders like Robert Walpole and through that lassitude the corruption or inept work of customs officers in the American colonies of Great Britain.

These older statutes, the Navigation Acts, were designed for structural control of the imperial advantage, not so much to produce revenue to the Crown. Thus, shipping between the mother country and her colonies had to be in British ships only or those of the colonies and with crews made up largely of British nationals. Similarly colonial exporters to other countries could not trade certain items of trade, those deemed essential to the British economy, at all. And coastal trade among the colonies was only to be carried in British ships or those of British colonies. In the seventeenth century, before New Amsterdam became New York, that prohibition was particularly inconvenient for New Englanders and, as one might imagine, widely ignored.

With the new monarch on Britain's throne and with the success of British arms in defeating the French in their long war of two continents, George III's ministers were determined not only to tighten up the reins of empire but also to find new ways to assist British taxpayers in bearing the financial burden of an expanded empire. Early estimates of the cost of maintaining regulars of the British army garrisoned in North America after the peace treaty with France ranged up to £200,000–300,000 per year. The colonies could not be expected to defray this cost alone, but they could be obliged to pay some of it, perhaps half.

The Stamp Act of 1765 was the considered answer that the ministry of George Grenville gave to the question of how the colonies might do their part. Just the year before Grenville, upon the recommendation of Charles Townshend chairman of the Board of Trade, had Parliament pass the Sugar Act of 1764. It was designed, through a reduction from six pence per gallon of molasses to two or three pence, to eliminate or at least discourage smuggling and thereby produce some actual revenue after thirty years of blanket protection of the West Indian British planters. But the effort, while not as controversial in New England and the other colonies as what would come next, simply produced too little new revenue. Another approach was needed.

The idea of a tax on official paper stamps had been considered in the cabinet since at least 1763. Its enactment occurred only after Grenville had consulted with colonial agents, including Franklin, as to alternative measures that Parliament might consider. The minister said "no" to the suggestion of a self-imposed subscription of funds by the colonies themselves. And nothing more was forthcoming from the colonial side. Revenue to the tune of over £250,000 annually was being raised in Britain at this time through a stamp tax enacted much earlier. The stamps were required for most printed matter including newspapers as well bills of sale in commerce and legal documents such as conveyances and bills of lading. It was expected that such a tax might raise at least a considerable fraction of the domestic sum in the colonies. The revenue so raised would go directly to pay for the army in North America. At least that was the original intent.

Another feature of the Stamp Act was probably meant to be a concession to colonial sensibilities: the use of local people as administrators of the stamp tax system to distribute the stamps and collect the payments for them. This certainly gave a nod to the patronage and loyalty of local governors and others in their company, but it also built in a very fundamental flaw in the proposed system. By the time the Act was set to go into effect, November 1, 1765, there was no local collector ready and willing to handle the stamps.

Resistance to the proposal of a stamp tax, floated in London by Grenville over a year earlier, grew in Boston, as it did in other colonies as assemblies drafted petitions of protest. None of these proved effective to prevent passage of Grenville's bill, and the announcement of its adoption, seemingly heedless of colonial opinion, provided the spark to violent demonstrations. One in Boston on August 13, 1765, destroyed the office of Andrew Oliver and seriously damaged his home. By that time it had come to be widely known that Oliver was to be the stamp tax collector in Boston. Perhaps that connection, Oliver's familial and political ties with Hutchinson, more than any other single cause, led to the sacking and near destruction of the Boston ancestral mansion of Thomas Hutchinson, too, just twelve days later. What most dismayed Hutchinson, and many others at the time, is that he was opposed to the proposed Stamp Act. He had even chaired the committee (while he was lieutenant governor and presiding officer of the colony's Council or upper house) that drafted the final petition sent to London prior to the Act's passage. Hutchinson's losses were so extensive, not limited to family silver, furniture and valuable paintings, that in the next day's court session where he presided (Boston probate), Hutchinson appeared in borrowed clothing and robe.

In Philadelphia that same season collectors nominated by Benjamin Franklin backed down, and rioters tried to force their way into Franklin's family home but were held off at gunpoint by his wife Deborah and some neighbors.

Violent opposition to the Stamp Act had not been anticipated in London, although it was clear that the Grenville government intended to assert Parliament's authority to levy any tax on the colonies. Grenville would not limit the scope of the ministry's taxes to merely external ones as many had thought would be tolerated. Just as emphatically he intended to raise a substantial amount of revenue from the colonies with this legislation.

Although it was the clean-up work of the next administration and not Grenville's, Parliament was ready to vote repeal of the Stamp Act in 1766. Franklin played an important part appearing before a committee in the House of Commons and answering probing questions about the effect of the tax and about the attitudes of his fellow Americans toward Britain. The act of repeal, though it angered Grenville's supporters in Commons, was thought to be one of practicality or prudence and not a surrender of the principle of Parliament's authority. And before the successor revenue measure, the Townshend Duties, was enacted, Parliament, lest there be any doubt about the matter, adopted a formal declaration of its right to tax and legislate in any manner for the whole of the British Empire. This significant, if face-saving, corollary to the repeal of the hated Stamp Act went largely unnoticed in the colonies.

The Townshend Duties Act, named for the Chancellor of the Exchequer in the Pitt-Grafton cabinet (of 1766–70) Charles Townshend, was passed by Parliament in 1767. The act comprised a fairly straightforward set of import taxes on the colonies covering a variety of seemingly isolated items: china, glass, paint and paper plus tea. The levy on tea was to be three pence per pound, and it was estimated that this alone would raise about £20,000 per year for the royal treasury; another £20,000 could be expected through the duties on all the other commodities combined. This was not as much as had been projected under the now repealed Stamp Act but a significant £40,000 nonetheless.

Believing that his legislation was playing to the colonial distinction between external and internal taxes, a distinction he himself thought to be nonsense, the Chancellor went on to add a feature that would prove to be just as troubling to the colonial mind as parliamentary supremacy itself. The Townshend Act's revenues were to be used to pay civil authorities in the colonies and not the regular British army troops stationed in the colonies as part of the post-war attention to the needs of an expanded North American empire. This feature served to undermine the authority of colonial assemblies just at the time when popular resentment was already growing in response to the very fact of the new taxes themselves. Abandoning the earlier justification for the new revenue—sharing the costs of continental defense, poisoned the atmosphere further, for the switch suggested that other motives were in play in London. There is little doubt that this plan for direct payment of salaries to executives in the colonies would strengthen their hands in continuing struggles with the representative assemblies and by that means make the colonies more compliant with royal authority. This was a radical change of policy from the laxer days of Robert Walpole and the older Whigs, that is before George III had come to the throne determined to find new and firmer hands through which to conduct his reign.

Colonial reaction to the Townshend Duties was slow to develop, and the merchant-led boycott of British goods was not uniform from one colonial port to another. As that effort faltered, two things happened to complicate the next phase of relations between London and its colonies. One was that the ministry was moved to reconsider the wisdom of the duties, especially in light of the importance to British manufacturers and exporters of most of the covered items: china, glass, paint and paper. A compromise was struck allowing these products to be removed from the taxable list but leaving the much more lucrative tax on imports of tea, which was not a commodity produced in Britain. This was the way, the ministry maintained, and Parliament readily added its approval, to assert the principle of broadest authority to tax the colonies, without causing further harm to the commercial interests of the mother country.

While these developments were proceeding in London in those years, 1768–70, efforts to enforce the customs in the port of Boston had encountered such resistance that a call for army troops was initiated by customs officers, not by the Governor, Francis Bernard, who had pointedly declined to ask General Clinton in New York, headquarters of the army in America, for troops, fearing further popular resistance and friction. And so for the first time since the late war with France and for very different reasons, units of regular army troops were dispatched to an American port city, not for defense against foreign enemies but to restore civil order. These units were reinforced later so that by the end of this short period, 1770, there were about two thousand Redcoats garrisoned in and around Boston. It is a wonder that it did not happen sooner, but after about eighteen months of this occupation there was a fatal clash between the troops and civilians. Some called it a "massacre" of five civilians and others saw it as a contrived provocation by a mob with sticks and stones. London held its breath over the news. In Massachusetts thereafter the event would take on overtones of patriotic martyrdom as the event was memorialized in public ceremonies on all subsequent anniversaries of the event, March 5, 1770.

The next few years, 1770–73, down to the time of the Hutchinson letters affair, saw a return to the calm of earlier periods, those before 1765 and the Stamp Act. Conceivably the very intensity of the period of turmoil had produced its own need for a lull. The non-import agreements, never fully adopted everywhere in the colonies, were softening their hold further, for it is rarely convenient to keep up self-denial for very long. Moreover, the compromise in the ministry lifting the Townshend duties on most imports (except tea) seemed a masterstroke of political brilliance or the sheerest good luck. For the moment at least, it appeared that way. Further, his majesty's government diverted by larger imperial concerns, such as an imminent war with Spain (over the Falkland Islands!), was content to leave well enough alone in colonial matters.

There was great relief in London that the trials in Boston of the soldiers implicated in the deadly shooting had apparently been conducted fairly (John Adams had been one of the defense counsel), and there was no conviction for murder. Thomas Hutchinson, too, was worried over the trial of the soldiers and began preparing for a storm. While the event was to have lasting effect on the psyche of Americans, public protests about those results at that time were peaceful.

Comparative calm did not mean, however, that controversy had disappeared. After Francis Bernard resigned in 1769 and returned to England, Thomas Hutchinson was formally appointed royal governor the next year and took his oath of office in March 1771. (In that same year, as one of his more enduring official acts, Hutchinson, issued the charter for the still thriving town of Whately in the central part of the colony in honor of his old friend and political confident, Thomas Whately.)

Hutchinson had actually succeeded to the problems of the office as acting governor upon Bernard's resignation two years before that formality. And those leaders of the House determined to test the new governor did so at once and often. For his part, Hutchinson did not seek to avoid controversy either. In an evidently self-confident way the new governor, steeped in the history of the colony and by temperament a somewhat stiff and humorless man, chose to meet the House on its own terms and turf. His speech to the House and Council in 1772 turned into a lecture on constitutional principles, the only ones Hutchinson could conceive, the traditionalist view of Britain and its colonies developed in law and practice for a century and a half.

His address to the House and Council, "the Court" of Massachusetts, was Thomas Hutchinson's way of responding to claims for local autonomy and accountability over the whole range of legislation, especially with regard to raising revenue for any purpose. What seemed to be needed, the governor must have thought, was some straight talk about how things had been and should remain. There was, he felt, no way to bridge the divide that had opened up between those who violently challenged what London was doing on the one hand and complete independence, which he thought would bring the ruin of the colony.

Agent Franklin meanwhile in London was trying to smooth things over, advising the colonial secretary of the time, the Earl of Dartmouth, to pay no attention to the recent claims of the House for more autonomy; "they're merely words."

Bostonians certainly did not appreciate the governor's bluntness, but those like Sam Adams who indeed were bent upon the "extreme" option that Hutchinson posited, independence, welcomed the clarity of the picture. Important ministers in London, North and Dartmouth, were miffed about Hutchinson's speech, for they could see the folly in such ill-timed frankness. Even imperial hawks can see the wisdom in now and then folding their wings. For the new governor and his elected assembly, the speech was to mark the beginning of the end of his turbulent term in office.

Lincoln's Inn in 1760. Courtesy of The Honourable
Society of Lincoln's Inn.

CHAPTER 4. HARVEST OF SPITE: REACTION IN THE LONDON PRESS

The written word held such power for Franklin that he virtually composed his life through it. He resorted to the pen as easily as most men to
speech. And much of what he wrote found its way to print—and much of
that during his own lifetime.[17] Moreover, "[n]early everything he wrote that
was published in his lifetime—except the scientific papers, the almanacs,
and sundry pamphlets—first appeared in a newspaper or a magazine."[18]
From his boyhood apprenticeship to an older brother, a printer in Boston,
to the very last year of his life in 1790, Franklin was writing, writing for publication. In between those times, he was himself an independent printer,
publisher of newspapers, and frequent contributor to the papers, both in
America and England. During his second and third residencies in London,[19]
this experience as journalist and publicist would find increasing utility in
the life he created for himself in the center of the empire he so admired.

---

17 Few if any other American statesmen of the time have left as compendious a paper
   record of his life as Franklin. The collection on which much of this book's reporting and interpreting of the events under scrutiny rely, *The Papers of Benjamin
   Franklin* (sponsored by the American Philosophical Society and Yale University),
   now numbers 37 published volumes. Several more are contemplated for future
   publication.
18 Verner Crane, Ed., *Benjamin Franklin's Letters to the Press, 1758–1775* (UNC Press,
   Chapel Hill, 1950) page xi, from the Introduction.
19 Franklin lived in England first as a young man in 1724–26 working in printing
   shops; in maturity 1757–62 for his first stint as agent for the Pennsylvania House;
   and in 1769–75 when he served multiple agencies.

Increasingly during the 1760s Franklin found political journalism the prime element of his informal "work" as commentator, information source and spokesman for all things American. The English public, he felt, was very poorly informed about the North American colonies on the widest range of subjects. His very first letter to the London press, in 1758, soon after his arrival there on behalf of the Assembly of Pennsylvania, opened up his campaign to express the widespread dissatisfaction of the colonists there with the power and the privileges exercised by the Penn family. Under the original proprietary charter from the Crown, the Penns appointed the governor of the colony and they kept their own family lands from being locally taxed, to name a pair of grievances. Gradually Franklin's writing branched into a wide variety of topics and concerns. He defended Americans against "'angry reflections' and ... often against opprobrious epithets; charges that they sought independence; against misrepresentation in Parliament; he defended their ancestors; their virility and even their diet. More rarely he defended his own conduct."[20]

And this time, late December 1773, was such a rarity, when Franklin had to defend or at least explain himself. His Christmas Day letter in *The Advertiser* had several purposes. It was a last minute third-party intervention to save a life or lives. It was a public disclosure of a major political gamble clandestinely undertaken. It was also a kind of testament to the complex of loyalties and roles that its writer had woven around himself over the previous decade.

Whatever Franklin had intended or expected from his Christmas Day letter to the press, its significance cannot be overstated, for him personally and for the cause he served. It provided for those in power already frustrated with developments on the ground in the colonies, especially in Massachusetts, a ready confession with which to condemn its writer and through him the colonists whose agent he was. It is not too much to say that the Christmas Day letter of Franklin was the tipping point for a determination in London to take more decisive action, action to stop the drift of the colonies into further lawlessness or worse. All of this becomes clearer as the next formal steps of this story of Franklin's trial unfold in the next several chapters.[21] That this reaction was being formed in London, although there is no official

---

20 Crane, *Letters to the Press*, page xxxv.
21 Even though the coming news of the Tea Party was yet to reach London, it would do so before these formal steps were finished. Thus, it is not free from doubt that Franklin's Christmas Day letter in the press was itself so powerful

statement thus far about these developments, can be inferred from the spate of letters to the press that were published following Franklin's Christmas Day surprise. Letters and "paragraphs"[22] attacking Franklin for his misuse of the Hutchinson letters poured into print in the weeks following his own revelations and they continued through 1774. Quite a few are unsigned or attributed to names with stylized appearance. So many were unsigned in fact that collectively they suggest an organized effort to discredit Franklin.

One such letter, published in early January, 1774, made several hard-edged points in a very few lines of doggerel:

> To: Dr. Franklin:
> Thou base, ungrateful, cunning, upstart thing!
> False to thy country first, then to thy King:
> To gain thy selfish and ambitious ends,
> Betraying secret letters writ to friends:
> May no more letters through thy hands be passed,
> But may thy last year's office be thy last."[23]

Betrayal of royal office carries, the writer concluded, its own just desserts. Not only is such a person ungrateful for that honor, but he is also himself selfish and ambitious. The writer suggests that Franklin's motive was not what his own public letter had claimed, although there is no suggestion here of what that motive otherwise might be.[24]

---

a goad to official action, yet together the two events seemed to many merely to confirm the worst fears about each of them.

22 The newspapers of the time carried signed and unsigned pieces, whether of news or opinion or sometimes both in one. The smaller such items, typically unsigned, were identified then in common parlance as "paragraphs."

23 *General Evening Post*, London; 11 January 1774; reprinted in Verner W. Crane, ed., *Benjamin Franklin's Letters to the Press, 1758–1775* (Chapel Hill, Univ. of N.C. Press, 1950, page 239. The style of these lines of verse bears a surprising resemblance to that of Robert Burns, most beloved of Scots poets who also lived in the 18th century. Consider, for example, this poem of Burns' entitled "To a Louse" (On Seeing One on a Lady's Bonnet at Church): "Ye ugly, creepin, blastit wonner, Detested, shunn'd by saunt and sinner; How daur ye set your fit upon her— Sae fine a lady! Gae somewhere else and seek your dinner...." See www.About. com.Quotations. Burns' writings, songs and poems, emerge in print themselves in the next decade after these events in London. Perhaps it was a style that had already captured popular attention, at least among the Scots of whom there were quite a few in London. Notable among them was Alexander Wedderburn, the man Franklin would later face in his trial. See Chapters 5 and 6 below.

24 It will be useful to bear this point in mind when at trial the solicitor general claims that Franklin wanted to be governor of Massachusetts himself. See Chapter 6, "Showdown in the Cockpit." What might the writer have meant by "false to thy country first"? Would there be any point in distinguishing "King"

Some of the shorter, unsigned pieces repeat epithets perhaps heard in the streets and coffee houses of London, such as the "Old Treachery of Craven Street" and "The Hoary Old Sinner." Almost a full year later another contribution to the press calls the agent "the great Dr. Franklin, the American Seer" who protests in the "prints" of London against taxation on the colonies "but spirits up the Americans by his letters...to throw off their allegiance."[25]

OTHER ADVERSARIES

If there were any readers of London's papers in January of 1774 who thought what Franklin had done was an understandable action, let alone a commendable one, it was not reflected in the pages of these papers. His friends and admirers would have been at least nonplussed, if not shocked, by what he had revealed.[26] They would not be sending off letters of support, certainly.

It is plausible to suppose that the principal themes of these letters of outrage would reflect the views of official London. Perhaps then some or many of these stridently negative letters in fact did come from the desks of ministers, sub-ministers or their associates.[27] Verner Crane in his landmark study of the London press in the 1760s to 1775 labels such writers "ministerial hacks" and points to one in particular who used the pseudonym "SAGGITARIUS" in one paper, *The Public Ledger*, frequently to "flay" the Bostonians and their agent, Franklin.[28]

As it turned out, the writer using Saggitarius as his nom de plume was a man named John Mein who had been printer of the *Boston Chronicle* some years earlier where he was much abused for his opposition to the efforts of

---

from "country" if England were the reference? If "thy country" meant colonial America, the writer was making a more subtle point of political significance: namely, that Franklin's dispatch of the Hutchinson letters could only serve to create or augment tensions, not quiet or compose them, as Franklin had said he sought to do. All in all, it was a concise summary of what would become the solicitor general's rationale for the charges against Franklin.

25 *Public Ledger*, December 10, 1774, p.1, col.3. Reported in Crane, *Letters to the Press*, id. at xxxii.

26 See Chapter 8, "Circles of Support," for some of the friends' private letters about the affair.

27 That so few chose to use their real names, though, is puzzling, but a few notable writers did so. For example, Ben Johnson and Horace Walpole.

28 Verner Crane, Benjamin Franklin Letters to the Press, 1757–1775, id. At page xxvii–xxviii.

the locals to boycott British goods made more expensive and objectionable under the Townshend Acts. The example of Mein suggests that there were people in London apart from those with ministerial authority at that time who were just as ill disposed toward Franklin or what he apparently represented. Indeed there were and any number of them might have been responsible, directly or not, for the outpouring of castigation Franklin experienced after his revelations over the Hutchinson letters.

An Arc of Resentment

While any number of "ministerial hacks" could have been at work in publicly condemning Franklin, there is no known evidence of any concerted effort of the kind. As we shall see, the events of January of the next year speak for themselves well enough as to the government's attitude toward Franklin. But if there was any deliberate and sustained effort to "try" him in the press before the formalities were carried out, the evidence to support the existence of such plan is sketchy at best.

It is just as plausible to suppose that at least some, perhaps much, of the negativity toward Franklin was spontaneous. Not necessarily from "every day Londoners" but from those few (thousands) who did read either the daily papers or the trice-weeklies. Among these would have been persons who Franklin would recognize were not his friends. What is significant about them, of ones we can readily identify, is that their experiences with Franklin over the years of his second and third London residences, 1758–62 and 1764–75, reflect the breadth of his dealings and the cross-currents swirling near him.

The nucleus of any cluster of enemies or detractors of Franklin would include three influential persons or their associates and followers. First among these would be George Grenville (d. 1770), formerly prime minister and chief sponsor if not architect of the Stamp Act of 1765. A likely second was Lord Hillsborough, predecessor to Dartmouth as colonial secretary for North America. Then there is Thomas Hutchinson himself, the much troubled just replaced royal governor of Massachusetts.

Grenville had had to swallow hard at the repeal of the Stamp Act in 1766. It is said that he greatly resented the fact that while Franklin had gone along with the tax at its inception—and Thomas Whately, Grenville's principal assistant at the Treasury, had even solicited names from Franklin of likely distributors for the stamps in Philadelphia—in the end Franklin's bravura performance in the House of Commons that year insured its repeal.[29] While George Grenville died in 1770, those associated with him as hard-liners of the ministry in the 1760s, had not forgotten the role that Franklin played in their parliamentary defeat. Among those still in Parliament and waiting their opportunity for return or revenge would include Charles Jenkinson a staunch Grenville supporter and close ally of Lord Bute before him. Any of them would have been capable, certainly motivated, to seize on the Christmas Day disclosures to disparage their adversary and nemesis.

Just as plausible, perhaps more so because of more recent scores to settle, would be Lord Hillsborough himself. Lately resigned from his post as colonial minister for the American colonies, it is no secret that he was bitter about what happened in the Privy Council only a couple of years before. That was the occasion when Vandalia [or Grand Ohio Project, a.k.a., the Walpole Company] project, a very large grant proposal south of the Ohio River, was being considered after so many years of delay. Franklin was one of the stockholders. Hillsborough's recommendation to deny royal approval of the grant because the Grenville ministry had determined to restrict or close settlement west of the Alleghenies was soundly rejected in the Privy Council on July 1, 1772. The outcome was attributable in no small measure, or so Hillsborough believed, to the machinations of Franklin.

If that were not enough to embitter the former colonial minister, there were other incidents in which the two men had rubbed each other decidedly the wrong way. Personally significant was the occasion when upon presenting his appointment as agent for the Massachusetts assembly to Hillsborough Franklin encountered a haughty rejection from the minister.[30] The agent's reaction was an angry one, calculated to sting. Franklin, reaching with his hand for the letter of appointment so far unread by Hillsborough,

---

29 Indeed it was this timely and authoritative speech, really a series of questions and lengthy answers, which most singularly accounts for Franklin's reputation as an effective spokesman for the colonial "cause" up to the time of the events in this study. It was probably helpful to him in gaining the Massachusetts post five years later. Equally ironic just prior to this success in the House of Commons, Franklin's stock in both Boston and Philadelphia was at a low ebb owing to his participation in the start up of implementation of the Stamp Act the year before.

30 While this encounter between Franklin and Lord Hillsborough occurred at a very heated moment in the affairs of Massachusetts, riots in opposition to the Townshend duties, it is likely that the earl's irritable disposition was also responsible. See Chapter 9, "Other Perils and Aftershocks," for information about Hillsborough's reputation among other peers.

said: "I beg your lordship's pardon for taking up so much of your time. It is, I believe, of no great importance whether the appointment is acknowledged or not, for I have not the least inception [*sic*] that an agent can at present be of any use to any of the colonies...."[31]

Hillsborough subsequently shared with others his indignation over Franklin's jab. It seems not a little likely that Hillsborough would have shared the sentiments expressed in those letters of rebuke of Franklin published in late 1773 and early 1774.

Then of course there were the London friends of the Massachusetts governor himself, Thomas Hutchinson. He was not yet in London by December 1773, but he would arrive there, having been relieved by General Thomas Gage as governor of the colony, in early summer of 1774. Even prior to that arrival, however, and just after the news broke about publication of Hutchinson's letters in Boston, many angry letters had appeared in London papers denouncing their theft and publication. Indeed, these letters had led to the accusations and denials between the heirs of Thomas Whately and William Temple. But for these public accusations against Temple, it seems probable that the duel would never have been demanded and accepted.[32]

Like Hutchinson, too, Francis Bernard, before him, had been forced out of office by the efforts of the Massachusetts malcontents, and he was also present in London at the time the letters affair came to light. Bernard had been personal agent for Hutchinson in London for a time.

One additional candidate for inclusion in the short list of influential Franklin enemies would be Thomas Penn, senior heir of the founder William, who for many years had been able to resist his efforts on behalf of the House of Burgesses in the proprietary colony of Pennsylvania to have the charter changed in important ways or, more ambitious still, have the charter re-issued as a royal one, under the direct charge of institutions of government not controlled by a single family. Franklin bore the brunt of the

---

31 From enclosures of personal notes in Franklin's letter to Samuel Cooper of February 5, 1771, *Papers*, vol. 18, page, as quoted in Van Doren, pages 384–87.

32 At least one scholar has paid particular attention to the weight and character of letters in this the age before telegraph, telephone or radio. See Christopher Looby, "Franklin's Purloined Letters," *Arizona Quarterly* vol. 46, no. 2(1990), at page 2: "If words were the form that the exercise of imperial power had to take, then resistance to that power also necessarily took the form of linguistic performance. Franklin's interference, in the affair of the Hutchinson letters, with the transmission of messages between colony and crown is a promising site for the examination of these issues."

irritation generated in London in the pursuit of these aims, for there were powerful family interests arrayed against him and few ready openly to support them.

Whether in fact any of these groups included the writers of these particular letters, it has to be said, has not been established. All the same, such sentiments were certainly present among members of all three camps.[33]

How very swiftly conditions had changed in that London autumn of 1773. While his hand in the Hutchinson letters affair was hidden, Franklin could contemplate the larger effects of his risky initiative with detachment. Popular reaction in Boston had been sharp and immediate and not a little alarming. Mob violence was always frightening to Franklin,[34] yet he trusted that those in high authority in the end would act reasonably when not provoked too much. In December, provocation in the government was not yet evident. For the moment what the fuss in London was about was the sanctity of private correspondence and papers.[35]

Now with his very prominent part revealed by his own published admission, Franklin endured a furious barrage of criticism. It would have comforted him very little to suppose that some, even many, of these attacks were from persons already ill disposed toward him. Even so, judging by his personal papers and letters, there is no evidence of any considerable disquiet in Franklin during this time, late 1773 and early January 1774. In fact, of the several letters he composed in January prior to the showdown in the Privy Council on January 29, only two contain some treatment of the affair.

---

33 There is more. Scholarship about the colonial agents themselves, while limited, does examine the irritation arising in London about them, Franklin plus a handful others, during this period. See, for example, *Rope of Sand: Colonial Agents, British Politics and the American Revolution* by Michael G. Kammen (1968).

34 Living near but not on the frontier in Pennsylvania, especially during difficulties between settlers and the native-American tribal communities there, Franklin was alert to the fragility of order in such a society. More recently he had heard from his own wife Debbie about the threat to her security and that of their home brought on by the riots against the Stamp Act and his own willingness to help with its implementation by naming friends to the position of stamp officers.

35 The opening of other people's mail was not that rare in the age of letter writing, perhaps not a routine practice but not uncommon either. It was not yet publicly acknowledged, apparently. But see Horace Walpole's experience as reflected in a letter to a friend in 1764: "As my letters are seldom proper for the post now, I ... am forced to trust to chance for a conveyance." *Horace Walpole's England as His Letters Picture It*; page 175; edited by Alfred Bishop Mason (1930). Nor was it acknowledged at the time that private letters and other papers were sometimes copied and sold in the city's black market. See Bernard Fay, *Benjamin Franklin: Apostle of Modern Times* (1929).

He wrote one letter to Thomas Cushing in Boston and one to his son William, both dated January 5, 1774. The letter to William contains the more direct admission of some discomfort: "This [sending the Hutchinson letters to Boston] has drawn some censure upon myself, but as I grow old, I grow less concerned about censure when I am satisfied that I act rightly...."

In his letter to Speaker Cushing his concession is more guarded: "I am told by some that it was imprudent in me to avow the obtaining and send-ing those letters, for that the administration will resent it, but if it happens I must take the consequences."[36]

THE TOLL FROM OTHER WRITINGS

Shocking as it was, Franklin's revelation in the Christmas Day surprise cannot by itself account for the quick and numerous condemnations pub-lished in its immediate wake. A considerable disposition to distrust or to resent the writer must have already been present in that London press read-ership of late 1773. Reasons are not far to find.

Indeed Franklin's pen had been at work almost continuously in the ear-lier months of that year. Much of his outpouring centered on the news of events as they unfolded in the colonies, especially Massachusetts with its very assertive protests to the changes in imperial policy. Three composi-tions in particular underscore the extent to which Franklin had taken his commentary even while maintaining that his fellow colonials remained loyal subjects of the British Crown. They were ready to resume their affec-tion, the agent contended, and respect of the King's authority. What was missing was a better understanding of the American view of things and a willingness to respect the older traditions in colonial governance.

To move that understanding along, to promote that respect, he was will-ing to try some very distinctive literary devices as variations on his usual po-lemical essay style. Whether the agent succeeded in those aims is doubtful, but the work certainly garnered attention and comment. In neither of these essays did the agent use his real name, but it was no secret in the London of those autumn days in 1773 who the author was in fact.

In his "Rules by Which a Great Empire May be Reduced to a Small One" Franklin adopted a bitingly satirical style in the fashion of Jonathan Swift.[37]

---

36 Vol. 21, Papers of Benjamin Franklin, pages 5–9.
37 Printed in *The Public Advertiser*, September 11, 1773; BFP, Vol. 20, page 391.

The frame for the piece was an imaginary set of rules that a minister for the colonies might have adopted for himself upon assuming that office. Franklin's reference without naming him was most probably Lord Hillsborough, minister for the colonies from 1768 until 1772. In this lengthy composition the agent goes over a complete list of accumulated grievances that the colonies, especially Massachusetts, were building ever since the Townshend Duties were put into place and the various attempts thereafter to see to their effective enforcement. Here is a sample of the "rules," which numbered twenty altogether.

> IV. However peaceably your colonies have submitted to your government, shewn their affection to your interest, and patiently borne their grievances, you are to suppose them always inclined to revolt, and treat them accordingly. Quarter troops among them, who by their insolence may provoke the rising of mobs, and by their bullets and bayonets suppress them. By this means, like the husband who uses his wife ill from suspicion, you may in time convert your suspicions into realities.[38]

Several of the "rules" dealt with taxation, for example one admonishes the minister:

> ...never to regard the heavy burdens those remote people already undergo...for their own provincial governments...for roads...bridges... and other public edifices.... [And] forget the restraints you lay on their trade for your own benefit.[39]

> XII. Another way to make your tax odious is to misapply the produce of it [so that if it was intended to pay for defense, then apply it instead to augmented salaries or pensions of governors and thereby make the colonials more unwilling to pay it and thereby induce quarrels with those who collect the taxes and so on, contributing] to your main purpose of making them weary of your government.[40]

The colonies previously were accustomed to paying the governor from their own legislative appropriations thereby making the executive more responsive to the people's representatives. London abrogated this arrangement in 1769, as we saw in the previous chapter, at the time of Francis Bernard's resignation as governor of Massachusetts and at his urging. The matter remained a sore point throughout the run-up to independence.

---

38 Id at 392.
39 Id at 394.
40 Id at 396.

There was even a rule given over to the demeaning employment of regular naval personnel in aid of enforcement of an aggressive customs policy, thus:

> XV. Convert the brave honest officers of your Navy into pimping tide-waiters and colony officers of the Customs. Let those who in time of war fought gallantly in defense of the commerce of their countrymen, in peace be taught to prey upon it. Let them learn to be corrupted by great and real smugglers; but (to show their diligence) scour with armed boats every bay, harbour, river, creek, cove or nook throughout the coast of your colonies, stop and detain every coaster...tumble their cargoes ... and if ... pins be found un-entered [i.e. without customs declaration], let the whole be seized and confiscated. Thus shall the trade of our colonists suffer more from their friends in time of peace than it did from their enemies in war....[41]

From "insolence of troops" to "suspicions of revolt" to "pimping tide-waiters ... of customs," it is clear that Franklin was not holding back his frustrations. He neatly converted well-known complaints and grievances into slingshots of invective that even in the robust journalism of the time must have shocked or offended many of his readers. Not least, we may suppose, those who occupied positions of authority in the government. At that time, however, there was little done or said—publicly—by the ministry. Not immediately, anyway.

Less than two weeks following publication of the "Rules," there was another essay, this one altogether different in style, not a sarcastic reframing of the issues but pure allegorical satire. Probably the cleverest of his journalistic essays, this was a brilliant hoax entitled "An Edict of the King of Prussia."[42] In it Franklin pretends that Frederick II has reclaimed an ancient title by way of settlement or colonization in Britain by Germans and thereby seeks to enforce upon the current inhabitants of these islands the duties and allegiances due him as sovereign of their land. Franklin in effect turns the posture of the current imperial impasse on its head and puts the British in the place of the Americans as "colonials" who without any representation in Prussia nevertheless owe certain duties to its king.[43] We do not have to imagine what the immediate effect was in London, at least among

---

41 Id at 397.

42 Printed in *The Public Advertiser*, September 22, 1773.BFP: Vol. 20, page 414.

43 What apparently gave the frame of the piece credibility and currency is that Frederick, as reported in the London press, had really acted this way toward certain portions of Poland and Holland in recent times. See editors note in BFP, Vol. 20, page 413.

some readers, for in a letter written later to son William, Franklin describes the scene he was part of when the newspaper was brought in and shown round to his companions, causing shock giving way to wry amusement in the course of some minutes.[44] The newspaper edition that printed the essay sold out and there were repeat printings in days to follow. It was a notable publishing success.[45]

The author and his cause, whatever the momentary notoriety, could not have been so fortunate. Franklin himself expressed the view later that the official resentment at these essays[46] was every bit as responsible for the heavy-handed treatment he would receive after the disclosure of his involvement in the Hutchinson letters affair as that episode itself.[47]

> The two essays had a single purpose, to induce the public to take a fresh look at the American problem. When Parliament reconvened in the autumn, that problem promised to be a major subject of discussion; and the sensational demand from Massachusetts for the removal of Hutchinson and Oliver was sure, when it came before the Privy Council, to provoke a storm. Moderate counsels could never prevail unless the folly of past measures was exposed, and Franklin devoted himself to exposing it.[48]

Thus do the editors of the Franklin papers interpret the moment and the cast of mind of the agent. But of course purpose is one thing, effectiveness of the effort is quite another, so we may concur with the editors:

> Satire is a poor instrument of persuasion. The open-minded are likely to be entertained—perhaps shocked—rather than convinced [while] the close-minded [are likely to be] angered.[49]

---

44 Letter to WF, October 6, 1773. *Papers*, vol. 20, page 436.

45 "These odd ways of presenting matters to the publick view sometimes occasion them to be more read, more talked of and more attended to." Letter from Franklin to Thomas Cushing, September 23, 1773. Papers, vol. 20, page 419.

46 The third piece was not nearly as sensational but did serve to put Franklin very squarely on the side of the dissenting views of the Bostonians on disagreements then coming to a head there between the royal governor on the one hand and the Boston Town meetings and eventually the House of Representatives as well, on the other—this in the summer of 1772. The Preface to the Resolutions of the Boston Town Meeting, published in London in June of the next year. *Papers*, Vol. 20, page 82.

47 Letter printed *in The Pennsylvania Gazette*. April 20, 1774; *Papers*, Vol. 21 at page 96, attributed to Franklin, although it did not bear his name. The writer reasoned that the ministry had not earlier taken public offense to these writings in an effort to avoid giving their excesses additional notice and scrutiny.

48 Editors, *Papers*, Vol. 20. Page 390.

49 Ibid.

Chapter 5. Preliminary Hearing

The Empire Strikes Back

The blustery December storms of outrage cleared dramatically in January. It soon became apparent that more was taking place off-stage, so to speak, than the sentiments expressed in the newspapers would suggest by themselves. Along with the clearing, Franklin would soon face the much colder effects of official action and plans.

John Dunning by Joshua Reynolds. Courtesy of National Portrait Gallery, London. ©National Portrait Gallery, London

Scarcely three days after he had written to his son William in New Jersey and to Speaker Cushing in Boston, disclosing what he had done, the Lords' Committee on Plantations of the Privy Council issued a summons informing Franklin that the petition from the Massachusetts House would be heard forthwith. The notice was dated January 8. The hearing was to be held on the eleventh. It directed Franklin to attend.

From its presentation to Dartmouth in August until now, Franklin had been in the dark about the course the petition for the governor's removal had taken. It had lain for some months with one of the King's secretaries before it was lodged with the Privy Council on December 3, 1773. The Christmas season slowed the process somewhat, but in January official processes moved along with uncharacteristic speed.

On the 10th of January the agent received an additional jolt. One day before the scheduled hearing another notice arrived informing Franklin that he should expect to face lawyers for the governor in that proceeding. One Israel Maudit, London agent for Governor Hutchinson, had elected to be represented by counsel. Franklin was now on formal notice that this was to be no ordinary administrative hearing. Maudit explained at the hearing that he was not acquainted with conditions in the colony, nor did he feel equal to the abilities of his adversary, the representative for the House of Representatives of Massachusetts.

If he had not seen before this time what was coming, Franklin certainly reacted appropriately now. What actually occurred on the 11th of January proved to be an anti-climax. Arriving without a lawyer of his own, Franklin was informed he could retain one for himself or elect to proceed without assistance, as he might choose. Seeing for the first time that counsel for the governors would be the Crown's solicitor general, the agent said he desired to have counsel. How much time would Dr. Franklin require? Three weeks was the answer, and the matter was set then to be heard on the 29th of January.[50]

Just prior to this event, the first formality in the chain of serious confrontations with colonial disobedience that the ministry and parliament would stage in the first three months of 1774, Franklin had consulted with long-time colleague William Bollan. Bollan was his counterpart as agent in London for the Massachusetts Council or upper house of the colony's legislature. Before coming to the preliminary hearing on the 11th, Bollan had

---

50 Actually, there was an experienced lawyer with him that day at the Privy Council on the eleventh. William Bollan, a London solicitor, was also the agent in London for the Council of Massachusetts, effectively an upper house of the legislature or an advisory body to the Governor. He had previously served as agent for the colony's government as a whole, having been approved by the House, Council and the governor. Franklin had conferred with Bollan right after his first notice of the eighth of January. Bollan had suggested then that counsel not be retained in that the matter was political in nature and not legal, hence there was little help a lawyer could render. On the other hand, Bollan did offer to appear and offer support of the Council to the cause of Franklin's client, the Massachusetts House. Interestingly the chair of the Privy Council Committee ruled that Bollan could not speak for the House in that he was agent for the Council, which had not joined in the petition for removal.

advised Franklin that legal counsel would not be of any particular utility in connection with the petition. And Bollan had plenty of experience with matters coming before the Privy Council, although he had probably rarely if ever encountered the Crown's second chief legal officer there for any purpose.

Something more, beyond the solicitor general's presence, occurred at the hearing on the 11th that moved Bollan to change his advice to Franklin and urge the retention of counsel. That was the explicit reservation by the barrister for the governor, Alexander Wedderburn, until the postponed hearing, of an opportunity to inquire into the details of the Hutchinson letters themselves, notably how they were acquired and to whom they were sent. Here, Mr. Bollan could see more clearly what was developing.

While Wedderburn had waived any demand for proof of authenticity that might be made as to the copies Franklin would present as the foundation for the House's resolution and petition, the way was being prepared for more strategic moves. Bollan could readily see that Wedderburn was determined to lay bare who had obtained them and perhaps other details of the cooperation necessary for the letters to be received, circulated and published in Boston. That determination would of course involve the agent more deeply in the scandal than his own disclosures to date had done.

As a friend or at least a colleague in the affairs of the colony, Bollan knew that Franklin would be facing no ordinary advocate in the person of Alexander Wedderburn, the Crown's own solicitor general. Moreover, the solicitor general's presence there was not the only sign that the wind was up. Whatever initiative had brought this particular barrister (member of Lincoln's Inn, often an advocate in the King's courts, and a royal office holder) to the Cockpit that day, there was a sizable attendance of lords as well, presumably due to the notoriety of the case. The crowd of members was larger than anyone could recall for meetings of the Privy Council or one of its committees.

Two seemingly minor points in the developments of January are worth underscoring. One is that the notice to Franklin of January 10th indicated only that the agent for Governor Hutchinson had elected to be represented in the proceeding by legal counsel. The notice did not say who that lawyer would be. The second point is that we do not know when or how the choice of the Crown's legal officer (second only to the Attorney General in rank and authority) was made. Yet, there he was when the Privy Council committee opened its proceedings on the 11th of January.

Israel Maudit was the personal London agent for Governor Hutchinson, and in that capacity he could speak for him. Instead, Maudit said he had elected to have legal representation. Why he said anything more than that, we are not told, but Maudit explained, according to the transcript, that he knew well "Dr. Franklin's abilities and wished to put the defense of my friends upon a parity with the attack. He will not wonder that I chose to appear before your lordships with the assistance of counsel...."

It is doubtful that Maudit really meant to flatter the agent with such words. Franklin, we know, was not trained in the law. It seems likely that he was as aware as others present that the election to engage counsel was extraordinary for such proceedings and so some explanation was called for.

Why did Maudit choose this particular advocate? Did he act under directive of his principal, Governor Hutchinson? Did Maudit ask the ministry for assistance? Did the ministry or one of its chief officers like Dartmouth suggest the choice? Did Wedderburn volunteer for the role? Does it matter?

Carl Van Doren's answer is straightforward: "That the solicitor-general had been chosen to defend the governor was evidence of what the ministers wanted. He was the government's master of abuse."[51] If that is an accurate assessment, the question of Maudit's involvement melts away of course. Perhaps events simply moved so swiftly that the cast of characters necessarily changed with the events.

Perhaps, too, early on the agent for the governor had in mind a choice of private counsel. And it is certainly possible that Governor Hutchinson had already instructed his agent about such a choice, although that seems unlikely given the uncertainty, earlier, about the progress of the petition and the rapidity with which the matter came to a head once the process started.

The greater likelihood is that the choice of counsel for the governor was indeed that of the ministry, as Van Doren has claimed. That assessment seems supported by contemporaneous developments of late December. By the 23rd, the government had received reports from the East India Company in American ports of preparations being made to resist the landing of its tea cargoes. Then, on December 25th, Franklin's own surprising revelations

---

51 Van Doren, p. 464. Wedderburn's reputation for ill-temper likely came early in his career as illustrated in the incident described in Chapter 6, "Showdown in the Cockpit," note 5.

appeared, in full view of the public, in the very face of imperial authority at its core. Why would not those managing the petition for removal of its royal governor in the Massachusetts Bay Colony opt for strong and experienced counsel to defend collective interests of authority? Why not indeed.

Additional assaults on authority were already underway. Two portentous developments, independent of each other, revealed themselves between the preliminary hearing of the 11th of January and the full hearing scheduled for the 29th. One demonstrated how much legal trouble the agent was in already. The other added tremendous weight to the gravity of the unrest in Boston and likely compelled the government in the direction that soon it took.

If nothing else had set the ministry full tilt into a strongly coercive mood, the news of the Boston Tea Party, reaching London on January 27th certainly would have provided the extra inducement. As it was, news that the colonists had destroyed a considerable amount of private property in front of helpless royal customs officials and in apparent contempt of the authority of Governor Hutchinson was only the last of a string of outrages flying in the face of the ministry in just as many weeks.

It would have been of little reassurance to the ministry that the agent for the Massachusetts House was himself stunned by the violence in Boston harbor. So chagrined by the resort to destructive protest was Franklin that he offered not long thereafter to pay for the tons of tea himself, if that gesture would restore the balance of things. But the offer would have little or no effect on the climate of opinion in January of 1774.

Troubled though he was by the nasty turn of events back in Massachusetts, Franklin had to be more immediately concerned with his own fate. The prospect of being arrested or otherwise held accountable in a new and totally unexpected way suddenly loomed before him. Between the preliminary hearing on the 11th and before the full hearing on the 29th, a private lawsuit was filed naming him as defendant. *Whately v. Franklin*, a "bill in equity" could provide the Whately family scarcely anything in a monetary award, yet it might force Franklin's hand in a way he could not have prepared himself for up to this point.[52]

What is significant for present purposes is that while a private person brought the proceeding in Chancery Court, coming as it did at the same

---

52 The Chancery Court case will be discussed more fully in Chapter 9, "Other Perils and Aftershocks."

time as the Privy Council hearing was immediately in prospect, the appearance of a coordinated effort to corner Franklin begins to emerge. He begins to look more and more like the symbol for, if not the central actor in, the increasing effrontery of disloyal or seditious British subjects. Not merely in the colonies, but right under the very noses of imperial authority and within the circle of trusted officials.[53]

Was this in fact what the ministry was thinking in January of 1774? Key ministers had clearly become alarmed by events, not least by Franklin's own revelations. That he chose publicly to explain, rationalize, or defend what he had done in the Hutchinson letters affair may have served to compound his misdeed. If the agent's acts were not motivated by a desire for personal advancement, as the Crown's lawyer would argue before the Privy Council, they clearly looked to some ends beyond those which would uphold the authority of government as then established. The authority of British rule now seemed so directly challenged that anything less than a forceful reaction would be unimaginable.

Franklin Chooses Counsel

Initially it was not clear to Franklin how legal advice or representation could help him or his cause. After the preliminary hearing of January 11, 1774, it was a bit clearer to him and certainly to friendly on-lookers that he himself might need assistance even if the petition to remove the royal governor would not likely be advanced in any way.

The coming proceedings themselves could not result in a conviction for any crime, for Franklin had not been charged with a crime, and this was not the Court of King's Bench. Nevertheless, if he gave any testimony on the issues that Wedderburn had opened up in the "preliminary hearing," that testimony could well lead to filing of charges not only against him but also others that Franklin's testimony might implicate. At some level of understanding, Franklin sensed this. At least one person present on January 11th urged him to obtain counsel for what was to come.

The way was being prepared for the agent to have to go beyond his Christmas Day surprise, admitting that he had sent the letters back to Bos-

---

53 The language of the time had, like our own, several names or degrees of disloyalty, short of treason itself. Our modern equivalent of "sedition" would likely be subversion, though they are not of course quite the same thing. For convenience and consistency the political vocabulary of the time will be preserved here.

ton, and thereby make a prosecution more likely or at least facilitate one if the ministry later chose to initiate it. At the very least, Wedderburn hoped to learn the names of others involved. In either case, Franklin was decidedly on the horns of a dilemma. If he played along with Wedderburn, he would betray friends or allies and breach his promise of confidence. And should he decline to do that, there could well be other consequences, which he could not foresee.

The very question of what "playing along" might mean, however, was apparently never brought up, certainly not with correspondents or even, as far as we know, with legal counsel. In today's settings of trials, political or routinely criminal in nature, such a dilemma would likely generate at least an inquiry from the "defense" counsel to the "prosecution" to see what that side might accept in return for cooperation with the government.

All of this, however, merely illustrates one way in which counsel might assist or could suggest such assistance to the agent. That is why people in jeopardy of course do seek legal advice, when they become aware of it. Franklin's problem at this point was simpler. To whom should he turn in the first place?

In the following days Franklin was hemmed in by a number of factors that made his choice complicated and contingent. The time it took to make the choice and relate his activities to prospective counsel used up a great deal of the interval he had left before his scheduled second appearance before the Privy Council. The search itself demonstrates how awkward all of this was for him and also affords some little window on the ambiguity of the legal context of the whole episode.

Actually, there were three distinct stages in Franklin's search for a lawyer. In the first, the agent was unsure, almost indifferent, as to whether he would indeed secure counsel at all. During the preliminary hearing itself Franklin had addressed members of the Council on his own, after Bollan had been denied the privilege of speaking for him or the Massachusetts House. In these remarks he told the Council that he was not prepared for the use of counsel, nor did he see any good purpose legal counsel would serve given the nature of the resolution from the House of Representatives, which was already before them here in this panel of Lords.

The disallowance of Bollan's appearance, coupled with Wedderburn's reservation of the freedom to inquire as to how the letters came to be in the hands of the House of Representatives, combined to usher in the second stage of the process. Bollan then explicitly urged Franklin to secure counsel for the final hearing.

The agent had been instructed by Speaker Cushing (of the House of Representatives) to employ Mr. Arthur Lee, his alternate and successor, who was a lawyer. But Lee was not available; he was out of the city. That being the case Franklin would approach Lee's own favorite, Sergeant Glynn (1722–79), who was presently Member of Parliament for Middlesex. He had been prominent in the defense of John Wilkes some years previous. Glynn, the agent discovered, was not available as he was out of commission with disabling gout and unable to get about.

Stage three. Left without the potential services of Bollan and of Arthur Lee, and Lee's choice, too, Franklin did two things. He had already retained for other business in the past a solicitor named Thomas Life. Through him and upon the urging of friends the agent went to John Dunning, a success-ful barrister in Lincoln's Inn and a former solicitor general under a different ministry.

In the small world of English barristers John Dunning was known as quick-witted and articulate, though not particularly attractive in frame, face or voice. (The portrait of Dunning by Joshua Reynolds or one of his stu-dents was said by contemporaries to be a most "flattering" one.) His reputa-tion for success in the court room had brought him attention and referrals by an increasing number of solicitors and other barristers, not least Serjeant Glynn, too, who may have mentioned his name when Franklin's solicitor Thomas Life called.

Very close to the time that the agent had need of these services Dunning had appeared in two historically significant cases, the latter one being Som-erset v. Stueart (decided in the King's Bench in 1772), the decision that more than any other to that time determined the legal status of persons brought to the England as slaves of British subjects. Perhaps it says something about the man as barrister that Dunning appeared for the losing side in both cases, the slave in the first and for the owner in the latter one. Clearly John Dun-ning was accustomed to controversy, including wry commentary on his willingness to speak on both sides of a given issue for a fee.[54]

---

54 For a fuller exploration of Dunning's legal career, especially as it relates to the slavery cases, see *Though the Heavens Fall, The Landmark Trial That Led to the End of Human Slavery*, by Steven M. Wise (2005).

For Franklin's case Dunning saw his role as limited to two fairly narrow undertakings. He would be present at the final hearing to raise objections to Wedderburn's expected inquiry about Franklin's custody and handling of the letters. Dunning must have thought that questions along this line would be impermissible on grounds of a privilege of the agent's in respect of his promise to the others involved to keep their involvement private and confidential. In other words, the barrister conceived of something akin to the journalist's protection of his sources as the basis for his objections. Since this was not a prosecution for a crime, a claim of privilege of that sort would be problematic, although a privilege against self-incrimination could be raised.

The second part of Dunning's representation, as he conceived it, had even smaller professional scope. He would in effect repeat Franklin's contention that the basis for the Assembly's resolution was self-evident—the governors of the colony had lost the respect and confidence of his fellow colonists. There would be no effort to prove the accuracy of the developments recited in the resolution. Rather, the Lords of the Privy Council, Dunning would point out, would simply see that confidence had been lost and it would serve the purposes of the sovereign—good order in and the affection of the colony of Massachusetts—to grant the request for removal. And this is evidently what Dunning told Franklin would be the substance of his representation during the latter's visit to Dunning's Lincoln Inn chambers one day between the 11th and the 29th day of January.[55]

Mr. Dunning's view of it certainly served to streamline Franklin's case. There would be no offer of proof on any of the various gaps in what the letters had claimed was happening in the colony on the one hand and the version of reality that is portrayed in the resolution for removal on the other. Dunning evidently thought that the accuracy or truth of what was asserted in the resolution could not be established under the usual rules of courtroom evidence. These claims were too much colored, he believed, by the partisan posture of the assembly on the one hand and the governors on the other. What mattered more, Dunning implied to Franklin, were the "political reflections" of the writers of the letters—their "sentiments of government, their aims to extend and enforce the power of Parliament"—these

---

55 *Papers*, vol. 21, page 91.

would "never be considered here [in England] as offences but as virtues and merits."[56]

Dunning's estimate of Franklin's case seems overly cautious, even defeatist. We know that Dunning had himself stood where Wedderburn now stands; he was the solicitor general under an earlier administration. This, of course, was one reason, presumably, Thomas Life, Franklin's solicitor, thought that his appearance could help Franklin. Taking this case certainly would make him no friends at court or in this administration. Having agreed to appear for Franklin, however, he might have done more for him. True, political points of view were involved in the case, much more so—arguably—than any strictly legal claims and counter claims. Indeed, the whole proceeding was about sovereign prerogative or discretion, not claims based on legal right. So, it is not altogether a surprise to discover that a barrister who had served in a position of royal authority would take a narrow view of the role of counsel in such a proceeding. On the other hand, there are other points of reference with which to see the way the advice unfolded.

One is to contrast what Dunning thought and advised in comparison to what Franklin's solicitor Thomas Life thought and did. We are told that Life in his brief for use by the barrister took a more expansive view of the matter. "By this opinion [that of Dunning], great parts of the brief became unnecessary."[57] Unfortunately, copies of that brief do not survive, as far as we know. We do not know whether Mr. Life wanted to have testimony taken in Boston or in London on some of the main claims about the nature of the government actions and when various initiatives were begun, for example. Nor do we know that Mr. Life suggested that argument be made on any of the constitutional claims or assertions made by the colonists and resisted by the governors in their letters.

If we can read "constitutional" for "sentiments of government" (the latter words used by Dunning to his client), then suddenly the tone or quality of the lawyer's understanding of his case is transformed. Never mind that only Parliament and the Crown could resolve such differences of understanding. What would matter, if we assume that Life's brief was more challenging than Dunning was willing to be, is that the colonists differed on these matters from the conventional London view not a little and these differences lay at the heart of this proceeding. If those issues could be explored,

---

56 *Papers*, vol. 21, page 91.
57 *Papers*, vol. 21, page 91.

Life might have suggested in the brief prepared for barrister Dunning, at the very least, the Lords of the Privy Council could have a far wider perspective from which to consider what their advice to the King should be. If any particular issue, whether factual (what did occur on certain dates or times relevant to the rise of the King's subjects in protest there in Massachusetts) or constitutional or even political (what ministerial action was the antecedent, and when, to activities in the colonies), could be raised and argued far enough to be understood for its role in the standoff between the governor and the representative bodies in Boston, then the hearing could have been postponed. Additional time allowed for the collection of such testimony or documentary forms of evidence would have slowed the process down.

Given all we know about the times and the institutions involved, the petition probably would have been denied ultimately. Yet that delay of the proceedings could have been a huge benefit to the agent, if not to his principal in Boston. That would be a gift of time, time in which tempers in London might have subsided from the shocks of, first, Franklin's own published revelation; and, two, of news of the Tea Party shortly thereafter.

Ironically, just such a scenario did take place in 1769–70 when then Governor Francis Bernard was the subject of a similar removal petition in Massachusetts.[58] In that instance while the petition was not formally granted, eventually Bernard did resign and asked to be replaced. And of course in our case the petition was denied and Hutchinson ultimately asked to be relieved; and he was. The facts on the ground in Boston in both instances were the most powerful forces at work in deciding the fate of the royal governors. The fate of the colonial agent, however, could well have been very different had the juggernaut then in motion been interrupted on or before January 29.

In fairness it must be said that Dunning did not seem up to the job at hand, not just physically, as we learn in the next chapter, but also not suited for it either temperamentally or by conviction. It would have required a barrister much more attuned to the perspective of the colonies, as in the case of Mr. Lee whom the House leadership favored, or someone like Serjeant Gwynn more accustomed to trials with strong political overtones (like the one involving John Wilkes some few years earlier or the one for Somerset, the slave, more recently in which Gwynn appeared) and not averse to risking the displeasure of the powers-that-be. But as it was, the agent's solicitor saw something more in the case and for that Franklin seemed appreciative.

---

58 See *Papers*, vol. 21, note on page 38.

Perhaps Franklin remembered an earlier encounter, in 1758 during his previous residence in England, he had with the Privy Council when as agent for the Pennsylvania Assembly he appeared there with counsel to respond to the appeal of William Smith, a prominent supporter of the proprietary government in Philadelphia. Smith had been convicted of publishing a libel of the Assembly and was jailed briefly. The arguments on both sides of the case were broadly political. Public criticisms of the House said that they were soft on defense, owing, the defendant claimed, to the dominance of the House by Quakers. Denials by the House's lawyer of that state of affairs were coupled with the very interesting assertion that this case was really a smoke screen for the Penns, who were critical of the House for its efforts to tax their lands. The constitutional issue in the case centered on the powers of the House under the charter of the colony and how if at all those could be changed.

In the end the Council did not decide these issues, but at least it heard them. The significance for Franklin in his 1774 contest is this. Had he been represented by counsel as innovative or flexible as those he obtained for the 1758 proceeding, the fate that awaited him in the Cockpit on January 29, 1774, could well have been less the personal calamity that it was. At least his solicitor had seen the possibilities. The popular barrister, on the other hand, could not, or chose not to, take them seriously.

"Franklin Appearing before the Privy Council" by Christian Schussele. By courtesy of the Huntington Art Collection, San Marino, California.

Chapter 6. Showdown in the Cockpit

> "What marks of resentment the parliament will show, whether they will be upon the province in general or particular persons, is extremely uncertain, but that they will be placed somewhere is most certain." Thomas Hutchinson's letter of 20 January 1769 to Thomas Whately.[59]

If the term had existed in 1774, the press would surely have called this a *show trial*. Like its modern-day counterparts, the outcome could not have been in doubt. The "guilty" would indeed be punished, of course. But more importantly, the majesty and authority of the state would be re-enforced for all to see. And, to ensure greater notoriety, there could be some memorable moments of drama and entertainment, even levity. Declarations about the sanctity of traditional virtues, like loyalty and honesty, would serve to remind all of the wisdom of the collective inheritance and the endurance of institutional custom.

Caricature of Alexander Wedderburn by Robert Dighton. Courtesy of National Portrait Gallery, London. ©National Portrait Gallery, London

In all these ways, the proceeding that cool January Saturday in Whitehall, London, was certainly such a trial. Technically it was not a trial at all. It was neither criminal nor civil in legal character. Not one of the royal courts of justice, King's Bench or Common

---

59 *Papers*, vol. 20, pages 549-50.

Pleas, this was the oldest governing institution of the realm—the Privy Council of the sovereign of Great Britain and its Empire. In point of fact, this particular group of members of the Council made up only its Committee on Plantations, but it would report its findings and views to the King and full Council promptly.[60]

THE SCENE

While this was only a committee meeting of peers, and not the entire Privy Council, a casual observer could be forgiven for thinking it was a great occasion of state. Into the modest-sized building known since Stuart times (but named for Henry VIII's earlier "sports arena") as the Cockpit, where the Council held its meetings, streamed more than thirty peers (at least one duke and eight earls among them) and a considerable number of others who would be onlookers at what everyone must have expected would be a rare spectacle. Quite a few making their way into the hall would be recognized by any Londoner: the Archbishop of Canterbury, head of the Church of England, for example, and Chief Justice 1st Earl of Mansfield. Also attending was the irascible Irish Lord Hillsborough, who believed himself to have been forced out of his cabinet position by the machinations of Franklin and his partners in the Ohio Valley land grant scheme. The young Earl of Dartmouth, Hillsborough's successor for colonial affairs, was there as well as the Crown's chief minister Frederick, Lord North. Among all the peers present, only Lord Despencer, frequently in social contact with Franklin, could be counted as a friend at court that day. If they had attended, two other peers would have been upset by what was to come, Lords Shelburne and Camden, both having positive ties with Franklin.

Others who managed to get in as spectators included some of current or promising distinction. Two of these knew Franklin well: Edmund Burke,

---

60 Conceptually it is an anomaly in modern political structures, yet in Britain the Privy Council remains with limited function as a testament to that country's attachment to ancient traditions. In its time the Privy Council exercised some of all the major elements of government: legislative, administrative and judicial. Its existence goes back to at least Norman times when its members were nobles loyal to the crown whose advice, counsel and judgment served sovereign purposes in most matters of state. By the eighteenth century the Council imprimatur added weight to royal decrees as by "Orders in Council" and by affording collegial oversight to appeals of all sorts from imperial possessions beyond the seas. It reviewed colonial legislation; it provided appellate review of criminal convictions and civil judgments from the colonies in unusual cases.

M.P. and since 1770 agent for the colony of New York, and Joseph Priestly, sometime dissenting minister and scientist. Young Jeremy Bentham, legal scholar and critic, best known later in life for his espousal of utilitarianism as ethical and political philosophy, also found his way into the hall.

While it seemed certain to be a significant public occasion, exactly what lay in store no one could say with any certainty, save perhaps a few of the principals. Of these, Alexander Wedderburn, appearing as advocate for the Massachusetts governors, would have the best foreknowledge. Lord Gower, too, the president and presiding officer, would have a pretty good idea of what was to come. It is quite likely that North as well as the Earl of Dartmouth, the minister most directly concerned with colonial affairs, would have known what, in general terms, to expect. Indeed, just the previous evening, the cabinet of ministers met at Lord Gower's home.[61] Lord Camden, "who knew what was planned, refused to come" according to Carl Van Doren's recreation of the event.[62]

It is fair to conclude that what was to happen in the small meeting hall was indeed planned, if not in detail, then in outline and general thrust. The solicitor general would lead the council through a review of the sobering events of the last several years, including the destructive riots and assaults on Crown agents plus the various provocations of the radicals both in the Massachusetts House and in quite a few town meetings around the province, that led up to the current impasse with the governor in Boston. The review could be expected to lead to a motion or recommendation to the panel that the petition be denied, that the governors be commended for their steadfastness to duty in the face of continuing strife and challenges to authority and that the agent for the House should at least be reprimanded and called to account for his part in bringing the province to its current stormy state.

Whether the Crown's advocate would seek any other objective, such as a more punitive confrontation with the agent, is uncertain. We can suppose that the cabinet might have left the solicitor general to his own devices with few if any guidelines. Their restraint would be based on the fact that Wedderburn's appearance in the matter was nominally to represent the governors personally. In that role he would be free to use his judgment as to how

---

61 No correspondence or personal memoir of that cabinet meeting has come to light. Formal minutes were commenced in 1815.

62 Carl Van Doren, *Benjamin Franklin*, page 467 (Penguin Edition 1991).

best to proceed and take full advantage of the occasion. It is unclear whether the cabinet tried to take precautions with respect to what would unfold in that day's proceeding. It appears likely that Wedderburn must have had his mind set on how the thing would go. After all, he was an experienced and assertive barrister, and it would be unlikely that anything that happened in the Cockpit that day would or could happen without his willing it. The only uncertainty was whether the man's temper might get the better of him. Those who knew his courtroom or parliamentary reputation could predict that Wedderburn would go beyond where prudence would dictate.[63]

We do know that at the preliminary hearing on January 11, Wedderburn had taken pains to reserve the right to inquire into how the Hutchinson letters disappeared and by what means and to whom they were returned in Boston. Most probably Wedderburn had a strategy to elicit this informa-tion from Franklin, whether for the Crown's interests or for those of Gov-ernor Hutchinson and Lt. Governor Oliver. What that strategy might have been we can only guess now, for the proceeding did not yield the revelation of any new factual details nor any but a very last minute attempt to bring them out. Whether that aim was consciously abandoned or was simply the victim of Wedderburn's extended fury, with a corresponding loss of focus, may well be questioned. Yet the proceeding started routinely enough.

The Proceeding: "Just Deserts" or "Fall Guy"?

It began with the clerk's reading of the petition to remove the gover-nors, Hutchinson and Oliver. Since they were the foundation of the House's resolution and petition, the Hutchinson letters were also read aloud. Next the advocates would address the Council members, first John Dunning for the agent and the petitioner, the Massachusetts House of Representatives. By tradition and in deference presumably to their nobility, the petitioner's agent would stand before the panel of lords throughout the proceeding.[64]

---

63 Alexander Wedderburn was a Scot who initially practiced law as an Advocate in Edinburgh. One account of his leaving that city and coming to London has it that he lost his temper at the ruling by a judge before whom he was appearing. Asked to apologize for his incivility to the court, Wedderburn instead took off his advocate's gown, laid it down and walked out for good. There remains a firm of lawyers today in Edinburgh with his family name in it.

64 Franklin had been before the Privy Council on several prior occasions. In 1759 he was there to represent the Pennsylvania House in an appeal from a libel convic-tion of an outspoken critic who had maligned the entire House. And in 1760 he appeared before Council concerning the taxability of family lands belonging to

Franklin might have thought of other occasions when circumstances had thrust him front and center in the company of assemblies of authority, such as the time in 1766 he was "examined" at great length in the House of Commons when he supported a proposed repeal of the Stamp Act. That was a day of triumph for Franklin, however, and this one was not expected to be any such thing. Just how much of a trial it would be he could not know. Nothing like this had occurred in Franklin's life of 68 years. While he was aware of public expressions of anger at him in the press over his own acknowledged role in the letters affair and while he fully expected some official reaction, he had until this day no indication of its gravity or its very special resentment towards him.

Whatever his private mood that morning, he appeared calm and collected as he stood in the center of the hearing room. We are told that the agent wore one of his finest suits of clothing, a brown suit of Manchester velvet, and a full wig, not an adornment he often affected. Anticipating the formality of the place and in particular the robed and decorated lords before whom he appeared, the agent seemed disposed to grant whatever modicum of personal deference the occasion required.[65]

The reading of the petition by the Council's clerk would take only a few minutes, whereas the collection of letters would take a good deal longer. After that, a nod by Gower to counsel for the petitioner's agent would bring John Dunning to his feet. As it happened, Dunning spoke only briefly and with a hoarse or soft voice, barely audible more than a few feet away. Perhaps because of these conditions, Dunning did not finish what he was say-

---

the Penns in the colony. Yet another time he was there to support a request for a royal land grant in the Ohio River basin. In that case, too, Wedderburn opposed Franklin's interests.

65 The painting by Christian Schwende, 1859, now owned by the Huntington Museum of San Marion, California, purports to be a visual depiction of this scene in the Cockpit on January 29, 1774. It captures very well what we might imagine of the formality of the occasion plus an atmosphere of impending confrontation. The proceeding is about to begin. The center ground of the painting is held by the standing figure of Franklin, reasonably erect for a man of his years, his faced in composed profile. The others present are distinguished by their robes and decorations. Everyone is seated, more or less around a long table, save the agent and the crown's advocate. A few onlookers were standing in the gallery above the main floor of the hall. Some of the members and their guests are seen engaging in asides to one another. The second standing figure, presumably Alexander Wedderburn, off center to the right in the painting is bent over conferring with someone seated at the main table.

ing when counsel for Governor Hutchinson broke in and took the floor for the remainder of more than an hour of the public phase of the matter.

What John Dunning had to say in his brief statement was a simple recitation of the frame of his case: the petition consisted of a plea to the King to exercise his discretion in the interest of goodwill toward his loyal subjects in Massachusetts to replace the royal governor. Continuing, Dunning noted that the petition itself contained the only foundational material to be tendered in support of the claim that Governor Hutchinson had forfeited his legitimacy by suppressing the liberties of the King's subjects. No personal testimony or additional documents would be offered.

There was reason to believe that the petition itself would be dealt with rather more directly than it was. For example, counsel for Governor Hutchinson might simply have called for a vote of the Council, likening the state of the matter to a motion for summary judgment in a civil trial. In other words, while the petitioner might have alleged grievous wrongs, the proof was insubstantial and possibly even inadmissible as hearsay. The petition itself contained mere allegations, after all, and the accompanying letters of Hutchinson and Andrew Oliver (mere copies at that) contained opinion or sentiments, not a recitation of actions or measures implemented by either of them.

Under the circumstances, the vote on the petition might have been called for directly. Alternatively, Dunning as counsel for the petitioner's agent should have been asked whether he had anything further to offer or whether he wished to make argument on the petition as it stood. Instead, Wedderburn as counsel for the governors took over the proceeding and made a lengthy, detailed and at times highly animated speech. In it he first recounted the many disturbances in the colony since the Stamp Act riots of 1765, noting the role of the House leadership and their ties to town meetings beyond Boston in abetting these events. These misguided and irresponsible leaders, Wedderburn contended, were responsible for this contrived opposition to the royal governor that brought today's matter to the Council.

These points all led to the main thrust of the speech by the Crown's advocate, that the agent was himself at the core and center of these events. It was he who inspired the Bostonians to think of themselves as capable of their own great republic independent of Britain's authority and without him these activists in the colony could not have brought matters to their current state of civil crisis. It was the agent who sent those letters back, as he had publicly admitted, and he who thereby "set the entire province aflame."

In overall design the speech was brilliant: first, Wedderburn would show that the province had resisted British authority for some time and had done so violently; next, he would blame the local fire-brands who used their stations of local responsibility to generate disdain for the authority from which their colony sprang. Finally, he would close in on the self-disclosed boss of these radicals and show how Franklin acted dishonorably to fit his own selfish or ideological purposes.

It was a speech of much greater scope and scorn than likely would have sufficed to deny the petition. That circumstance serves to illustrate several things. First, this was no routine petition; this was no ordinary occasion. Second, there was little interest in Whitehall in finding in the petition any conciliatory opportunity, as might conceivably have been intended. Instead, the entire controversy was reduced to the simple question whether the Crown could appoint as its colonial officers persons of character who would be loyal and courageous enough to carry out the will of Crown and Parliament. If these stalwart governors were not to be backed up now, how could British authority be maintained anywhere?

Wedderburn made it abundantly clear that His Majesty was not, or those officers whose responsibility it was to advise the Crown were not, persuaded by the petition. Indeed the Crown's ministers had lost all patience with the trend of events in Massachusetts. And this displeasure would extend to the very person through whom the dissidents were represented in London. Given the strong tone of the harangue and its very personal focus on Franklin, it seems clear that the government understood the agent himself to be a principal contributor to the excesses of the outrages in Boston. The greater part of the speech, or at least the part that is most frequently denoted as heated as well as clever, was its extended attention to the agent and his duplicity and cunning. This part of the speech owes its memorable qualities to the personality of the Crown's advocate. It could only have been fashioned by a barrister of Alexander Wedderburn's temperament. He is said to have pounded the conference table quite hard with his fist during the tirade on Franklin several times, making the table "groan" under the blows.

That Wedderburn was permitted to conduct himself as he did, delivering a withering castigation of Franklin rather than focusing on the insubstantiality of the petition itself, suggests a couple of concurrent realities. One is that no member of the Council was concerned enough with appearances to intervene. Another is that for some reason Franklin's own lawyer did not raise an objection to the attack on his client as beside the point and out of order. Franklin and Dunning had not gone over the possibility of a raging personal attack as part of their forethought for the hearing.

Whether Dunning, who was hoarse with a cold, believed he could not be heard over the laughter at the spectacle or whether he thought it would be fruitless to raise an objection, we are not informed by any known account. Franklin's own recollection, in a letter to Thomas Cushing, soon afterward, serves the point well. "[N]ot one of their lordships checked and recalled the orator to the business before them, but on the contrary, a very few excepted, they seemed to enjoy highly the entertainment, and frequently broke into loud applauses."[66]

WEDDERBURN'S SPEECH

There remain several accounts of the speech and the reaction to it both in London that day and later among those who heard or read reports of the occasion. The speech itself was not published in full, but two substantial versions of it exist, one published in the same year, 1774, another five years later. The later one is thought to be more complete, although neither version carries the most outrageous of Wedderburn's words and insinuations as recalled by others who were there, including Franklin.[67]

---

66 BF to Cushing, February 15, 1774. *Papers*, vol. 21, pages 86,92. In another letter, this one to his Dutch friend, Jan Ingenhousz, who had learned of the trial and was shocked by the tone of the proceedings, Franklin seems to understand what happened. "On this occasion it suited the ministry to have me abused, as it often suits the purposes of their opposers to abuse them...." *Papers*, vol. 21, pages 147, 148.

67 The first printing was edited and published in London by Israel Maudit, Hutchinson's London agent: "The Letters of Governor Hutchinson and Lieut. Governor Oliver...with...the Proceedings of the Lords Committee of Council. Together with the Substance of Mr. Wedderburn's Speech Relating to Those Letters (1774)." The later one was edited and published by Benjamin Vaughan, "Political, Miscellaneous and Philosophical Pieces...written by Benjamin Franklin..."(London, 1779, page 341. Both versions appear, in substantial and relevant parts, in Franklin's Papers, vol. 21, pages 37-68. The historical importance of Wedderburn's speech is underscored by this estimate by the editors of the Franklin papers in our own time: "The speech constitutes the most thorough indictment in print of Franklin's conduct in the affair of the letters." *Papers*, Vol. 21, page 40.

The abuse heaped on Franklin by Alexander Wedderburn that day was extensive and intentionally demeaning. The editors of the Franklin Papers called the event "the one great public humiliation of Franklin's life."[68] Twentieth-century writer Catherine Drinker Bowen characterized the experience in these terms: "There has never, in my knowledge, except for the McCarthy hearings, been so public a disgrace of a good man more magnificently received and taken than when Franklin, nearly seventy...stood silent..."[69]

Although not much of it was relevant to the petition pending before the Council that day, Wedderburn's diatribe was loaded with political meaning. In fact a close reading of Wedderburn's hour-long speech (not unlike an opening statement by a prosecutor) reveals a set of inter-related points of substance.

Some of these were only rejoinders to Franklin's Christmas Day letter in the press. Others, the larger or more affirmative points, cover broader aspects of colonial affairs as then seen by more than a few in and around the ministry. Foremost was Wedderburn's claim that the hostility evident in the Massachusetts House of Representatives was the direct result of Franklin's sending the Hutchinson letters to the leaders of that group. In this context Wedderburn contended that: "Dr. Franklin...stands in the light of first mover and prime conductor of the whole contrivance against His Majesty's two governors...."[70] Indeed, the solicitor general rather pointedly claimed that Franklin was the origin or source of the hostility seen rising from the colony, the very hostility which produced the petition for the governors' replacement.

Faithful to his calling as an advocate and reflecting considerable preparation, the solicitor general did not leave the accusation of conspiracy with-

---

68 *Papers*, vol. 21, page 37.

69 Bowen, Catherine Drinker, *The Most Dangerous Man in America* (1974) at page 245. She was alluding, presumably, to the hearings on internal subversion in 1954, focusing in this instance on the Department of the Army defended by attorney Joseph Welch.

70 The allusion to Franklin's scientific work is one of the softer puns delivered in the speech. That work had gained the agent considerable attention among scientists—then called natural philosophers—well before this period. His experiments and proofs with the Leyden jar and with drawing electricity, lightning, from storm clouds were fully treated in a fourteen-page entry in the first edition of *Encyclopaedia Britannica* published in Edinburgh in three volumes in 1771. See Volume II, pages 471-85, facsimile edition. It was this work, principally, for which Franklin had been honored in various ways in Britain, not least by the award of honorary doctorate degrees by Oxford and St. Andrew's universities.

out supporting detail. Indeed some of the most carefully woven parts of the long speech were designed to construct a plausible account of how that conspiracy was formed and extended during the several years leading up to the affair of the Hutchinson letters. It began, so far as this sketch went, with a 1771 letter of the agent's, partially reprinted in the Boston press in September 1773, emphasizing that Franklin had intended himself to draw up a "memorial stating our rights and grievances" by which to keep alive the colonists' pleas for redress. From that beginning, Wedderburn connects Franklin to the famous Boston Town Meeting resolutions of November 20, 1772, which Governor Hutchinson characterized as a "declaration of in-dependency," upon its circulation throughout the province. Actually that document was not Franklin's work, nor did Wedderburn claim that it was, but the agent served, he argued, to inspire others in the province ready to undertake that which without the initiative of "the great man" would not have been attempted.

Some sixty or seventy town councils, according to Wedderburn's esti-mate, took up the paper and adopted various separate resolutions in sup-port. Wedderburn characterized the content of the Boston Town Meeting Declaration, soon published in Boston in pamphlet form, in these terms: it "told of a hundred rights of which they had not heard before; and a hundred grievances never felt before." Some of these resolutions were more extreme in sentiment than others, and of course the solicitor general called particu-lar attention to those. The town of Petersham had some of the most pro-vocative language looking to a redress of their grievances and support for their rights: "[T]he people are warranted in the use of every rightful art and energy of policy, stratagem and force." Wedderburn referred to this particu-lar resolution even though it did not appear in the London republication of the statement some months after its Boston printing.

Drawing the strands of his account together, Wedderburn then brought Governor Hutchinson into the matter, claiming that the governor certainly saw the folly in these claims and was determined to challenge them. And he did so on the occasion of the opening of the next (joint) session of the General Court, Council and House of Representatives, in early January of 1773, making a "very masterful speech in defense of the British American constitution." Hutchinson managed thereby, Wedderburn claimed, to stop the train of events for a time.[71] The leaders of the "faction" realized, Wedderburn claimed, they were up against a smart man in the governor and one they could not control, so they sought some means of embarrassing him! It was at this moment, the argument wound up, that the letters from Hutchinson, Oliver and the others became so useful. Making these private letters public would be the means by which the faction would topple yet another royal governor, as they had brought about the resignation of Governor Bernard several years earlier.

Here Wedderburn laid out the real meaning of the letters affair and challenged the agent's recent claim in the press. The letters, he contended, were sent back to Boston in order to provoke a sharp crisis in which the royal governor would voluntarily yield, because the King in council would not ask for resignation in the absence of any proof of wrongdoing or incompetence. Because the conspirators well knew that allegations and accusations without proof would be unavailing, they did not expect nor desire "a trial before your lordships" for "they meant to bring it before the multitude and to address their prejudices [for] [t]he mob, they knew, need only hear their Governors accused, and they will be sure to condemn."[72]

OTHER DETAILS OF THE SPEECH

That the irresponsible elements in the colony were being addressed directly from London is borne out by the fact the troops ordered into Boston a few years earlier were already on their way when the governors' letters reached London in 1768/9. Wedderburn was factually correct on that point. He was wrong, however, in claiming that the colonial assembly had not previously expressed any opposition to or frustration with the administration there.[73]

---

71 This was the same address that Dartmouth and others had found alarming and ill advised to make at such a juncture. Moreover, this is the speech which would have, we noted in Chapter Two, told his fellow colonists directly many of the things he was said to have revealed, by way of his own sentiments, attitudes and ideas, in the letters he had written earlier to Thomas Whately.

72 *Papers*, Vol. 21, pages 65-66: Speech of Alexander Wedderburn. Reprinted in *Verbatim C* following the Appendices in this work.

73 Just prior to the petition for removal of Hutchinson the Massachusetts House had sent another, complaining of the change to royal payment of the governor's salary. And before that there had been a petition about then Governor Francis Bernard's tenure. In another part of his speech Wedderburn refers to the complaint about Bernard to discredit the current petition then before Council.

Why would Franklin seek to do this, to stir up dissent and agitation where none existed? The agent had written that his purpose was to promote conciliation. The Crown advocate's second major argument was even more personal to the agent: perhaps, Wedderburn argued, Franklin had forgotten he was an agent at all and fancied that he might himself become governor in place of Hutchinson![74]

Moreover, Wedderburn went on, "Dr. Franklin's mind may have been so possessed with the idea of a Great American Republic that he may easily slide into the language of the minister of a foreign independent state."[75] Farfetched? Yes, at least as of that moment anyway. Feared? Perhaps.[76] The claim had immediate and practical use in the plan of the speech. Wedder-

---

74 While that even hypothetical claim has no known basis in fact as a foundation, it was no secret that Franklin was an ambitious man. Exactly the same thing had been said in Pennsylvania by the supporters of the Penn proprietary government when, as he did through the 1760s, Franklin as a member of the House sought to change that arrangement.

75 If there was anything grand in Franklin's ideas for the future of the American colonies collectively it is that he projected such a rapid growth in the American population the country would predictably be larger than the mother country in the span of another few generations. On that account he had sometimes written, both in his letters and in articles in the London press, that it could well be best if the colonies were recognized as a realm under the same king as that of England, sharing a union of the sort that comprised Great Britain of that time: Scotland, Ireland and England. He was not much of a political theorist, and there is no evidence that he ever employed the idea of a republic, until of course the writing of the federal constitution some fifteen years later. His thoughts were by and large conventionally monarch-centered, at least by implication. What was interesting about his ideas, though, is that increasingly during these years he emphasized how the empire he knew and regarded as highly as a "precious porcelain vase" could be composed of relatively equal realms with the same king but each with its own parliament. If there were then a heresy in his known views when Wedderburn spoke, it would be Franklin's antipathy towards and frequent contempt for Parliament, not the sovereign head of Britain and its Empire.

76 In their head notes to the report of the Cockpit proceedings of January 29, the editors of the Franklin papers call attention to the "underlying premise" of Wedderburn's speech: "It was that Franklin and his little coterie in Boston were conspiring to subvert the allegiance of the king's subjects and destroy the peace of the province. This conspiratorial interpretation of politics was widespread not only in America, where grievances were blamed on self-serving officials like Hutchinson and on evil counselors who had the King's ear, but also and to equal degree in Britain. Lord Bute [some years earlier and before North's ministry] had been and still was assailed for conspiring against the constitution, and the King had recently imputed protests from Massachusetts to the 'artifices of a few who seek to create groundless jealousy and distrust.' In Wedderburn's speech the concept of Franklin and his radical friends as a small subversive minority came to full flower." *Papers*, Vol. 21, pages 40–41.

---

burn pointed out that whatever politics Franklin "may teach the people at Boston, while he is here [in Britain], he is a British subject and answerable to the law" of Britain.[77] In other words, Franklin should expect in due course to be dealt with directly and be held accountable for his misuse of these letters.

More personal still, Wedderburn's strongest language was reserved for the means by which the letters were obtained. To do what the agent had confessed to doing, he must have either stolen them or obtained possession in some nefarious way, for he knew by whom the letters were written and to whom they were sent. And he obtained the permission of neither to thus expose them to public view. The only honorable thing he could have done, assuming he came by them innocently, was to return the letters to their recipient.

> "I hope, my lords, you will mark and brand this man for the honour of this country, of Europe, and of mankind....He has forfeited all the respect of societies of men, into what company will he thereafter go with an unembarrassed face or the honest intrepidity of virtue? Men will watch him with a jealous eye; they will hide their papers from him and lock up their escritoires. He will hence-forth esteem it a libel to be called a man of letters...."[78]

Clearly there were telling points scored in Wedderburn's tirade, as in the lines just quoted. Here the solicitor general is in effect daring the agent to explain, more fully than in his Christmas Day public letter in the news-paper, how these letters from the governors to their friend Thomas Whately could be anything but "sacred and as precious to gentlemen of integrity as their family plate or jewels." How could he possibly use them as he had done without the condemnation of honest men? And, Wedderburn went on, if the *writers'* desire to keep them secret be the test of guilt, then what of "Dr. Franklin's case, whose conduct in this affair has been secret and mysterious" and who "kept himself concealed until he nearly occasioned the murder" of an innocent man. Wedderburn was referring of course to the duel in Hyde Park in December. It is small wonder many of the lords present were moved to appreciative laughter and applause at such clever rhetorical flourishes.

Each time Wedderburn made a valid point of criticism for the agent's conduct, however, he also added an exaggeration of the facts or some gra-

---

77 Chancery Court would not, the barrister said, "much attend to his new self-created importance." Wedderburn's speech: See Verbatim C.

78 Wedderburn's speech. Verbatim C.

tuitous name-calling. Stripped of its sarcasm and meanness, Wedderburn's speech amounted, first, to a rejection of any merit in the colonists' claims. At most, in the solicitor general's view, the resolution amounted simply to an expression of unpopularity, nothing more, and that is no basis for the Crown to disturb its loyal and obedient officials in the colony. Indeed the governors stand justified by the support of the ministry's decisions in London. Second, the speech was a not-so-veiled warning of consequences to follow for this miscreant subject of the Crown who stood exposed, Wedderburn maintained, as ring-leader of the effort to discredit Parliament as though it had been preparing a plan to enslave the American subjects of the Crown.

It was of course the overlay of biting wit and condemnation by epithet that brought those present to uproarious appreciation. But for these colorful trappings the proceeding would have been pretty dull or merely serious. As it was, many of the councilors and perhaps also not a few of the onlookers must have enjoyed the whole experience. Perhaps it provided a welcome release of anger collectively building over the autumn of 1773, when one outrage followed another in the news from Boston. Franklin's Christmas Day letter to the press gave it all the little push needed to bring on the avalanche.[79]

Not everyone agreed that it was a fine show. Edmund Burke wrote that Wedderburn's attack was a "furious philippic" that transcended "all bounds and measure." Lord Shelburne wrote to Lord Chatham that it was "as agreed on all hands...scurrilous invective." John Bollan, the agent for the Massachusetts Council who was with Franklin at the preliminary hearing, recalled that the speech was "such a torrent of abuse...as never before took place within my compass of knowledge of judicial proceedings...incompatible with the principles of law...justice and humanity." A correspondent for the *Public Advertiser* in its February second edition, the following Wednesday, called Wedderburn an "unmannered railer" who employed the "coarsest language" and "licensed scurrility of the Bar."[80]

---

79 Twentieth-century British historian and Franklin biographer Esmond Wright estimated that in making his speech "Wedderburn fed on accumulated sentiments that had been building up to twenty years: of the Pennsylvania boss, of the critic of proprietary government...of the writer of anonymous articles, of the officeholder revealed as conspirator." Esmond Wright, *Franklin of Philadelphia* (1986), pages 226-27.

80 See *Papers*, vol. 21, pages 39-40, notes three and six and sources cited there.

Horace Walpole's lines of verse on the event have been frequently quoted:

> "Sarcastic Sawney, swol'n with pride and prate
> On silent Franklin poured his venal hate
> The calm philosopher, without reply
> Withdrew and gave his country liberty."[81]

Walpole's twin couplets are useful to the story in two significant ways. Whether or not its final point, "gave his country liberty," is anything more than a too large over-simplification or rhetorical flourish, it does reflect what for generations seemed a popular assessment of the episode. Namely, Franklin had been so humiliated that whatever sympathy and respect for the Empire he had possessed to that time, he realized he could do no more good; or after the trial he was merely unmoved to try.

Of secondary interest is the characterization in Walpole's lines of Wedderburn and the crucial role that he played in the grand political theater of the Privy Council. Was it merely the barrister's personal arrogance and verbosity on display that day? Perhaps the performance of the solicitor general embodied a certain degree of calculation as well. One commentator has suggested that Wedderburn saw in this trial a chance to move his political star higher: "[He had] the energy of a bold, bad man who saw a coronet [baronetcy] glittering in the eager eyes of the magnates he addressed."[82]

Of course the solicitor general was an ambitious man. Perhaps he was also unscrupulous.[83] Yet if the scene in the Privy Council reveals anything beyond self-seeking in a vain and ruthless functionary, it is that what transpired reflected settled choices of the government of Great Britain or at least those of its hardliners carrying the day.[84] And those hardliners could expect to carry some more days ahead—in Parliament as well as at court.

---

81 "Sawny" seems to have been a nickname for Alexander, as "Sandy" often is heard in modern Britain.

82 Quoted in Ronald W. Clark, *Benjamin Franklin, A Biography* (1983) at pages 241–45.

83 George III on learning of the death of his former servant some years later is reported, by the writer James Boswell, to have remarked: "My kingdom has one fewer knaves...." Boswell's source was Edward Thurlow, former attorney general and Wedderburn's superior in that office, who claims that he heard it from the King himself. See William C. Townsend, *Lives of Twelve Eminent Judges*, Volume One, pages 166–204 (London 1846).

84 "The ferocious tongue-lashing that Franklin received that day from Solicitor General Wedderburn ...was only a rhetorical exaggeration of the conclusion the government had already reached." Bernard Bailyn, *The Ordeal of Thomas Hutchinson* (1974) at page 255.

Carl Van Doren, in what was the best-known comprehensive biography of Franklin for much of twentieth century, concluded that the ministry meant to punish Franklin for it employed its own "master of abuse" in the proceeding.[85] There is no reason to believe that any other member of the bar would have been more effective in this way. It is important to consider one other reason why private barristers were not employed for or by Hutchinson through his resident agent in London, Israel Maudit.[86]

If the proceedings were expected to produce anything more useful than punishment by public humiliation, the expedient of having a Crown officer in the role could facilitate closer attention to the ministry's other needs. Wedderburn could not know that Franklin would remain silent. For all that could be anticipated, the agent might have responded with factual alternatives to the "theft" theory of the charge. If the ministry would smoke out the conspiracy some believed to exist, it could be very useful to press the one known participant while the opportunity presented itself. To discover names of others in London who assisted him would be a considerable step in exposing all those who would undermine British imperial authority.

If this tactical advantage had been a consideration in the decision to engage Wedderburn, the barrister's own excesses likely defeated that possibility. If Wedderburn expected Franklin's cooperation or that the agent might spontaneously reveal new details about the affair, the manner and length of his speech served instead to silence Franklin. Not only had Franklin stood alone and unmoved throughout the Privy Council hearing that day, he also endured frequent laughter from Council members at Wedderburn's thrusts and barbs. He could have had no illusions of any sympathy or patience remaining in that company, even if he had by the time Wedderburn was finished the energy or voice to speak.

When finally Wedderburn wound down his long and sometimes highly animated address and the applause had subsided, still on his feet he turned to the panel of lords and indicated that he was ready to "examine" the agent

---

85 See Carl Van Doren, page 464.

86 If the choice had been that of Mr. Maudit, uninstructed by the governors, he could well have chosen Wedderburn simply because he was already familiar with colonial affairs and knew some of the principals personally, such as Thomas Whately. The important remaining question is whether any other officer of the crown was involved in the decision, and the record is silent on the matter.

at that point.[87] According to Maudit's transcript, Franklin "remained silent but declared by his counsel that he did not choose to be examined."

And so the lords of the Privy Council adjourned on that anti-climax. Presumably this body would not compel the agent to answer any questions. Wedderburn did not contest the point, content by then to rest on his laurels.[88]

---

87 Maudit's semi-official version of the proceeding's transcript reports that just before indicating his readiness to examine the agent, Wedderburn concluded the speech by referring to the cover letter that accompanied the Hutchinson letters as being "anonymous" and that it was "directed to be shown to six persons only" and then: "I am prepared to enter into proof of this. I call upon Dr. Franklin for my witness..." Papers, Vol. 21, page 68. Wedderburn was manifestly wrong about the first point and incomplete on the second. Franklin did sign his cover letter, although he preferred that Cushing not identify him as the sender when showing the enclosed letters to others. While the agent had named several specific individuals to whom the letters could be shown, he explicitly left it to Cushing's discretion to identify others who could see them.

88 It is curious that Wedderburn worded the introduction to a possible exchange with Franklin the way he did. See the previous note. There was no need to establish the authorship of the cover letter, for Franklin had already publicly admitted that he was the sender. Perhaps Wedderburn wanted to make sure that the record of the proceeding included a finding of that fact established there and then, yet the copies before the Council would display Franklin's signature or name and they had already been accepted as authentic at the preliminary hearing. A couple of possible explanations can be identified. First, after such a long and wide-ranging oral argument or statement, the barrister believed he needed a technically sufficient foundation, one narrow enough to put the witness on notice of what the questioning would cover. Alternatively, Wedderburn could have used this device to shock Franklin into a denial of the obvious falseness of the barrister's assertion. In either case, had the inquiry gone forward, there surely would have been a greater scope to Franklin's examination than this opening would suggest, one thing leading to another.

CHAPTER 7. THE VERDICT

It was all there. The Crown's lawyer delivered his personal best demonstration of forensic fury and brilliance. In taking care of the King's business so demonstrably and conclusively, the ambitious barrister certainly secured his own advancement through official favor. Wedderburn could, if he allowed himself, reflect, too, that he upheld the honor of the much-maligned royal governors of Massachusetts. A former governor, Francis Bernard, was in the chamber that day and would likely have appreciated the litany of challenges of the kind he too had endured while in Boston. Perhaps the trial's featured speaker also imagined that he spoke directly to the reckless radicals of that colony and let them know that His Majesty's government would not be intimidated nor undermined through cabals and secret maneuverings.

Whatever else was intended or accomplished, the impact of that day's Privy Council proceedings fell most heavily on Benjamin Franklin. The reputation of a proud and internationally famous man of science was deliberately reduced to that of a common thief. He might just as well have been in the dock of a criminal trial as standing before Council that Saturday afternoon in January. It was all too obvious to one and all the proceeding was meant to humble a royal office holder before both the peers of the realm as well in front of some of the philosopher's own real peers, London's men of learning.

Anything that followed could only be a formality. Before documentation could be finished, however, those present that day in the Cockpit—both the principals of the drama, as well as Council members, and spectators— would pass close to one another in the ante-room of that hearing chamber before emptying into the streets of London's Whitehall. In that brief, small passage were crowded some very sharply contrasting human emotions. There was Alexander Wedderburn, glowing with self-satisfaction, standing in the midst of a clutch of well-wishers. These several score of people of rank or recognition were fresh from witnessing a stunning one-man show of ferocious indignation and political outrage laced with not a little verbal cleverness.

Meanwhile, but a few feet away, Franklin coming into the hallway spotted Priestly, took his hand briefly and without a word moved on toward the outer door. Priestly reports that he soon followed and brushed past Wedderburn as the barrister sought to speak with him. It could not have been a hurried pace, the room being so full. Even one who was intent on leaving at once could not have pushed through very quickly. But Franklin made his way deliberately, and Priestly followed him. It seems likely that his close friend accompanied Franklin back to Craven Street, given this brief encounter and their rendezvous the next day. Otherwise, he left the place as he had come—alone, but more solitary than ever he had been in all the long years he had called London his working home.

At times like these it would be understandable for anyone in Franklin's shoes to want most to be outside, even in winter, in the open and away from the close confines of that crowded meeting chamber, to breathe more fully again, striding as deliberately as accumulated fatigue would allow. There would be time enough later to recall feelings and compose reflections. Surely this slightly rotund man of 68 years, having stood still for an hour and more, would be tired, of legs if not of mind. Yet he would have walked on, cane in hand, the half-mile or less from Whitehall to Charing Cross, the Strand and down to Craven Street.[89]

---

89 At least he might have walked that distance. Given the state of London's often muddy or scruffy streets of the day, Franklin might just as well have taken a hackney cab or sedan chair, two of the customary modes for any Londoner of means. See Kirsten Olsen, *Daily Life in 18th Century London* (1999). In the previous period of his residence in London, 1757–62, he would likely have had his rented carriage wait for him, staffed by his then attentive all round personal servant Peter.

We know the state of his spirits after that exit from the Privy Council chamber and the half hour required to walk home. By that time, Franklin was composed, reflective and careful in what he wrote. And by the time of his first writing about that day, the second shoe had dropped.

Within twenty-four hours, on Sunday, January 30, Franklin received his discharge. In a brief note from his old colleague Anthony Todd, secretary to the Post Office Board, he was told very starkly that the ministry had directed he be discharged from his office as deputy postmaster for the colonies, a post he had held for twenty years. Disgrace by public abuse and humiliation—that was the real punishment, yet the firing itself was not insubstantial, even if it was predicted. Indeed, Franklin noted earlier that this is what he expected once it was revealed what role he had taken in the affair of the Hutchinson letters.

Not only did the annual stipend of his post office appointment provide principal financial support for his life in London. His work in improving and making the postal system in America profitable for Britain was a source of considerable satisfaction and pride for Franklin.

To his son, William, in New Jersey, Franklin wrote:

> This line is just to acquaint you that I am well, and that my office of Deputy-Postmaster is taken from me....You will hear from others the treatments I have received. I leave it to your own reflections and determinations upon it.[90]

And to his sister Jane Mecom of Boston who worried about his loss of income, he wrote reassuringly:

> You and I have almost finished the journey of life...and have enough in our pockets to pay the post chaises." Beyond that, though, he said: "Intending to disgrace me, they have rather done me honor. No failure of duty in my office is alleged against me; such a fault I should have been ashamed of. But I am too much attached to the interests of America and am an opposer of the measures of administration. The displacing me is therefore a testimony of my being uncorrupted.[91]

On February 15th, Franklin wrote to Speaker Thomas Cushing an extensive report on all that had happened in these last weeks. It was a remarkably nuanced letter in which he showed some personal anger over the treatment he had received. Yet, writing perhaps for history, he felt greater loss "for the public" whose "grievances cannot be redressed unless they are

---

90 Ltr. to William Franklin of February 2,1774. Papers, vol. 21, page 75.
91 Ltr. to sister Jane Mecom of February 17, 1774. Papers, vol.21, page 103.

known." "[W]here complaining is a crime, hope becomes despair," has to be one of Franklin's most quotable lines written in this whole period. More revealing, in this same letter is this kernel of prudential advice for those in authority, though it is likely more often observed in the school room than in councils of state: "Wise governments have...generally received petitions with some indulgence, *even when but slightly founded*. Those who think them-selves injured by their rulers are sometimes by a mild and prudent answer convinced of their error."[92]

Here then is at least a hint of a concession by Franklin of the weakness of the case for removal against governors Hutchinson and Oliver. All the same, he coupled that admission with larger claims and ideals: that he ex-pected more of Britain in this hour, deservedly or not. Clearly, he reckoned, this was not as prudent a government as he had hoped it would prove to be.

In these days closely following his ordeal in the Cockpit, we see Frank-lin displaying a fairly full range of emotions. In his letters home he is more philosophical than defensive. In a breakfast with old friend Thomas Priest-ly on the very next day, however, he is defiant, claiming that if he had the whole thing to do again, he would, and that this was "one of the best actions of his life."[93]

THE PETITION DISMISSED

Even as Franklin, months before, handed the petition to Lord Dartmouth, there was little or no expectation of its plea being granted. Royal governors did not acquire their positions by popular consent or even through consul-tation. Their removal, too, would be brought about only by very exigent circumstances of state need or necessity. There certainly was no such need with regard to Thomas Hutchinson or Andrew Oliver, who had served hon-orably, faithfully and done so through trying events. Such was the view, at least, of those most responsible in London for colonial oversight.

If it were not already clear by implication in earlier exchanges with the ministry, even in spite of Dartmouth's distaste for the governor's bluntness the year previous, that Thomas Hutchinson enjoyed the confidence of his

---

92 Ltr. to Speaker Thomas Cushing of February 15, 1774. Emphasis added. Papers, vol. 21, pages 86–96.
93 This comment is attributed to Priestly, as he recalled the event some years later, by the editor of Franklin's *Memoirs*, William Temple Franklin, Volume I, page 185. Cited by the editors of the *Papers of Benjamin Franklin*, Volume 21, page 37, 42.

majesty's ministers, even before or as he became the governor of his province, it must nonetheless have been reassuring to have Lord Dartmouth's letter to him of February 5, 1774.

Anticipating that it would take some days before the Order-in-Council on the Assembly's petition could be issued, "it will be a satisfaction to you to know," Dartmouth wrote, "that there has been a Hearing upon it before a Committee more numerous than was ever known to attend upon any occasion and that their report to the King is conceived in terms that reflect the highest honor upon your conduct, and express very just indignation at the falsehood and malevolence of the charge brought against you."

On the seventh of February the (full) Privy Council approved their Committee's report, which meant that the King had formally rejected the petition. Israel Maudit published the letters from the governors with an account of the proceedings and Wedderburn's speech so far as it touched upon the letters. "This part of his speech," Franklin wrote to Cushing on the 15th, "was thought so good that they have since printed it, in order to defame me everywhere, and particularly to destroy my reputation on your side of the water; but grosser parts of the abuse are omitted, appearing, I suppose, in their eyes too foul to be seen on paper, so that the speech, compared to what it was, is now perfectly decent."[94] Only a few of the worst things Wedderburn actually said were ever printed, and that by Benjamin Vaughan five years later, as well as they could be recollected.[95]

The Lords' Committee on Plantations gave its report the same date as the hearing itself; thus, we may suppose they met privately that same afternoon once the roasting was finished. They were of the opinion, the report recounted, that the petition was "founded upon Resolutions, formed upon false and erroneous allegations" and that it was "groundless, vexatious and scandalous...calculated only for the seditious purpose of keeping up a spirit of clamour and discontent" in the colony of Massachusetts Bay. The petition in their opinion to their majesty ought to be dismissed. And so it was, then, on February 7th, when George III met with his full Privy Council (there were fewer in attendance, the minutes reflect, than on January 29th) and the Council adopted the same "vexatious" language in formally dismissing the petition from the Assembly of Massachusetts.

---

94 BF's ltr. to Cushing on Feb. 15, '74. *Papers, vol.21*, pages 86, 92–93.
95 See Van Doren, page 176, for one summary of Benjamin Vaughan's fuller account of Wedderburn's speech.

Nothing appears in the minutes of these meetings (either of the Committee on Plantations or the entire Council) about Franklin's office. Yet the bureaucracy operated with incredible dispatch, in view of the fact that the letter of firing arrived (according to Franklin) the very next day, on Sunday, January 30th. Perhaps, as one biographer suggests, the matter had been previously decided somewhere and only awaited the conclusion of the public confrontation to support the move.[96]

Deeper Impact?

In many works about Franklin, in the centuries following those events and down to the present time, a notable legacy of the Privy Council humiliation, virtually conventional wisdom, is that this was the turning point if not the principal cause in Franklin's re-direction from a supporter of empire to that of a partisan for American independence. Some of his biographers have been more cautious. In a wide survey of these scholars, the estimate that seems most balanced in assessing the crisis, both for Franklin personally and for the place of the event in the history of the time, is that of a British historian writing near the end of the twentieth century. Following is an excerpt from the work of Esmond Wright in 1986:

> In one sense...it is an over-simplification of the causes of the Revolution to trace many of them to Franklin's ordeal in the Cockpit...
>
> Yet in another sense Franklin's ordeal of January 29 is a microcosm of the causes of, the moment of truth. [sic] To him the gulf then became obvious and unbridgeable. A moderate who had worked for peace was made a victim by ugly and irrational forces, rooted in the certainty of their prejudices. The language in which he was attacked was vindictive and savage; he was presented as an organizer of rebellion, which—until then—he certainly was not. The attack on him was foolish, for many of his ties and interests strengthened his natural caution: his crown office, his son's governorship, his wish to replace the Proprietors by a royal government, his hope for a vast land grant in the West, all made him, and might have kept him, loyal. The arrogance of Wedderburn in 1774 was in some respects an index of national arrogance.[97]

For a variety of reasons the story did not suddenly end with the trial's immediate outcome. Perhaps most important is the fact that Franklin himself was, some months later, offered and accepted opportunities to do a bit

---

96 Van Doren, page 476.
97 *Franklin of Philadelphia* by Esmond Wright (1986) at page 228.

more on behalf of reconciliation. However remote and foregone that possibility seems to us more than two hundred years later, the relevant historical record remained "open" for a bit longer with Franklin still present, and still writing, talking and biding his time. Indeed it probably seemed to Franklin, too, in 1775, just a little more than a year later when he did finally take ship for America, that the door to possible reconciliation had been closed earlier. But in those intervening months, curiously, there were other interesting prospects and a few more perils as well. These too are part of this story and some of these provide the subjects of succeeding chapters.

Up to this point the focus of the story of Franklin's political trial has been on the public events immediately surrounding the showdown or those reflected in the Hutchinson letters, their treatment and what they reflected about the times. Little or no attention has been given to the private life of Franklin in London. The narrative shifts in the next chapter to do just that.

The 2d Earl of Dartmouth by Nathanial Hone. Courtesy of National Portrait Gallery, London.

View of the Treasury and Cockpit on the left. Engraving by Benjamin Green, first published by R.Baldwin, 1773.

Chapter 8. Circles of Support

The Closest Circle

If he was alone by choice it would be for writing, to read or invent something, for Benjamin Franklin was a gregarious man. He made friends wherever he lived or traveled. Sometimes the friendship was limited to correspondence. Once begun that way, some relationships grew into something more personal. Franklin kept a number of friends over great distances and considerable time. Among those he could count as close friends in London of 1774 were those who shared the house of his lodging for all the time he lived there, sixteen years in all.

On that Saturday evening in January of 1774 when he returned from the exhausting episode in the Privy Council chamber to his home in Craven Street, it is almost a certainty that he chose to spend the evening in the company of one or more of a small group of intimates who had become his London family. Of all the attachments that Franklin established during his adult life, these would be among the most enduring. Certainly few could have been more personally supportive.

Mrs. Margaret Stevenson, a widow, was both his good and trusted friend and also his landlady, the role in which Franklin first knew her. Knowing that her famous lodger had been before Council that day, she might have prepared dinner for him, trusting that he would not likely go out that evening. Perhaps to be included for some part of the meal or tea would be her daughter Polly Stevenson Hewson, her husband the physician William Hewson and perhaps the latter's two very young children. They all lived within a stone's throw of one another, Franklin and Mrs. Stevenson in one of her two Craven Street leased properties and the Hewsons across the street in the other.

From his earlier London stay, that of 1757–62, Franklin had established his residence in the lodgings of Mrs. Stevenson of Craven Street and to her house he returned in 1764 for his final decade there. "I lodge in Craven Street near Charing Cross, Westminster; we have four rooms furnished and everything about us pretty genteel," he wrote to Debbie in the early weeks of 1758, "but living here is in every respect very expensive." Staying initially in London in the suburban home of his long-time correspondent Peter Collinson, who, like William Strahan, seemed genuinely delighted finally to meet him and his handsome son, Franklin evidently found the Stevenson house by asking round the area close to government offices and adjacent to the Strand with its coffee houses and shops. The location might have seemed as agreeable to him as Market Street was back home.

In the same letter to Deborah he told of going shopping with "Mrs. Stephenson" to select presents for Debbie and the Franklins' daughter Sally, to be wrapped and prepared for shipment through the lady's assistance. The letters to Debbie after that would often contain references to Mrs. Stevenson's good services for him, and Debbie sent her appreciation and compliments in response. Among other routine responsibilities she assumed for Franklin was looking after his abundant mail when he was out of London, as he often was after settling into a routine of traveling in the summer. At such times she paid bills for him as well.

By 1774 and the time of his trial, on the order of seventeen elapsed years following his initial arrival in the Stevenson household, Franklin had become not merely her most prominent and favored boarder but a very appreciative friend and confidant as well. The several dependencies, cheerfully discharged, might by themselves have given all the sticking power a loyal and appreciative friendship needed, but Franklin's generous affection for the Stevenson household probably lay more in the special rapport that Franklin developed with the daughter of Margaret Stevenson, Mary, known as Polly to all who knew her.

The younger Stevenson was nineteen when Franklin entered the lives of that family and she flattered him with her attentiveness and the engagement of her mind. She sought answers to puzzles of the natural world from him. Why, for example, does a candle flame "prosper" with some air yet go out when too much is applied? How can a barometer measure the pressure of the air as its column of mercury is surrounded by glass? Polly more than once in her letters referred to Franklin as her "preceptor." Some of his explanations were extensive, for example, about tides, rivers and phases of the moon. One of his letters to Polly on the subject of electricity found its way eventually into his published work. Occasionally, practical advice was sought and given, such as how to deal with a crotchety aunt for whom Polly was a live-in companion and, when the time did come much later, whether to accept a proposal of marriage.

The fondness that Franklin had for Polly can be read from many of his letters, but none is more explicit than this one from Franklin on the eve of his departure from the port of Portsmouth for the colonies in August of 1762, his five-year agency for the Pennsylvania House concluded. "Adieu, my dearest child; I will call you so; why should I not ... since I love you with all the tenderness, all the fondness of a father..." Franklin refers impliedly here to an earlier possibility that William might wed Polly and make her his daughter (-in-law) in fact.

Polly, for her part, a few days before, when neither was sure he would return to England, wrote that it was just as well she missed seeing him off from Craven Street since, as her mother informed her, "I made you unhappy with my tears."

Franklin did return two years later, armed with a new commission from the legislators of Pennsylvania, and the friendship continued to flourish. A few years later Polly, serving Franklin as a transcriber for his new phonetic English alphabet [e.g., "alfabet," "difikultis"], expressed her willingness to do the work; but she also spoke her mind very directly. In a 1768 letter Polly wrote: "I see many inconveniences as well as difficulties" with his new system, notably "all our etymologies would be lost," plus words of different meaning but similar sound would be "thrown down," not to mention that all the existing books in print would have to be re-written! This candor is surely a mark of friendship, one that had grown in scope and texture over the years.

In 1770 Polly at thirty found a suitor worthy of her respect and pass-ably so also by her honorary father, it would seem, though she was not so sure at first of Franklin's blessings. Her choice was one William Hewson, a fellow who seemed every bit as curious about the natural world as she. Franklin did attend and took part in the wedding, giving the bride away (as she reminded him in a letter noting their anniversary). The couple was blessed with two children within three years—one of whom, Billy, would become Franklin's godson. By 1774, the time of the trial or soon thereafter, another was expected. William Hewson, a few years younger than Polly, was beginning to make a name for himself as a research surgeon and teacher. Especially interested in problems of the vascular system, Hewson was in the same year as his wedding elected to membership in the Royal Society. In modern medical scholarship he is regarded as the father of hematology.

Hewson's promising professional activity likely reinforced Mrs. Steven-son's decision to make room for the young family in her Craven Street loca-tion, closer into the center of London than where the Hewsons had been living initially. In the summer or autumn of 1772 she took a lease on a build-ing across from Number Seven and there moved Franklin's set of rooms, an "apartment." She turned much of the first house into the living space for the Hewsons and a medical office plus a teaching theater for students of surgery.

Franklin had arranged to be away during the move, staying with an-other friend and frequent host, Jonathan Shipley, Bishop of Asaph, at his country house in Twyburn, near Winchester. It was in this quiet setting that Franklin commenced writing his autobiography. When things were almost ready for his return, Polly wrote to him and extended an invitation to stay with them, the Hewsons, for a few nights while his books and other possessions were moved across to the new dwelling. She cautioned that he might like to avoid the actual moving itself, knowing both her mother's ex-haustion by that point and the likely distress or discomfort to him in all the activity of the move. It is really a mature version of the younger Polly, often playful with her mentor and friend, when she added in this letter of October 1772, "I know that you need courting, so let me repeat the invitation to stay with us" those few days upon (your) return to Craven Street.

Two points of reference will prove useful in "seeing" this domestic scene as it must have existed at the time of Franklin's troubles over the Hutchin-son papers, his trial and its aftermath. One is that its details are taken directly from the correspondence of Franklin and the Stevenson–Hewsons during this period and earlier. Second, this correspondence (between Polly and Franklin) stops after the 1772 letter; it does not resume until Franklin has left for America in March of 1775, just over a year after the trial. The reason for the interruption emerges from this circumstance. Except for when Franklin himself was out of town, or earlier when Polly, in her twenties, was with the lady for whom she was a live-in companion at her home some distance from London, there was no need for letters as the friends lived, during that three-year break in the correspondence, on the same street, if not under the same roof.

No record remains of what they did or how they spent those hours and first days after the trial, but it seems safe to imagine that there were distractions of the sort that any extended family, especially one with very young children, has in some degree even in times of great disappointment and anguish. If the hour was not too late after the meal, a glass or two of Madeira might have been passed round. Given the strains of the day, however, it seems likely that everyone turned in early.

FRIENDS AT LARGE

> [Dr. Franklin] has had the satisfaction to find that he has lost no friends by this attempt to disgrace him; his house has ever since been filled with visitants who come purposely to show their regard for him and express their indignation at the unworthy treatment he received. [98]

Whether by earlier arrangement or not is not certain, but in his own later writing about these events Joseph Priestly tells us that he came to Craven Street and shared breakfast with Franklin the next morning, Sunday, January 30th. Although he does not mention this detail, it is quite possible that Priestly, following the proceedings in the Privy Council on Saturday, accompanied Franklin to Craven Street. If not, he could well have sent a note that evening to him and set up the rendezvous for next morning.

Those times that Franklin did choose to be alone would include some considerable number of hours composing drafts and final versions of a vast correspondence, now making up most of the thousands of pages in thirty-seven volumes of his published papers. Because he left so many letters with

---

98 Anonymous "Letter from London" published in *The Pennsylvania Gazette* on April 20, 1774, believed authored by Franklin. See Papers, Vol. xxi, page 112, n. 5.

so very many correspondents, there are no fewer than ninety different entries of names in his papers for 1774 (Volume XXI), perhaps history can forgive Franklin for not keeping a regular diary as many of his contemporaries did, men like Thomas Hutchinson of Boston, for example. While diaries might be more complete and detailed when rigorously tended to, letters are probably less subjective involving as they do the sensibilities of at least one other then living person.

It would be doubtful that Franklin on the evening of his ordeal in the Council would have chosen to do anything but collect himself, perhaps over tea with Mrs. Stevenson, if not dinner with the Hewsons, and go to bed early enough to be fresh for the breakfast with his friend Priestly. By that next morning, he exhibited not only the vitality of a man refreshed but also the spirit of one satisfied that he had acted honorably.

He did not, so far as their letters reflect, often discuss politics with either Margaret Stevenson or his friend and protégé Polly. Still, both women would have been anxious to hear something of their friend's experiences that day, if they had not heard already through the grapevine how he was treated. He might well have said just enough to avoid seeming indifferent to their feelings, yet not so much as to open up the full range of what he had endured. As he would report soon thereafter to son William, Franklin might have told Margaret Stevenson that he expected his post mastership would be taken from him; of that he was sure. Indeed it was, as he learned the next day.

Franklin's friendship with Thomas Priestly grew out of their common interest in experimental science. It began, so far as the correspondence itself reveals, from the earlier Franklin London sojourn, 1757–62, with a letter from the younger man, then living in Yorkshire, seeking information about experiments in electricity. That request led in turn to a long collaboration on all manner of scientific and technical issues. Priestly's history of electrical experiments would shortly be published in book form, and it would include an account of the episode in Franklin's scientific career more famous than any other, flying the kite and catching lightning.

Their closeness was reinforced by the evident skepticism they both shared about religious dogma, among other subjects they shared with fellow members of the Club of Honest Whigs at their meetings in St. Paul's coffee house.

Priestly, best known in modern times for his discovery or isolation of oxygen, remained interested also in theology to which he was drawn earlier in life. He is credited with influencing Thomas Jefferson, twenty years later, after settling in America following his unpleasant encounter with British reaction to the French Revolution (for which Priestly had expressed sympathy), on aspects of the Christian faith that Priestly managed to keep. In the winter of 1774 both men were more urgently concerned about the drift of imperial policy into more rigidity and the plight of colonists with whom men like Priestly came increasingly to identify. Both men would have to have concluded that the proceedings in the chamber the day before gave the clearest sign that official sentiments were harder than anything yet made public.

At least two other good London friends could well have had contact with Franklin in this period: William Strahan and Sir John Pringle. Strahan (1715–1785) was a printer and supplier of press equipment for Franklin for years before they actually met. He was on hand to welcome and befriend the Franklins in 1757. Their correspondence extended over forty years, starting with a letter in 1743 from Franklin offering a position in his printing business to a journeymen London printer recommended by Strahan to a mutual friend in Philadelphia. Franklin offered to guarantee the young man's passage back to England if after a "twelvemonths' good work ... he enclines to return."

It was an auspicious start to a friendship that somehow managed to survive the War for Independence. They were continually in touch with each other about a host of things, public affairs as well as personal favors and business undertakings. Strahan became printer to the King in 1770, was a publisher, and near the end of his friend's time in Britain was elected to the House of Commons in 1774. Even with such ties to authority he seems never to have despaired of Franklin's friendship, although it was sorely tested during the hostilities as when Franklin was moved to write a letter, never posted, declaring to Strahan, after listing the varied destruction in the colonies at the hands of the British, "you were my friend, now you are my enemy." They never spared their letters the strength of their convictions, as is most clear from this time onward. Perhaps most notable in the Strahan connection, many of Franklin's essays and opinion pieces were first published in his friend's own newspaper. Closer than that to the "quick" of this friendship, the agent chose Strahan's newspaper to print his revelation about the Hutchinson letters on Christmas day in 1773.

With that much depth to their friendship, begun and maintained for more than a decade solely through correspondence but later layered and enriched by their personal association, it is difficult to imagine that Strahan, were he present in London at the time, would not have tried to attend the hearing in the Privy Council on January 29th. Equally difficult to conceive that some contact was not made in the days following the trial. The collection of their correspondence in the *Papers of Benjamin Franklin* reveals a gap from 1772 to 1775, the same time as in the gap in Franklin's correspondence with Polly Hewson.

Perhaps one clue to the friend's thinking, although it cannot be all the truth about it, may be found in a letter that William Strahan wrote in the April 1771, not to Benjamin but to William Franklin, then into his ninth year as the royal governor of the colony of New Jersey. The two of course knew each other from the start of the Franklins' arrival in England in 1757. Strahan wrote to the younger Franklin that his father "is not only on bad terms with Lord Hillsborough [then colonial secretary] but with the *Ministry in general*" [emphasis in the original.] His purpose in writing, Strahan continued, was to "put you upon your guard and to induce you to be as circumspect ... as possible, as it is imagined here that you entertain the same political opinions with your father."

Perhaps Strahan was of two minds about Franklin. He certainly liked and admired the man. Politically, Strahan had by this time very likely decided to keep his distance, looking to protect himself in the eyes of the court and ministry. One earlier relationship than that with Franklin, one that Strahan could well have still maintained, was that with Alexander Wedderburn. Both being from Scotland, Wedderburn had sought out William Strahan, an older man with capital connections, for referrals in his fledgling law practice, according to an early Wedderburn biography.[99] If Strahan chose not seek his old friend out after the trial, Franklin let the snub pass. After some desultory exchanges in that spring of 1774 about such things as bills owed by one or another mutual associate in Pennsylvania for books, their correspondence continued to be robust and extensive for a decade more.

---

99 William C. Townsend, *The Lives of Twelve Eminent Judges of the Last and of the Present Century*, pages 162 and following (London, 1833).

Sir John Pringle (1707–1782), a physician and like Strahan a native of Edinburgh, was not an amiable person, at least in the judgment of James Boswell, biographer of Samuel Johnson. When he encountered Pringle with Franklin during a coffee house chess game, the writer declared him, by way of his diary, to be of "sour manner" compared to Franklin's "jollity and pleasantry." On the other hand the two friends, Pringle and Strahan, together offered quite a range of complementary assets to their friendship with Franklin. Strahan enjoyed politics and was engaged in publishing; he wrote more extensive and personally expressive letters as well—once writing that he not only liked and admired Franklin but also *loved* him. Pringle was more reserved; his letters to Franklin were few and brief.

Pringle and Franklin did, however, enjoy one another's company. They traveled together with some frequency in these years, especially during summers. Following one trip the friends wrote about an otherwise inconsequential excursion by skiff they had shared in Holland. It seems that Pringle was curious about the comparatively slower speed of the boat through the water on that occasion. The boatman had explained that the water was shallower than it had been due to insufficient rain. Having confirmed that the boat was not actually scraping the bottom of the canal, and not content to leave the phenomenon unexplained, Franklin conducted his own experiments. As he wrote to Pringle later, he could confirm that, because of the differential force of the wave action from the bottom of the waterway, a boat could be propelled with greater ease in deeper water.

Pringle was also a fellow of the Royal Society, making his mark principally through experimental efforts to inhibit the spread of disease based on his work in military hospitals. He introduced Franklin personally to the members of the Society upon his arrival in England, though Franklin had been formally tapped for membership in absentia while still living in Philadelphia.

Curiously the surviving collected correspondence between Franklin and Pringle stops well before the time of the trial, the last such communication of substance being a note in 1772 when Dr. Pringle arranged a meeting with Franklin at William Hewson's home and offices in Craven Street, presumably to examine Hewson's collection of medical exhibits and discuss their respective professional experiences.

But for a letter Pringle wrote to David Hume after the trial, we would be left to wonder whether they met at all then. As was noted in a preceding chapter, Pringle reported his dismay over the Hutchinson letters affair when Franklin's role in it became known. But he also defended his friend, too, noting that Franklin had done all he could to promote reconciliation. Writing to Hume that he had urged Franklin to respond to the Wedderburn attack in print, there is a reasonable inference that they did meet sometime following the trial.[100]

Two other gentlemen of substance who occupied a position of recipro-cal respect with Franklin in these same last years of his in England warrant inclusion here, even though it is not known whether they were in contact with their mutual friend at this season of trial and challenge. Certainly they would have had sympathy for his plight and probably at least one of them also sympathy for Franklin's cause. Richard Price, 1723–1791, dissenting clergyman and writer on a range of ethical and political matters, was a fel-low member of the Honest Whigs society. They had a rich correspondence from the 1760s right through the War and afterward. He, too, was a friend of Joseph Priestly, and like Priestly, was appreciated by Franklin as "a preacher of *rational* Christianity" (emphasis in the original letter of Franklin to Price of September 28, 1772.) Franklin had told Dr. John Pringle of Price and they sought him out on occasion to hear his sermons. Price was so supportive of the American interests that later Congress, presumably on Franklin's initia-tive, offered him citizenship and an invitation to help them with oversight of their finances (this in 1779 and during the contest for independence)—an offer he respectfully declined, saying that he was not qualified and was re-luctant to leave the country of his birth at so advanced an age. Reflecting the sentiments that had made his bond with Franklin both personal and politi-cal, Price wrote that he "looks to the American states as the hope and future refuge of mankind" (Price letter to Franklin, and other commissioners from Congress in Paris dated January 18, 1779).

No less significant to Franklin was the friendship he enjoyed with Rich-ard Jackson, 1721–1787, during the late colonial era if not during the War itself. Jackson, a well-known and respected lawyer and Member of Parlia-ment for 22 years, was an agent for Pennsylvania, and for two other colonies at times, with Franklin and had served in such a role prior to Franklin. Their correspondence goes back to the 1750s and includes abundant detail about

---

100 *Letters of Eminent Persons Addressed to David Hume*, John H. Burton, editor (Edin-burgh and London, 1849), pages 270-271, as cited in *Papers*, vol. 21, page 113, note seven.

colonial issues with London, such as how to deal with the Penns in England. Jackson as an MP was opposed to the Stamp Act of 1765 on prudential grounds but defended Parliament's authority on such measures. Franklin and Jackson shared an extended trip to Ireland and Scotland in 1771 when both men were desirous of learning whether the semi-autonomous regime each of those nations enjoyed might provide a model for the American colonies within the empire.

While Jackson had aided Franklin in several of his efforts to promote the cause of fair treatment for the colonies, some of them controversial, it seems doubtful that Jackson would have smiled on Franklin's exploitation of the Hutchinson letters. He was too much a traditionalist even if he openly criticized the ministry's policies for the colonies. Whatever contact the two had in the period of the letters affair crisis, it cannot be gleaned from their letters, as there is a gap for this entire period in the collected papers of Franklin. The final letter in the collected letters of Franklin for their series was one from Jackson in 1785, in which he congratulated his old friend and his new country on the conclusion of peace; and he expressed the hope for renewed amity and goodwill between the Britain and America.

The Circle of Kinship

If the Stevenson–Hewsons composed Franklin's family-away-from family, then the one in which his own offspring and theirs were members occupied a constant if more distant outer ring of significance throughout this whole time. Wife Debbie never left Philadelphia all those years. Franklin gave up trying to get her to cross the ocean after his first years away. Somewhat curiously, however, William Strahan, who had never met Debbie, wrote a surprisingly personal letter to her in the autumn of 1764 urging her to reconsider so that she might be on hand to protect her interests, so charming had people found her husband to be.

She kept the home, and his growing library and selected furnishings he sent from London from time to time, the newer house Franklin had not seen completed and the one to which he fully expected to retire to in time. Debbie held Franklin's power of attorney over property and business matters and received a portion of the Post Office stipend that her husband earned. She also kept Franklin informed, and sought his guidance, about such developments as their daughter Sally's social life. Debbie once wrote to her husband that she was a bit worried about some of her associates, or at least one fellow in particular whom she did not name. Having talked with their old friend and fellow political ally Joseph Galloway about this, she had decided to treat the person "as a friend" lest she "drive her to see him somewhere else." She hoped that she had acted "to your satisfaction" and she had used her best judgment, as she was "obliged to be father and mother" for Sally.

Some time later Debbie wrote to Franklin about their daughter's desire to contract a marriage with an Englishman not long arrived from New York named Richard Bache. He was lukewarm about this match, principally on grounds of insubstantial material promise. In the end Franklin did not forbid the marriage, as he was in no position to judge from where he was, but he cautioned Debbie to keep the expenses to a minimum. The wedding took place without him. Sometime later Franklin warmed up to Richard and actually received him in London on a trip to visit his family of origin in England.

Franklin's dependence on Debbie for keeping their home and family in good shape is obvious, yet his emotional engagement with her during these absent years is noticeably limited. While he often referred to his wife as "my dear child" or signed his letters "affectionately, your husband," it is clear that most of the topics were simply reports on his travels, encounters and expressions of good health. There is little to indicate that he truly missed Debbie's presence in the life he was leading in England. There was little of substance about the issues he was dealing with in his work as agent for the several colonies, or his scientific and literary pursuits. Pretty clearly the old couple had grown accustomed simply to *being there* for one another and little more. Yet Debbie, ever loyal, was as devoted to her husband as she could be, expecting him some season to return to her and their home. She apparently did not, until the near the end of her life in 1774, despair of seeing him again.

Franklin's reports about the trial and its aftermath to family members back home were written over the course of three weeks in February. Interestingly, his first such letter, dated February second, three days after the trial, was addressed to son William, but it was terse: "This is just to acquaint you that I am well and that my office of Deputy Post Master is taken from me.... You will hear from others the treatment I have received." Then on the seventeenth of the month Franklin wrote letters to his sister Jane Mecom in Boston and to son-in-law Richard Bache in Philadelphia. To Bache the information was almost identical to that written to William, "you will have heard that I am displaced" and consequently not in a position to help him with the postal service. To his sister, Franklin he wrote a bit more, admonishing her not to have "any uneasiness" about his loss of position for he was secure enough. And, finally, he wrote to Debbie on the twentieth of the month, but the text of the letter does not survive.

William at least had had some inkling of what might happen, both because news of the Hutchinson letters' publication in Boston had reached him and because his father on January 5th had written to him about the duel and his Christmas Day letter of responsibility for sending the letters to Boston.

None of Franklin's letters to Deborah from this immediate post-trial period survive, nor are there any from her. There are, however, letters from both son William and sister Jane Mecom. William's first letter of relevant substance, written on the third of May on a short visit to the Franklin home in Philadelphia (to be with his adoptive mother and his half-sister and her family which by this time included two young children, Benny aged four and Billy, just about a year old), let his father know two things. His "popularity in this country, whatever it may be on the other side, is greatly beyond whatever it was," William wrote, and "when you return here [there will be shown] every mark of regard and affection." William's letter also tried to reassure his father about the security of his own office, perhaps heeding, implicitly anyway, the earlier advice from William Strahan to watch his step.

Letters from sister Jane in that same season reveal how complicated matters were for Franklin, despite the positive news from Philadelphia by way of William. In Boston, she related, there were rumors that the agent was prepared to sacrifice his own countrymen to keep his post. Franklin's response dated July 28, 1774, is blistering: "an infamous falsehood ... for God knows my heart, I would not accept the best office the King has to bestow while such tyrannic measures are taken against my country....They have done me honor by turning me out, and I will take care they shall not disgrace me by putting me in again."[101]

Whether Franklin relied on the other family members at home to break the news of the trial and firing to Deborah seems doubtful, given all that they had been through and had shared vicariously over these years. But if Franklin did find it too difficult to write such news to Debbie directly, such a decision would have been no more patronizing than the paucity of real

---

101 BF Ltr. to Jane Mecom of July 28, 1774; *Papers*, vol. 21, page 264.

news about his work over the years had been in his letters to her in those years.

The tie between Franklin and his son William, closer earlier in life than later, was not limited to politics or their careers. The two had lived together in Craven Street for the first residence there, in 1757 to 1762, the time of the young man's coming of full age and attainment of a profession. William traveled with his father in those years, met men of distinction like David Hume in Edinburgh, saw him honored at Oxford and St. Andrews. Once they hurried back from Holland in a bad storm on the North Sea, arriving just in time, William wrote to his sister Sally, to attend the London coronation of George III in 1761.

After William was appointed royal governor for New Jersey and the senior Franklin went back to Pennsylvania for a two year interval in 1762, their lives were never really close again, however much they corresponded. They saw each other only three more times: while the agent was on "home leave" in Pennsylvania (1762–64), again upon Franklin's return a little more than a year following the trial and after the skirmishes at Concord bridge and Lexington, the summer of 1775, and finally after the War as Franklin was making his way back to America after his Paris mission was completed in 1785, his voyage home interrupted briefly in Southampton.

And a Grandson

The tension and political distance between father and son only increased as this series of reunions played out. But there was more to the meetings than politics and diverging loyalties. There was also the presence of another Franklin. And that presence, alas, served to make the two competitive in a whole other realm. William Temple Franklin was the London-born illegitimate son of William. He lived for most of his young life under the auspices of or with his grandfather, first nearby him in London during the third and final stay in London, 1764–75. Temple, as he was called, would become the kind of companion that William had been previously.

During his governorship years William did not try very hard to have his son united with him in New Jersey, although the grandfather did not make the matter easy for him, insisting on his schooling in England. Temple's father did contribute to his support, as sometimes Mrs. Stevenson would attend to the boy's medical needs and send the bills to William.

It is one of the notable ironies of the story of Franklin in London that while the relationship of the first two generations of these Franklin men foundered on the rocks of revolution or the drift toward it, the relationship between the first and *third* was cemented by the same set of circumstances. It is as if Temple took the place of the son "lost" to the other side in the War and its antecedent strains. Clearly the senior Franklin held most of the cards when William and his new bride, Elizabeth Downes, left for the New World without the infant, whose own mother remained out of the picture altogether and whose identity is lost to history. That is not to say that Franklin took the child in with him at Craven Street. For the first years of the boy's life he resided with foster parents, then in a Kensington boarding school that was recommended to Franklin by his friend William Strahan.

Gradually the youngster was brought into the fold of the Craven Street household, however, and he would spend holidays and other special days there. His formal status would remain something of a mystery, the Stevensons referring to him as Mr. William Temple, a young friend of Dr. Franklin who was kindly looking after the boy's welfare. Only after their departure for Philadelphia, when Franklin took Temple from his school and left on the voyage home, was it made clear that Temple was indeed a Franklin. Polly wrote sometime later that she had always thought there must be a kinship, but she would have been too polite to ask. Temple would have been fourteen or fifteen by then. It seems doubtful that he shared much about the public events surrounding his benefactor that winter. Still, the very presence of the youngster, his own kinsman, in England at the time must have been of some small comfort to the old man. Franklin would have the boy with him on the voyage home and, except for a season or two with his father and step-mother in Amboy, New Jersey, until manhood and into the trials of his own about his destiny and place, whether in the New World or old.

No Stranger to Ambiguity

If nothing else this sketch of Franklin's private life during these hardest of his days in London reveals that he was no stranger to ambiguity. Nor did he seem uncomfortable with it. That he could adjust to changes, even starkly unwelcome ones or ones that might embarrass other men, certainly adds depth to our appreciation of his character and personality. That said, however, Franklin was not as forthcoming as we might like about details of his life that must have complicated it a good deal. Or, if they did not do so, they certainly leave us over two hundred years later scratching our heads.

Among the prominent questions remaining would be the one about the "two-family" reality of Franklin's London years. What was Debbie's working understanding of her husband's relationship with the Stevensons? Was there anything more between Franklin and Margaret than met the eye? While there are abundant objective possibilities for some considerable unease on Debbie's part, she never exhibited it so far as their letters reveal or those of other family members. Indeed judging by the solicitudes each woman extended to the other in letters, often passed on through Franklin's correspondence, one might believe they were the best of friends or sisters. And while his associates in England often invited Margaret Stevenson along with Franklin to dinner or other social gatherings and thus treated them as a couple, there seems no evidence that the connection was anything more than what they both represented it to be, a solid friendship based on mutual respect and service. Not without abundant fondness, but lacking, so far as anyone knows, any romantic surrender.

PERSONAL SERVANTS

An account of the British years for Franklin, even a brief one like this, would not be complete without a mention of two members of his household who, while not present with him in London in these last years, were with him for all or part of the previous period, from 1757–62. These were two men, Peter and King by name, who are described as servants brought with him from America. In service they were, but within the law of Pennsylvania they were slaves who had been part of the Franklin household in Philadelphia. Peter was there for the senior Franklin and King for William. A few references to these men are found in the letters of Franklin during the period. One of these describes a trip that Franklin and William made to the ancestral village of the Franklins, where, after Peter had cleaned the moss from them, William wrote down the inscriptions on the tombstones. Another reference appears in a letter to wife Debbie who had inquired about the two men. Franklin reported that Peter continued to be a more or less satisfactory servant, though he was prone to turn a deaf ear and see with only one eye all that went on in his service, whereas King had left the household and was last known to have been befriended by a family in Sussex. Presumably,

Franklin made no effort to have him returned. At that point we do not know what Peter's fate was, or even whether he returned to Philadelphia with Franklin in 1762. Perhaps he, too, decided to stay in England.

The matter of slavery in the American colonies, at first little touched upon in Franklin's writings, became a subject of more prominence in the England of the 1770s. And Franklin was a little defensive about the issue, minimizing the prevalence of the practice in the colonies. Eventually, Franklin would come out more resolutely against the institution and become prominently associated with abolitionist groups in America and abroad. He was especially critical of the maintenance of the slave trade itself even from this time. In this evolution of view and conviction two prominent Quaker friends from Philadelphia were influential, Anthony Benezet and Dr. Benjamin Rush.

The presence of slaves resident with their owners in Britain was a fact of life in the 18th century, not only in the company of resident Americans (mostly, we should expect from the southern colonies, but not all, as Franklin's case suggests) but also in the company of British planters returning from stays in the West Indies. In a recent study of American colonials living or visiting 18th century England, Julie Flavell has given a rich account of the prevalence of blacks in London during this period. (See *When London Was Capital of America*, 2010.)

Inevitably, an instance would arise when the law was invoked to assist such "owners" with the return of slaves who did not wish to leave Great Britain. Such a case arose in 1772.

Somerset v. Stueart reached the court of the era's most renowned jurist (and formerly a respected political principal as well) William Murray, 1st Earl of Mansfield, Chief Justice of the Court of King's Bench. Mansfield was in his time as important a figure for common law growth in the colonies as in England. His ruling in *Somerset* was the first to declare that the law of England did not permit a forcible removal from England of anyone under bondage according to the law of another country. To that extent, then, the ownership of one person by another would not be recognized in English law.

By itself the ruling was not a declaration of the end of slavery anywhere. It remained for this development to be followed, moreover, by the abolition of the commerce in slaves that Parliament enacted in 1813 for the Empire, a development that in two years would find its way into international law by way of a multi-lateral treaty with other European powers. (See "Amazing Grace"—the film story of William Wilberforce's long campaign of protest.) In that special moment of 1772, however, Franklin added his own memorial of its importance. In the *London Chronicle* he authored an unsigned article, "The Somerset Case and the Slave Trade." It is not an unqualified endorse-ment of the ideal of human liberty so much as a spur to more comprehensive action: "Pharisaical Britain! To pride thyself in setting free a single slave [i.e., Somerset] that happens to land on thy coasts while thy merchants ... are en-couraged to continue a commerce whereby so many hundreds of thousands are dragged into slavery that scarce be said to end with their lives, since it is entailed on their posterity!"[102]

As in so many other substantial issues of his time, Franklin was not writing with a broad sweep of a single ideal or theory or a completely clear purpose. He moved with his best lights as far as they took him at the time. The evils of the bondage of slaves he plainly condemned and the trade in human beings repulsed him, but he found it difficult to conceive how blacks (in America) once freed would be assimilated. Start with the children of slaves; make sure they would be free when they came of age and provide them with education. Stop the import of slaves to America. Eventually, he seemed to be saying, the issue would fade away. In the meantime, he tempo-rized. As colonial agent for Georgia in London (his agencies for three other colonies—Pennsylvania, Massachusetts and New Jersey—did not impose a similar burden), he had to present a newly enacted slave code for approval by the British government and, in that regard, he even published an essay entitled "Conversation on Slavery" in which he again took imperial govern-ment to task for not keeping slaves out of the colonies. An individual colony must therefore protect itself "by such Laws as are thought necessary to gov-ern them while they are in it."[103] Ever the pragmatist, he did and said what the occasion seemed to demand of him.

Affability Versus Closeness

The complications of Franklin's personality, however puzzling at times, do appear to present patterns in the view of some of his biographers. For

---

102 "The Somersett Case and the Slave Trade," essay in *The London Chronicle,* June 18–20, 1772, reprinted in *Papers,* vol. 19, pages 187-188.
103 "A Conversation on Slavery," printed in *The Public Advertiser,* January 30, 1770; re-printed in *Papers,* vol. 17, page 37.

instance, here is what Walter Isaacson in his 2003 comprehensive biography writes about Franklin's capacity for closeness in personal relationships:

> Throughout his life he had few emotional bonds tying him to any one place, and he seemed to glide through the world the way he glided through relationships.... He was a sociable man who liked clubs that offered enlightening conversations and activities, but the friendships he formed with his fellow men were more affable than intimate.... His relationship with his wife was a practical one, as was the case with his London landlady, Margaret Stevenson....[104]

Perhaps Franklin simply had less need than other men for sharing either successes or reversals of fortune with close friends or family members. He was by all accounts an exceptional individual, complex beyond appearances, too. Franklin, moreover, had lived independently for some years at this point in his life and seemingly managed well within a limited range of emotional expression. He would find his way. Affability would not long desert him. Engagements of a practical sort would be pursued. His mind would find its voice again in letters and essays. In the process, however, there would be other challenges before he left England one more time.

---

104 Isaacson, Walter; *Benjamin Franklin, An American Life* page 487 (2003).

36 Craven Street, London, in recent times. Courtesy of Benjamin Franklin House Foundation, London.

Joseph Priestly, portrait by Ellen Sharples, 1794.

Chapter 9. Other Perils and Aftershocks

A Private Lawsuit

Of the several other hazards Franklin was to face because of his role in the Hutchinson letters affair, none was potentially more serious than the private proceeding against him in Chancery Court. On January 7, 1774, just four days before the preliminary hearing in the Privy Council, William Whately filed a "bill in equity"—*Whately v. Franklin*—the equivalent of a lawsuit in English courts but in a particular kind of court, "Chancery" or "equity" practice, to obtain results not available through an ordinary civil suit for damages. Franklin's correspondence of the period takes no notice of this filing until after the Privy Council proceedings had begun less than a week later.

The uniqueness of Chancery's jurisdiction would allow the court to compel the surrender of the letters wrongfully taken from the Whately's or from someone else without their permission and to disclose what, if any, other letters to the late Thomas defendant might have and return those as well. The court could enjoin the defendant from any further publication of Whately's correspondence. For all William knew, Franklin might have acquired letters to his late brother other than those published recently in Boston.

Of these possibilities, Franklin would have few fears. The originals were in Boston and he did not, so far as we know, have any other of Whately's letters. Nor did he have any plans to print any of the letters. Indeed, as we know from Franklin's own cover letter to Thomas Cushing, he had not intended that those be published. Indeed, he was explicit in directing that they not be printed.

Should it ever go to trial, however, other aspects of the suit would be a major problem for Franklin. The court was asked to compel him to reveal how he came to possess the letters, from whom they were received and to whom they were sent in Boston and with what instructions or restrictions. These demands could be very difficult for Franklin in view of his promise of secrecy to his source. He could be forced to choose between his own liberty and the embarrassment, or worse, of those who had supplied the letters.

At first blush this might seem to be the whole point of the proceeding, for it suggests that the ministry was behind this court proceeding somehow and that what was in name a private lawsuit was being used for political ends. But, as the editors of the Franklin papers have observed, "[William] Whatley, whether or not he was serving the administration, had reasons of his own to seek redress for the wrong done his brother and himself. Rumor about the Hutchinson letters cast doubt on Thomas Whately's carefulness ... in guarding the confidentiality of his correspondents, and involved William in the public argument that culminated in his duel with Temple."[105]

The threat that he might be compelled to testify about these details hung over the agent for the entire time he remained in the kingdom, more than a year. That was the particularly bad part for Franklin. The one beneficial thing for him was that delays in Chancery were commonplace, and the course of its processes was notoriously slow. Franklin and his counsel filed their answer only after more than three months had elapsed after Whately's suit was filed. That would not be the last time that the snail's pace of Chancery benefited the agent. When the respondent's initial answer was opposed as being insufficient, there was one more opportunity for the threat to be carried out. Yet counsel for Franklin managed to secure more time to amend his answer.

At some point in the proceedings, though, Franklin could be faced with incarceration for failure to answer fully what the Bill asked, a form of civil

---

105 Papers, vol. 21, page 14.

contempt of court. How did he manage to avoid it? Any answers have to be tentative, incomplete and largely conjectural.

What is known about the Chancery proceeding, however, may give some clue. One aspect about it that stands out is the very timeliness of the initial filing itself. It bears repeating, the Chancery proceeding was initiated against Franklin on January 7, 1774. This was but two weeks from the time that the world discovered that the agent was the sender of those letters to Boston! An obvious question arises, how could William Whatley have decided to take legal action, engage counsel and have the matter drafted and filed so quickly?

We may agree with the editors of the Franklin papers who have concluded that it "defies probability" that Whately could have moved that swiftly had his first notice been Franklin's Christmas Day surprise. He "must have known of the American's involvement long before the public did, probably before the duel."[106] But "how he knew is one of the mysteries that still cloud the affair."[107]

Not to put too fine a point on the mystery, but there seem logically at most two sets of people who could have known and could have communicated with the executor early on. One set would include those in London involved in the original delivery of the letters to Franklin or who were associated with or who had facilitated that delivery somehow. The other obvious suspect group would be those in Boston who learned from Thomas Cushing or through intermediaries that the agent had sent the letters. We know that the latter group was one of some size and grew larger as the Massachusetts House became aware, at least of the presence, of such letters even if they did not know for certain that the agent was the sender, and that was months prior to the filing of the suit in London. There would have been ample time for a letter to reach Whately or someone in touch with him in London.[108]

Of the possibilities in London any sustained effort to try to identify someone or ones would prudently begin with a survey of the likely sources for Franklin himself. Inasmuch as that exploration is covered in detail in the

---

106 Id. at 14–15.

107 Id.

108 Thomas Hutchinson, it is known, had been worried that his letters to London might be used in this fashion, the way Governor Bernard before him had experienced. His suspicions might well have included Franklin, although he is said to have first fingered John Temple for that role. See Bailyn's *Ordeal of Thomas Hutchinson*, pages 222 to 223 and correspondence cited there.

after word of this book, for now we might limit ourselves to this one fact. And it brings us back full circle to the high possibility that there was some ministry support for or at least more than passing interest in Whately's suit against the agent. In his hour-long dressing down of Franklin in the Privy Council chamber on January 29, Alexander Wedderburn made an explicit allusion to the agent's being "answerable" to law in England. Unlike a foreign ambassador while resident there, Franklin would find, the Crown's advocate predicted, that the "Court of Chancery will not much attend to his new self-created importance."[109] Of course the filing in Chancery was three weeks old by the time of the Cockpit showdown and, formally at least, it was a matter of public knowledge. Certainly it is as possible that Wedderburn was informed only after the filing as that he knew before. Nonetheless, the fact that he alluded to the matter demonstrates the range of his analysis of the situation facing the agent and a certainty that by one means or another Franklin might be required to fill in the missing links of the saga of the Hutchinson letters. And those unknown elements could indeed be very important to the government.

Would There Be an Arrest?

Is it plausible to think there might have been one? Decidedly, yes. In either of two ways, the civil context of the Chancery proceeding, to compel a more definitive answer to the Bill brought by William Whately or to answer questions in that court demanded in it, such as who gave him the letters and whether he had possession of any others from the same source. Alternatively, the agent could have been taken into criminal court custody through charges brought by state prosecution for sedition or treason or conspiracy to assist in such crimes. In his Privy Council tirade Wedderburn, speaking as the government's lawyer, even as he spoke on behalf of the royal governor that day, characterized activity surrounding the abuse of the Hutchinson letters in just those terms.

> "These men [Franklin and his 'party' in Boston] are perpetually offering every kind of insult to the English nation. Setting the King's authority at defiance, treating the Parliament as usurpers of an authority not belonging to them and flatly denying the supreme jurisdiction of the British Empire.[110]

---

109 *Papers*, vol. 21, page 59.
110 *Id.* at 60.

"[In all the] arts ... made use of to incense the colonies against the mother country... no one I fear has been a more successful proficient than the very man who now stands forth as Mr. Hutchinson's accuser. My Lords, as he has been pleased in his own letter to avow this accusation, I shall now return the charge, and show ... who it is that is the true incendiary, and who is the great abettor of that faction in Boston, which in form of a Committee of Correspondence, have been inflaming the whole province against his Majesty's government."[111]

Clearly the Crown's solicitor general by this time was thinking sedition or treason.[112] Inflaming a province against its royal governor, whatever the incendiaries themselves might claim for their intentions, amounts to defiance of the whole of "his Majesty's government." The empire is unitary, so an assault on authority in any of its parts is to be treated as made on the whole of it.

That he was never held to answer in the Chancery proceeding owes as much to that court's ponderousness as much as it does to the skill of Franklin's legal representatives.[113]

---

111 *Id.* at 60-61.

112 Being doubtful of the sufficiency of admissible evidence of the agent's role in the Boston troubles, some in the ministry had it in mind to locate the originals of his letters as court-worthy proof of the agent's complicity (as through aiding and abetting, provoking and soliciting seditious acts). Notably, the secretary for American affairs Lord Dartmouth reportedly had seen copies of two letters (one from Franklin in July 1773 and another from Arthur Lee in December of that year) that he characterized as "dangerous correspondence" between people in England and "leaders of the faction at Boston." Dartmouth asked General-Governor Gage to locate originals of these letters so as to provide "the grounds of a proper proceeding." Clark, pages 251-253. Not until the summer of 1775 was such a search successful, and BF's letter to Thomas Cushing was found in the latter's trunk of papers hastily abandoned in his house when the speaker left Boston while he still could. The general eventually presented King George with the original of Franklin's letter as being of at least historic import, and it so it became part of George III's legacy of books and papers which formed the core of the British Library collection at the end of his reign. It is housed in the Rare Books division of the Library and has been read by the author.

113 Franklin employed Thomas Life as his solicitor who in turn retained several barristers to appear in Chancery for him. These included Arthur Lee, his colleague on the Massachusetts agency (by this time presumably qualified as barrister), and John Dunning, the advocate who had lost his voice the day of the Cockpit hearing. They were joined, in name at least, by the well-known Richard Jackson and by Charles Sayer. Sayer's name appears on the last substantial filing made on Franklin's part in the case, the answer to Whately's original filing that began the case. After the answer was submitted, issues were raised as to its adequacy and a hearing was set for argument on these issues before the Chancellor. The respondent had left the country by that time and thus that potentially decisive stage of things was never reached. Presumably on the urging of the plaintiff's

Good fortune seemingly worked on the agent's behalf in avoiding criminal charges, too. Not only was there uncertainty as to the sufficiency of evidence on any possible charges, but also there was a reported split of opinion within the ministry about the prudence of such a move. While Solicitor General Wedderburn apparently did want to have Franklin placed under arrest, his senior, Attorney General Thurlow, was cautious. The cooler heads in the ministry were evidently persuaded that nothing salutary could result from imprisonment of this most famous of all Americans and could well make matters worse for British authority in the colonies.[114]

THE FORMER GOVERNOR FLEES BOSTON, COMES TO ENGLAND

As if the scene were not already menacing for Franklin, the arrival there in London in the summer of 1774 of Thomas Hutchinson would likely have added to his sense of unease. The very man whose letters, views and status lay at the center of the trial had come to England. Although he was thoroughly vindicated in London, the last American-born royal governor of Massachusetts no longer felt secure in his native Boston of 1774. And so it was, Hutchinson had resigned and taken his family to England. It was only the second time Thomas Hutchinson had left his native land. He arrived in London that summer and received warm and supportive welcomes from the court and cabinet. Within days of his arrival in London, he was presented personally to the King by Lord Dartmouth and stood for a two-hour interview in depth on a range of issues. His majesty, Hutchinson's diary reports,

---

barrister, the court would force the issues about the adequacy of Franklin's answer. It issued a warrant to the sheriff of Middlesex to arrest the defendant. Eventually the court's process server reported back that after a diligent search the defendant was not to be found. See *Papers*, Vol. 21, pages 197-202; editors' notes and primary sources cited there.

114 While Franklin was worried about the possible effects of the Chancery proceeding and its cost to him in lawyers' fees, there is little to suggest that he felt immediately threatened with arrest. There is, however, one account published later by one of his occasional correspondents that Franklin following his humiliation in the Cockpit did leave town for a short time. It is said that the agent took a trunk of his papers from his Craven Street home, between the Strand and the Thames, and went by boat up river to Chelsea, there to stay for a few days in the home a friend, David Williams. Williams was a clergyman of dissenting views with whom Franklin had met sometimes to discuss reforms in the Book of Common Prayer. In his autobiography published late in Williams' life (he died in 1816), he sets out his recollection of such a visit. The editors of the Franklin Papers have concluded that "the story of his flight to Chelsea leaves us skeptical," finding no contemporary support for it. *Papers*, Vol. XXI, pages 119–120.

---

was particularly solicitous for his health and that of his family after their ordeal. By this time the former governor had become a London celebrity, much sought out for his knowledge of and views upon events in America. There was a good deal of interest in the impact of the Coercive Acts, about which the newcomer could only know that the first of them, the Boston Port Bill, was burdensome and much resented.

> And everyone, it seemed, had something to say on the background of the 'letters' affair, which according [to one important contact] had finally convinced the ministry to act against the colonial rebellion. The 'revelations' and sheer gossip about Hutchinson's letters, especially on the question of the identity of the person who had stolen them and given them to Franklin, were bewildering in their number and complexity.[115]

It seems surprising that Franklin and Hutchinson never encountered one another during this time, although they scarcely would have had the same social invitations. But it is likely that neither sought such a meeting. Franklin remained in the city for eight more months following the other's arrival from America. For his part Hutchinson was demonstrably interested in Franklin's activities. Indeed, he apparently sought information from several of his contacts; he was especially interested to learn about how Franklin had acquired the letters. Whether Hutchinson sought to influence official action against his adversary or to press for progress in the Whately suit we only know by inference.

So far as his own letters might reveal any disquiet, it is not apparent that Franklin was particularly concerned that his former friend had arrived and was perched in the catbird seat of imperial favor. Franklin could well have known about Hutchinson's probing. If so, he seemed disinclined to let it worry him. From the distance of two hundred and thirty years, the scene is overlaid with irony and is more than a little awkward. Perhaps it was as delicate for the former governor as for the former postmaster and agent. Both had suffered grievous blows to their fortunes and reputations in the months just passed. Both had to be uncertain if not anxious about what lay ahead for each of them. Hutchinson had not wanted to be in England at all and would be glad to leave when peace returned.

The other man certainly had wanted to be there, and he had been living in London, as we know, for a good number of years already. Among the ties that probably kept him there longer than perhaps was prudent, given all

---

115 Bernard Bailyn, *The Ordeal of Thomas Hutchinson*, page 285.

that had happened, there was one that was not formally related to any of his several "official" or public duties.

THE WALPOLE (OHIO) COMPANY

For several years prior to these events, back when Franklin's name carried more positive influence and association, Franklin was engaged with a number of prominent men in London in a great land grant proposal. The territory involved would be that of the present state of West Virginia. Chief among the leading front men for the proposal was Thomas Walpole, nephew of Sir Robert the long time leader of the Whigs earlier in the century, and he served as chairman. It was a stock company in which Franklin had purchased a few shares, as had a number of his friends like William Strahan and his son William. One of his fellow colonials, Samuel Wharton, came over to London to drive the effort, he and others already having worked out some sticky points with the Virginians who claimed their charter covered the territory and wanted to reward their veterans of the French and Indian War with grants as payment for their services. It was, formally at least, more than a request for an outright grant of Crown lands, for the investors offered to pay about ten thousand pounds as well as some "quit rents" based on tillable land after twenty years. The figure represented what the Crown had paid to Indian tribes in the area for agreeing to move the boundary between English and Indian territories. If the grant or "sale" were made, the owners would embark on the settlement of a huge new colony, incredibly twenty million acres, the first in those lands beyond the mountains of eastern America either ceded by France to Britain in the treaty concluding the Seven Years War or of disputed status among native Americans and the settlers of the European empires of France and Britain. The petition for the Walpole land scheme, known officially as Vandalia, in honor of the land of the queen's continental heritage, was pending for long periods before either the Board of Trade or the Privy Council. The former had ruled against the request on a number of different grounds, largely on the basis of the ministry's preference for restricting westward migration and limiting present colonial development to the seaboard of Britain's newly enlarged North American territories.

The Privy Council then over-ruled the Board, provoking Lord Hillsborough to resign his post in the ministry, as he had threatened to do if the

Council took that course. Some of the councilors apparently relished forcing Hillsborough, regarded by many peers as an unpleasant man, to that decision, whatever they thought of the scheme on its merits. The law officers of the Crown sat on their instructions to draw up the grant, and in the delay it was becoming obvious to the sponsors that Franklin's name in the company was a real detriment. Attorney General Thurlow is said to have told those who claimed that his office was trying to undermine the project that the grant would not be made while one of the potential grantees was a man who merited no favor from the Crown.[116]

Franklin had offered as early as 1771 to resign from the company directors, but Walpole had not accepted. By early 1774 everything had changed, and in January Walpole wrote to Franklin and asked for his resignation. He complied, at least formally. Franklin, not one to give up on any enterprise too readily, evidently remained a silent stockholder for a few more years, paying what was due on his two shares. Then in 1777, residing in Paris as the agent of the Continental Congress to the French court, he did surrender his shares and asked for a return of any unexpended balance on them.[117]

It is doubtful whether the grant would have been made even without Franklin's involvement. Hillsborough's views were widely shared in the ministry so that these coupled with those of the law officers would likely have prevailed to stop it. As it was, the prospective proprietor lost little, we can see now. The company never realized its ambitions. Its proposal for the land grant died a quiet death in the files of the ministry.

---

116 The attribution is in Franklin's own hand on a document bearing his signature, dated July 14, 1778, held in the New York Public Library. Papers, Vol. 21, pages 32–33.

117 *Papers*, Vol. 21, pages 31–32. Curiously, that was not Franklin's last move on the matter. In 1778, he wrote again to Walpole asking for his resignation letter back, noting that for his legatees the shares were still valid and would, he hoped benefit his descendants. His reason for resigning, he also noted, had been to obviate the Attorney General's objection to the grant. Ibid. Evidently the former agent had to consider that the Empire could still be in control of that part of the world by the time he died. Hedging his bets this way was not something that embarrassed Franklin, apparently, but of course no public notoriety accompanied these shifts in Franklin's attitude. We have seen before that Franklin endured ambiguity more easily perhaps than other men.

SUMMARY OF PERSONAL REVERSALS

Of all the losses and injuries he suffered in 1774, certainly the most severe were wrought by the verdicts of January. In that terribly fateful month, Franklin saw his place in the center of empire destroyed. It is true of course that his position had grown terribly complicated in the last several years, principally since he assumed the agency for the House of Representatives of Massachusetts in 1770. He had already acquired some enemies and detractors. His alienation of and from the Penn family was a significant factor plus the enmity of Lord Hillsborough. He also had called attention to himself as a very clever essayist, this in a day when cleverness in print did not translate well into other form of success, especially not diplomatic or political ones. Franklin could count on only a smattering of confidants and supporters, and not all of these were really important in the circle of authority and influence.

Yet what he did have was valuable, not merely to his constituents back home. Especially valuable was his attachment to the bonds of respect and cooperation (mutual dependence and uneven trust, if one prefers the more skeptical version) that held the American colonies and Britain together tolerably well for over a century.

Paradoxically Franklin was still seen, as we learn in the next chapter, by some significant people in London as the indispensable spokesman for America as a whole and believed to be in a position to influence events and attitudes there. For these, it mattered less how little influence he retained in London. What he had was knowledge and that might be put to good and conciliatory use in Britain, for sake of the Empire, if not especially for that of the colonies. The moderates would have a tough sell in the later months of 1774 and of course increasingly so in 1775. But they were game to try, at least to explore, compromise, while the opportunity was present before them.

Probably the most poetic of ironies in the whole saga of Franklin's trial, its origins and its consequences, is that while his status and stature in England had fallen precipitously in these last months, his popularity in America at large had increased just as rapidly. The effigies burned in Boston and Philadelphia of Wedderburn and Hutchinson provide a glimpse of the feeling aroused over the trial of this complicated man who by then was seen unambiguously on the right side of the widening divide between the colonies and Britain.

PARLIAMENT THROWS DOWN THE GANTLET

For the ministry the bad news from Massachusetts kept getting worse. The singular outrage to British sensibility that Franklin had committed, revealed as it were under duress, was followed closely by the riotous action of a score or more vigilantes, some of them barely disguised as "Mohawk" warriors, in staging their Tea Party on the wharfs of Boston harbor. To compound their insolence, the Bostonians refused to pay for the valuable cargo of tea that was the property of the British East India Company. Franklin himself had urged that the city of Boston offer to pay when its port was opened again. For his part Governor Hutchinson had urged Whitehall not to punish the entire province for the criminal acts of a few of its residents. The North administration by this time was in no mood for compromise and half-measures; nor was Parliament. The King's mood, too, had turned sour and he was willing to permit measures that just months before he would have refused.

Consequences for Franklin, as we have seen, were severe and swift. And some were still in the air. While the agent could be excused as preoccupied with these things, imperial authorities on the other hand went forward with initiatives of far greater magnitude. Scarcely two months following his dismissal from the post office position, Parliament passed and sent to the King for signature the first of a series of deliberately punitive measures. The Boston Port Bill became law on March 31, 1774. It compelled the closing of that port and thereby consigned the province and much of New England with it to certain economic strangulation. All commerce in and out would be stopped on June 1. Lifelines not only to and from Britain but also with all the other colonies were effectively shut down.

Then in quick succession during April and May Parliament enacted the Massachusetts Government Bill and the Administration of Justice Bill. Neither was as purely punitive as the first measure closing the port of Boston, but both were aimed at practices long complained of by British colonial officials and promoted by hardliners in London. The Government Act would end the tradition of election to the colony's Council or upper legislative body and mandate appointment by the King directly. It would also authorize the royal governor to appoint all judges and sheriffs replacing all community initiative and involvement. And, aiming directly at New England's town councils increasingly assertive in Massachusetts during the Hutchinson years, the Act would limit the number of their meetings to one per year, unless otherwise approved by the governor. Harsh measures against popular government, to be sure, were just what the distemper of the colony seemingly required in the ministry's view. Parliament readily agreed.

Bostonians, if theirs were shaky constitutional claims previously, would have substantial grounds from then forward. There was no question in London but that these steps amounted to an override or repeal of very significant portions of the Charter for Massachusetts Bay of 1691. George III had opposed such moves in 1769, during reaction to the Townshend Acts and related measures. Clearly, his majesty had by the spring of 1774 changed his views.

Similarly, the third parliamentary act in the series, the Administration of Justice Act, would confront the challenge of local jury bias against his majesty's customs officials and others who could be charged with criminal violations in the conduct of their enforcement activities. The Act provided for a change of venue for any such potential defendant in local courts. The parallel situation, of local juries or grand juries declining to convict or charge persons responsible for injury to the property of customs officers themselves, had been dealt with in another way. The Vice Admiralty Courts, originally set up at Halifax, Nova Scotia, were now authorized for Boston, Philadelphia and Charleston, South Carolina. These courts always sat without juries, so that their Crown appointed judges decided all contested facts and points of law.

An instance of jury "independence" was the subject of a complaint by one of the writers of the Hutchinson letters, an official in Rhode Island whose home and office were ruined by a mob. The more notorious *Gaspee* incident well illustrates the character of the challenge to royal authority. There in the sound below the Rhode Island city of Providence, a naval cutter pursuing smugglers ran aground, was boarded by civilians after nightfall and burned to the water's edge. An ensuing criminal enquiry failed for lack of witnesses against the local men responsible.

Collectively these statutes of Parliament were known as the "Coercive Acts," but in the colonies they were called the "Intolerable Acts." Orders-in-Council from Whitehall set other changes in motion. Most notably, on April 7, 1774, the replacement for the then resigned Governor Hutchinson was appointed, Thomas Cage, previously serving at New York as the commanding general of all British forces in the American colonies. New authority for assistance in housing and supplying the occupation forces came from Parliament's Quartering Act of the same spring. With so many newly arrived troops in Massachusetts, spare housing (such as in barns and warehouses under the existing rules) was scarce, so private homes could be pressed into service if need be.

As the new royal governor took up his duties in Boston, regular army reinforcements were sent in the form several fresh regiments of redcoats from Ireland. Boston soon became a garrison town, administered from Castle William in the harbor guarded offshore by ships of the Royal Navy and ringed with troops at barricades thrown up across the neck of the Boston peninsula.

Clearly Britain was preparing its authority for the severest of tests. The North ministry now considered Massachusetts to be in rebellion and set about to meet the challenge with enough force to intimidate its citizens. Whitehall did not expect that other colonies would actively sympathize with Massachusetts. In little less than a year, there would be unpleasant surprises. One was the successful call in Boston for a second continental congress. Another would be the encounter of troops with civilian militia at Lexington and Concord. And by that time, too, March 1775, that tireless promoter of all things American and most visible of colonial agents in London would himself relinquish his "station" and head for home.

CONSEQUENCE OR MERE AFTERMATH?

It is unconventional to claim, as this book does, that this series of sharp retorts to Massachusetts was a consequence of Franklin's actions in the Hutchinson letters affair. The continuous chain of events over the whole course of the Hutchinson governorship came to a head with the publication of the letters in June 1773 and the accompanying riotous demonstrations in Boston—these things formed a pattern, the ministry could see, especially once Franklin revealed his own pivotal role. To be sure there were other, longer-term influences at work already. But when a major colonial figure, no less than the one representing the most radical of the colonies, revealed his own hand in a scheme to unseat the governor and then there was a carefully staged mob action confounding local authority and destroying valuable property itself an instrument of imperial policy, it is plausible to see, as London believed it saw, conspiracy extending to both sides of the Atlantic.

Of course one cannot ignore the additional outrage to British authority in the episode of the Boston Tea Party just prior to Franklin's trial. For all its visual and material impact, however, and its considerable hold on modern imagination, the Tea Party was no greater a challenge than the affair of the Hutchinson letters and Franklin's admission of his own central role in it. Even without the brazen and unpunished act of spoilage of the East Indian Company's cargo in defiance of the tariff, London in January of 1774 was ready for a showdown with the radicals in Massachusetts.

The single best evidence of Whitehall's new determination is that at the "preliminary hearing" on January 9th, the solicitor general and the members of the Privy Council were ready to pounce on Franklin. And that was some days before news of the Tea Party reached London. Charles Jenkinson, MP and formerly close to the Bute ministry early in the reign of George III, concluded that the letters affair had finally convinced the government to act against rebellion in the colony of Massachusetts. He and most of his fellow parliamentarians were ready to do their part. Drafts of some of the Coercive Acts had been prepared by those, like Jenkinson and friends of George Grenville, still stinging from the rebuke of Parliament in repealing the Stamp Act in 1766. With the impetus provided by the provocations toward and forced retirement of Governor Hutchinson, a stiffened combination of wills at last emerged in Whitehall.

There is little doubt that the incident over the tea reinforced the ministry's resolve to confront the radicals, but it added little to the new "understanding" about the colony's disposition to oppose royal authority at every turn. The ministry's mind seemed clear by January 1774, when Franklin was put on trial. The Tea Party outrage was but an extension of the radicals' efforts of the last two years to confront royal authority and unseat its representatives in Massachusetts. There were, in the weeks to follow, unconfirmed reports circulating in London that John Hancock and Sam Adams, two of the more prominent figures of the Boston "faction," had actually been seen leading the mob of ill-disguised locals who boarded the ships and destroyed the cargo of tea.

Franklin's own impression at the time was that he was being given the blame "for all the misunderstanding" (BF Ltr to Cushing, October 12, 1774). Closer to the events he had written that "some part of the [wrath over the tea] has fallen on me..." (BF Ltr to Galloway, February 18, 1774).

CHAPTER 10. SECOND THOUGHTS

Moving on from the calamity of January proved more difficult for Franklin than he anticipated. He had written to friends that he expected to leave England by the month of May 1774, looking to have the accounts settled by then for the post office operations in America. Several complications intervened. Chief among them was that Arthur Lee was not prepared, apparently, to begin service independently as Franklin's successor agent for the Massachusetts House. In a letter to Thomas Cushing on April 2, 1774, Franklin harkens back to his letter to Cushing of February 2, immediately after the trial, in which he said that "after the treatment I received at the Council, it was no longer possible for me to act as agent, apprehending I could ... be of no further use to the Province." Yet, he added, "I have nevertheless given what assistance I could as a private man, by speaking to members of both houses [of Parliament] and by joining in petitions [of other Americans now living in London] ably drawn by Mr. Lee." The petitions or protests were against the Coercive Acts passed that spring and given the King's assent with uncommon efficiency and consensus.

Lee did not leave (for his expected tour of France and Italy) until the end of May, according to Franklin's letter to Cushing of June 1. "On his departure," Franklin reported, "[Lee] returned all the papers [of the agency] [to me], and I feel under ... necessity to continue" until the House can make other arrangements for representation in London.

Moreover, both New Jersey and Pennsylvania told him they wanted Franklin to carry on with his representation of those legislatures. Plus, Committees of Correspondence in the colonies were writing to him expressing solidarity with Massachusetts in a determination to resist and take some joint action through the upcoming Continental Congress set for September of 1774.

Called by necessity to step back into service for Massachusetts, asked to continue two other agencies, Franklin evidently tried to carry on much as he had before the trial. While he received no encouragement from the ministry, it must have given Franklin reassurance that what he was doing might be of service in the colonies. His presence in London at least provided hands and voice through which conditions and sentiments could be known there. Letters written by Franklin's ally Reverend Samuel Cooper, one on August 15, 1774, another on September 9, made clear that while there were hardships under the Coercive Acts, particularly the Boston Port blockade, there were gratifying examples of mutual assistance and solidarity among the colonies of New England as well.

> The act for blockading [Boston] has been executed with utmost rigor.... Our coasters with wood have been [made] to unload at Salem; fish from Marblehead may not be taken by water to Boston but must go overland by Roxbury (Cooper to BF, August 15, 1774].

> Besides the fleet in the harbor, there are four regiments encamped on the [Boston} Common, another at the Castle.... [Nonetheless,] the people endure all with astonishing calmness and resolution, supported and encouraged with the sympathy and good wishes of our brethren in the country and throughout the colonies. They have made our cause a common one. ... Large and generous presents to the indigent and distressed ... flow in from all quarters. [Cooper to BF, August 15] "And 1200 bushels of wheat ... have come from Quebec [Cooper to BF, September 9, 1774].

> Boston is not yet destroyed, nor the American cause desperate... Our rights may perhaps yet be redeemed and prove a means of saving the liberties of Britain [Cooper to BF, August 15, 1774]. We shall [Cooper added,] trust in our representatives at the Congress soon to be convened in Philadelphia, to propose either a "non-importation or a non-consumption of British goods resolution.

To the same effect is the message from James Bowdoin, another prominent man of New England (and father-in-law of John Temple). He wrote to Franklin within a week of Cooper's second letter:

> The spirit the [Coercive] Acts have raised throughout the colonies is surprising...; there is reason to hope it will be productive of a union that will work out for the salvation of the whole ... [and that union could be] the means of establishing on a just and constitutional basis a lasting harmony between Britain and the colonies [James Bowdoin to BF, September 6, 1774].

Two aspects of these developments could have lifted Franklin's mood in this, his last, autumn in England. One is that while the coercion from Britain was as formidable as he feared it would be when the infamous acts were being adopted, the reaction in American may well have surprised, or at least gratified, him. There were repeated acts of mutual community assistance; there was concerted activity to meet and present a united front; and a determination to try, once more, the favored strategy of economic boycott in response to British heavy-handedness. Equally important, there was as yet little or no violence or mob action reported. Americans were acting with restraint and determination. All the while, their common aim seemed to be toward reconciliation with Britain, not separation through civil war or rebellion. If his people back home could be that optimistic, under these trying circumstances, how could he not hold fast a bit longer? Long enough, he might have told himself, to see if there would be any reciprocal gestures from the British.

Perhaps Franklin's spirits were revived by these reports from the colonies. Somehow he gained a new, if very guarded, resolve to go ahead and assume, as many in the colonies appeared to believe, that reconsideration was possible in London. Franklin continued to have faith in the power of the economic boycotts in America; at least he encouraged the colonies to keep these efforts up and make them inclusive and effective.

As late as the summer of 1774, Franklin believed that a combination of colonial determination and British mercantile anxiety would produce meaningful political leverage on the ministry through the next Parliamentary election. But before that momentum could build up, the North ministry called a special election for October, well before it would normally take place. The friends of the colonies were caught off guard and were not yet organized. The election results were disappointing. Nothing changed in the alignment of members in the new Parliament. Lord North's hand would be as strong as before.

WHAT WOULD CONGRESS DO?

No one in London could predict the outcome of the great parallel political event of the autumn, the one that took place in Philadelphia in September. The very prospect of the Congress, deriving its presumed authority not from Britain but from the electorate at large in all the colonies, taking place was disturbing to court sensibilities in London. Ministry officials and the King himself were apprehensive that the Congress would be more provocative or confrontational than it proved to be. In that case, the hands of Whitehall would be tied even more tightly than they had become in the spring. The news of its deliberations, however, did not reach London until December, well past the time to have a bearing on Parliamentary elections. The tone of the resolutions of the Congress should have reassured England that the colonies were not bent upon separation, yet to many in the ministry they must have seemed high-handed: "the resolution of the Congress arrived and gave not a little umbrage to the ministry, as appeared by their conduct within and without doors" (Ltr of David Barclay, London, to James Pemberton, Philadelphia, March 18, 1775).

The aim of the Congress' resolution was to restore relations to those that pre-existed the Coercive Acts against the colony, first, of Massachusetts and, then, against all New England colonies. By repealing those laws and rescinding the orders of military occupation, the Crown and Parliament could be assured of the colonies' willingness to address remaining issues in a subsequent Congress of the colonies, issues such as how the colonies might tax themselves for their contribution to the joint defense of the Empire and the various charter and governance issues of individual colonies.

The resolutions of Congress "were laid before both house of Parliament" in late December or early January, but they were never taken up formally or in any direct fashion. Initiatives by individual MPs to force debate on one or another individual issue, however, were made in January and February 1775. The Earl of Chatham, one of a few avowed friends for the cause of the colonists in Parliament, introduced a motion in the House of Lords that the King be "humbly beseeched" to withdraw the troops from Boston as a conciliatory first step. After a "long and warm debate," the motion failed seventy-seven to eighteen. For their part ministers present in Lords declared their intention to enforce the acts (BF's Ltr to Thomas Cushing, January 28, 1775).

In the House of Commons, at about the same time, a petition was brought in by Sir George Saville, MP, at Franklin's request, seeking an opportunity for the London representatives of Massachusetts–William Bollan, Arthur Lee and Franklin—to address the House in support of the Congress' resolutions. The request was "rejected by a great majority" (Circular Ltr. to the Speakers of the Colonial Assemblies from Franklin, Bollan and Lee, February 5, 1775).

Private Overtures

The colonial cause was clearly going nowhere in the public and formal avenues of government. Yet, although his correspondence of these months makes no reference to them, there were some other initiatives afoot meanwhile. There were people in London, some of them close to, if not actually in the ministry, who felt something could be done to reconcile the colonies with Britain if these matters were approached quietly and out of public view.

In December, two private, unofficial initiatives began with overtures to Franklin. The first one had its apparent origin in a social invitation to Franklin. An offer of some chess games with the gentleman philosopher from a lady in a prominent family with whom he had not had any previous contact came to the former agent through a mutual friend of host and invitee. Whether the invitation was based on Franklin's certain recognition of her name, Caroline Howe, or whether it was merely the prospect of some amiable and diverting conversation with a lady in her home, he was eventually pleased to accept. He hesitated until a mutual acquaintance, a fellow member of the Royal Society, told Franklin he was ready to escort him personally to the lady's door. There was no thought, on his part anyway, that the engagement could lead to anything of political significance. We may assume, then, it was either sheer vanity or his natural sociability that led him to accept.

The lady was the widowed sister of Richard Howe, a rear admiral in the Royal Navy as well as a member of the House of Lords. At the second or third afternoon of chess, and following some little discussion of problems of mathematics, then a brief exchange over the differences besetting their two countries, Mrs. Howe inquired whether her guest would be willing to meet her brother who, she noted, was much interested in America. Of course, he would. And so began one of the so-called "secret negotiations" in which Franklin participated before leaving England on his way back to an America that had and would change every bit as much as he had during the last year.

What transpired in these weeks of December 1774 and January 1775 was not so much an exchange of views and positions as it was the submission of a series of lists or revisions of the first, by Franklin, of points of policy which, if they were modified, could bring about a return to normalcy in the colonies. Who exactly in the government ever read or considered these points has not been fully established, but it is certain that one of these "behind-the-scenes" conciliators was in direct contact with the Earl of Dartmouth and another with Lord Hyde.

Dr. John Fothergill was physician to the Earl of Dartmouth (and to Franklin as well, as it happens) and an associate of Franklin's since the 1750s when they pursued electrical studies together. David Barclay was a banker involved in trade with the American colonies. In that latter regard he was especially concerned to ease tensions so that exports of Britain to the American colonies would not be seriously affected. He proposed early on in these talks that a petition of merchants be submitted to Parliament.

Fothergill and Barclay were Quakers and held no public office of any kind. They could be considered neutral on the specific issues of the moment, neither hard-line Tory nor liberal Whig or sympathetic to the cause of colonists' grievances. Both men asked Franklin to record his views or suggestions (Franklin called them "Hints") so that they might share them with those who could be helpful in more direct ways. Neither claimed to be representing anyone in particular, yet the inference, at least for Fothergill, is that he had the ear of Dartmouth. Barclay's contact is not known, but he mentions in a letter of March 18, 1775, "two lords high in office"—one of whom was probably Dartmouth, since Barclay and Fothergill were acting together.

Howe's higher-level contact would be Lord Hyde, Royal Postmaster General, and member of the House of Lords.

"Principles ... [Too] Far from Each Other"

In both these mystery networks, that through Lord Howe and that through Barclay and Fothergill, what ultimately emerged was that on one major point both sides were simply too far apart for the gulf to be bridged.

Howe was blunt in his last report to Franklin: "[Lord Hyde] apprehends that on the present American contest, your principles and his, or rather those of Parliament, are yet so wide from each other that a meeting merely to discuss them might give you unnecessary trouble" (Ltr from Lord Richard Howe to BF, February 20, 1775).

On the colonies' side, it was Franklin's view, reflecting the resolutions of Congress, that Britain should renounce its authority in Parliament to legislate on matters internal to the colonies. No one involved on the British side in this weeks' long quasi-dialogue ever doubted that such a disavowal would be impossible.[118]

"The idea that a British monarch could reign over all but not rule in any of his territories was impossible to grasp in 1774," Esmond Wright once observed.[119] That was, he added, as strange a notion to thinkers of that period in Britain as the notion that powers of government could be separated would have been to Americans of that same decade.

Whoever stood behind these initiatives to draw Franklin out, one element throughout seems emblematic of the British establishment's assumptions about its late royal servant. And that is that Franklin somehow had authority to negotiate on behalf, not merely of a single colony, Massachusetts, but of all the American colonies. It was not that implausible an assumption in light of the Continental Congress' avowing the side of Massachusetts and the other New England colonies. Whether this inflated view of his status was based on anything that loyalists in America were telling London, or whether the British simply hoped Franklin could find a way to influence opinion back home, we cannot be sure.

Franklin himself was not a little responsible for the supposition about or misapprehension of his authority, given his writings plus his notable success in the previous decade with the Stamp Act's reconsideration and repeal. He often claimed that he knew American conditions very well. It is another of several ironies about this time of winding down in London that Franklin's knowledge of American conditions was consistently out of date and incomplete. The longer he stayed in England, the more steadily the currency of his information and understanding of events in the colonies declined. Given the relative rapidity of events, both in the colonies and in Lon-

---

118 Other biographers and historians have taken the view it was the insistence on dropping all the recent "intolerable acts" of repression before Massachusetts would pay for the tea that finally weighed down any possibility of compromise.

119 Esmond Wright, p. 234.

don, it could not have been otherwise. Yet by the time of his departure, he doubtlessly understood better than any other American how limited their prospects for any more conciliation, let alone reform, were in the mother country.

A Gratuitous Affront

One element in these unofficial dealings made them not merely unrealistic but distasteful for the agent. We have only Franklin's notes of what was said in the process. And so the weight placed on that account varies from one historian or biographer to another. At a couple of points Lord Howe more than intimated that should peaceable solutions be found between Britain and its colonies, there would be ample recognition from the Crown for those responsible for so happy an outcome. Moreover, to make the matter even stickier, Howe himself apparently entertained the prospect of personally leading a commission of conciliation to the colonies and hoped, he stated to Franklin, that he could accompany that delegation, perhaps as an assistant or advisor to Lord Howe.

Assuming these blandishments were indeed part of the message Franklin heard, one or two implications emerge at once. And neither is flattering to Lord Richard Howe. Either Franklin's mood (if not character) was badly misjudged, or, alternatively, the agent was being set up so that he could be defamed once more, this time on the other side of the Atlantic. If Howe or his "sponsor" had been correct about his mood or character, the other possible usage could be held in reserve, depending on the turn of events. To be fair to the other mediators, Fothergill and Barclay, it has to be said that there is no reason to believe they had anything but a high regard for Franklin and did not intend to use him for any ulterior purpose.

It was, conceivably, not mere bitterness which moved Franklin to write to son William and urge him to give up the dependency that accompanies the bestowal of executive appointment and lead a more satisfying independence, say by farming on Franklin family lands in Pennsylvania. That such a suggestion would not be taken seriously by this privileged son cannot really be doubted. William, thanks to his own father's success as a Londoner with visibility, had grown into his maturity in the Empire's capital and flourished there. He was as thoroughly British (and Tory) as his father was soon to become thoroughly republican, as well as clearly American, in identity.

Perhaps, on a more concrete level, the father feared for his son's future in an empire to which the father's loyalty was increasingly in question. If that were the case, he need not have worried about William's fate, at least at the hands of the British government. William was made to endure, however, a pretty rough time in the colonies. He was arrested by militia in 1776 and held in a prison in Connecticut for two years before being turned over to British forces in New York, and from there he returned to Britain.

Beyond injury to pride and self-respect, the blow to Benjamin Franklin at his trial seemed to have a much deeper reach. His considerable and considered respect for the institutions by which Britain and its empire were ruled seemed to have left him. It is as if the identity with which he saw himself as much British as American had been convincingly shaken loose. And these bribes, if that was what Howe was holding out, simply made losing that divided identity imperative and its retention distasteful.[120]

ONE MORE GESTURE: CHATHAM CALLS

If these "secret negotiations" of that winter were mysterious and clouded from history's view, one final overture Franklin received was not. This one was public, perhaps a bit too much so for its best chance to succeed. Word reached Franklin in late January 1775, that the former Whig prime minister William Pitt, the elder, now Earl of Chatham, desired to confer with Franklin. In plain view of the neighbors in Craven Street, the Earl's carriage arrived in front of Number 7 on the day appointed. England's most famous living political leader, no longer in ministerial office but a life member of the House of Lords, chief architect of the country's notable success in the Seven Years War, was making a call. Chatham wanted the American's opinion about current conditions in the colonies, as he was preparing proposals for reconciliation bills in Parliament.

The visit to Franklin took place on January 29th, exactly one year following his humiliation in the Privy Council trial; it served to cheer Franklin and afford him encouragement that things might go better than he earlier expected. Chatham, moreover, wanted Franklin to go with him and be present in Lords on January 31, the day he would deliver his speech in support of such a bill. That gesture must also have promised some vindication for

---

120 In his later reflection on these negotiations, Franklin colorfully characterized such an overture as "spitting in the soup."

a wounded pride. Franklin was in the gallery of the House of Lords on the appointed day.

What Chatham said in his speech that day was not as much as Franklin would have wanted, but it was far more than he could have expected at any time in the past twelve months.

In the end, the speech's reception in Lords brought all those newfound hopes crashing down at Franklin's feet. Dartmouth, who had plenary responsibility for the colonies in the cabinet, rose after Chatham's speech to give cautious support for its message. Then one of the hard-line members of the House of Lords present, the Earl of Sandwich, and one of Franklin's detractors, took the floor and denounced the speech in no uncertain terms. It was so offensive, he said, that he must conclude it "could not have been composed by an English peer." It could only, Sandwich threw out, have been authored by an American, and one whose face he was then looking into, as he stared at Franklin seated up in the gallery above the floor of the House. There were audible signs from other members that Sandwich's attack reflected widespread sentiment. On the vote, Chatham's proposal failed by a wide margin.

By his own account of that day, Franklin tells us that he remained outwardly unperturbed by what he heard, much as he had remained impassive at his trial just over a year earlier. Inwardly, Franklin was witnessing the final collapse of all the illusions of the intervening twelve months, and once again he stared at the open space that once held the admiration for and affinity with what had been great in the Britain of his long life.

The old liberal leader had had his moment to reclaim a calmer tone for British authority. It was not to be. He, too, must have been disillusioned if not bitter at the summary treatment by his peers. If so senior and famous a statesmen could have no greater influence than this, clearly matters of state, so far as the colonies were concerned in their defiance of imperial authority, were beyond deflection or reconsideration. Franklin might be excused for his illusions, given the twin identities between which he had not previously had to choose. That Chatham himself was so badly out of step with the times is the more remarkable aspect of the drama.

Just over a month later, in March of 1775, Franklin would finally sail for America. As if to add to the sadness of this leaving by political necessity, he had been informed a few weeks previously of another loss. In a letter from son William he learned that Deborah, his wife for these many years and mother of his children (including the one she only adopted), had died of a stroke in December. The substantial house on Market Street awaited him, but the gentle spirit tending it all during their partnership, in his absence and his presence, would be missing.[121]

Frederick North, 2d Earl of Guilford by Nathanial Dance. Courtesy of National Portrait Gallery, London. ©National Portrait Gallery, London

---

121 William Franklin wrote to his father on Christmas eve, 1774, to inform him of the funeral some few days earlier which he almost missed due to bad weather on the way from Amboy, New Jersey, to Philadelphia. It is a poignant letter and speaks of his (step-) mother's prior stroke as well as her despairing of ever seeing her husband again if he should not return home before that winter. *Papers*, Vol. 21, pages 402-405. While William was certainly reared as if he were Deborah's son, and his sentiments in this letter reflect his genuine affection for her, his biological mother remains unknown. William's half-sister Sally Bache and her husband, Richard, were of course at the funeral and they would be in residence on Market Street when Franklin returned.

Chapter 11. Going Home, Looking Back

The secret talks with the several surrogates of ministry that took place over three months—December, January, and February—of that last of Franklin's London winters had collapsed. Both houses of Parliament had adopted a resolution to the King declaring the province of Massachusetts to be in rebellion. The port of Boston had been closed under supervision of warships of the Royal Navy. Neither of Chatham's overtures for moderation had been seriously considered in Lords. Even so, as late in his stay as March 16, 1775, four days before he would leave London for Portsmouth and his trip home, Franklin attended a debate in the House of Lords to see once more whether the distemper gripping Westminster and Whitehall since his trial had abated. There was nothing encouraging about the experience. In fact he was so infuriated by what he heard that he drafted an angry letter to Dartmouth, a letter he never sent, thanks to the timely advice of friends, Thomas Walpole, a business partner, and Lord Camden.

There was something slightly hurried about these last days in London for Franklin. His turnover of the Massachusetts agency to Arthur Lee was by letter on March 19th, noting that documents for his successor were being left in the custody of his landlady. On the previous day he had a long talk with Edmund Burke. We do not know what they said to each other, but probably Burke spoke of ideas for a speech in Commons he would give soon on conciliation with the colonies. Franklin wrote a note to Mrs. Stevenson, his landlady and unique friend, about paying some accounts for him. But he spent nearly the whole of the day, that last full day In London, in the company of Joseph Priestly, a close friend and fellow scientist. They read recent newspapers from America and talked. Priestly later noted that he saw tears on Franklin's cheeks during those hours in his Craven Street home as they went over reports from the Philadelphia and Boston papers. Both could see how the gap between their countries was widening rapidly, and they shared regrets that there was no more for them to do for it.

When the departure was actually planned is not known, although intimations of impending departure had been around for some time. Franklin penned letters to correspondents in Britain, for example, one to Lord Kames, legal historian and contemporary of David Hume and Adam Smith, in Edinburgh on March 14, apprising him of his plans to depart. Nonetheless, there is the appearance of last-minute haste, not least that much of Franklin's books and furnishings in Craven Street would remain with Mrs. Stevenson until they were sent for after Franklin was again settled in Philadelphia. He managed then to get enough done to take some ease on the last day, a day perhaps of reflecting and pondering events with his old friend. It had to be a day of sadness for both friends.

TRANSITIONS

Then on the 20th of March 1775, Franklin left London for the last time in his life, and in a day or two at Portsmouth he boarded *The Pennsylvania Packet*, the small ship that would in six weeks bring him and his grandson Temple to Philadelphia. We are told only of two principal engagements during the long voyage. One was writing, in the form of a letter to his son William, an account of those mysterious encounters known in his biographies as "the secret negotiations" that took place in the last months before he finally departed. The other was a project of natural science, making observations of the Gulf Stream, by way of measuring variations in temperature of the sea, so as to place that current more securely in the charts of the time.

This would be Franklin's sixth crossing of the Atlantic. Accustomed to the sea that both separated and linked the major divisions of Empire, he knew about the Gulf Stream as one of its special features. Ships' captains based in New England knew from experience to avoid it when sailing west-ward and to stay within it, when the winds permitted, sailing east. Several days could be gained by respecting its powerful presence. Ever the prac-tical observer, Franklin recorded much and understood a good deal more. Perhaps he understood why Debbie, his late wife, had always avoided such crossings, preferring to remain in their home in Philadelphia, though she missed him and long had wanted him to terminate his stay in London and return home.

He would likely think of the risks of sailing in coastal waters, perhaps being reminded of his landing in 1757 after fog had kept his ship offshore and out of sight of land for a couple of extra nights. In his *Autobiography* he would later write of how relieved he was then to be, along with son William and two servants, safely on land again. Franklin noted also that while many of his fellow voyagers declared themselves so thankful to be safe that they wanted to endow the establishment of a chapel near the place of their land-ing, he himself would prefer to build a new lighthouse.

After the swells and shoals and tides and rocks that imperil a ship in its transit from harbor to open sea are left behind and the comparative safety of deeper water is reached, a vessel under sail moves forward more evenly and steadily. Finding a sustaining wind, the crew and passengers can then relax a bit. Some of them would turn again to their writing and not a little reflec-tion. There would be ample time in the voyage to conjure various anxieties over uncertainties about what lay ahead. The length of time for the passage could not be predicted, but given that this one took only six weeks, about average, it is likely that the ship was favored by the more northerly of the trade winds. In Franklin's previous westward voyage, that of 1762, the ship found its best initial course a southerly one, stopping briefly in Madeira be-fore picking up the winds favored by the Spanish and Portuguese from that point. Like that last sailing, this one was in the month of March, thirteen years later.

If Franklin had any concerns about his future in America, he did not re-cord them in letters or his notes during or after the voyage. But he did reflect on the recent past, composing his experience of those last few months in London with some fullness. It is the only known account of these tentative negotiations by any of the participants. In compiling such a report, Franklin could demonstrate that he personally had exhausted all reasonable possi-bilities for peace. And he had done so well past the moment when other men might have packed up and left—past the time, in other words, of his own humiliation and discrediting.

That "extra" year in London following the showdown in the Cockpit provided Franklin enough time to recover some from the personal sting of that drubbing. Enough anyway to be aware that there could yet be other possibilities. Having exhausted those, he could see more clearly what he must do. It was no longer open to him to hope; no longer open to him to temporize with his future. He had to choose to leave England, not an easy thing for him to do. Whatever the fortunes of his own native country might be, he must have been certain by March 1775 that his staying in England would be perilous. Franklin had said once that he would never resign from an office, and so he did not. That he abandoned Britain at the eleventh hour was merely prudent. By the time he reached the security of Delaware Bay and the harbor of Philadelphia, a warrant for his arrest would issue from the Chancery Court in London.

Looking Back at the Trial

Franklin observed, recorded, noted, but he rarely reflected or mused about what might have been. And although he sometimes took account of criticisms made of him by others, as he did over the Hutchinson letters affair, he rarely gave into a temptation to second-guess himself or to voice regret about what he has done, failed to do or might have done.

So it was with his trial in the Privy Council. Of course he was angry about his treatment and said so afterwards, but he had no misgivings, he said, for what he had done was the right thing to do. If there were any regrets, it was that his countrymen in America were afforded so little respect that their agent, their spokesman, had to be abused for his trouble in bringing their petition to the Crown. He lamented that if speaking up to one's rulers was itself punished in this way, there was little hope that wrongs could ever be righted. Wise rulers could not rule for long in such circumstances, he warned.

We do know that Franklin began sometime in 1774, but apparently never finished, an essay or memorandum on the charges made against him in the course of Wedderburn's tirade. Friends urged him to take on such a task, perhaps with a view to publishing rejoinders for the world to see. That was not to be, and his "Tract on the Hutchison Letters affair," as it came to be called when published posthumously by his grandson William Temple Franklin, scarcely went beyond what he had already written on the subject in letters immediately after the event.

What is notable about Franklin's few written comments is that they concentrate on just two features of the events under review here in this work. They leave unexplored a number of other areas of concern both to his contemporaries and to history. The abusive nature of the proceedings is well covered and its failure to come to terms with the petition from Massachusetts itself. So also do Franklin's letters and draft (the "Tract") emphasize his understanding of the character of the batch of Hutchinson letters and his perception of the letters' relationship to his purpose in making use of them as he did: that was, his intention of promoting reconciliation through a broader understanding of recent political history.

Given the precariousness of his position in London in 1774 and the complexity of his remaining engagements there until his departure in 1775, Franklin can certainly be forgiven for not saying more about these matters. Moreover, he was, as soon as he landed back on American soil, immersed in the urgent business of crystallizing a revolution and garnering allies for it. If he lacked the time to complete his reflections on these two years while he was still in London, he certainly would likely have lacked incentive or inclination to do so as he focused on the immediate future of what was emerging as both his and America's singular cause.

It is of course quite possible that Franklin never had any real desire to write a fuller account of these events. The reasons would not be far to see. He was, as already noted, not a man to dwell on the past, certainly not his own record of choices, poor ones or good. Yet he had during his middle years begun an autobiography, a work not published until after his death. The first part, written in England in 1772, brings his young life down to starting out in the printing trade and contains a handful of minor regrets, or "errata" as he called them, over a few youthful indiscretions. When he was later living in France, Franklin resumed the work, whose second section deals with his active public life in Pennsylvania and brings him to London on his first agency mission for that colony. In this section of his memoirs there is scarcely any language of regrets, mistakes or errors. A third part was begun back in Philadelphia after his service in France, which would have covered the years of his second, longer and concluding agency service in Britain. Illness and death intervened and the work was not completed.

Had he lived a bit longer, Franklin could well have had more to say about those final few years in London. He was at work on completing his autobiography during his last illness. "His greatest years would have to stay unwritten. He might truly have reflected that this was not altogether the loss it seemed. Plenty of other men could find materials for the story of his latest years. Only he had known about his obscure youth, which could never again be obscure."[122]

Indeed that has been the case; other men have found materials aplenty, not least Carl Van Doren who authored the most complete and probably most authoritative biography of Franklin in the twentieth century. Yet the materials, plentiful though they are, do not by themselves complete a thorough understanding of the Hutchinson letters affair and the climax of it in the Privy Council. Notable questions and concerns arising out of the materials still go unexplored in the main. It is to some of these this work now turns to complete our study.

REMAINING QUESTIONS ON THE LETTERS AFFAIR

To be sure the events themselves, the characters, the issues and the immediate outcomes are fairly easily laid out. It is the matter of their significance in the history, and histories, of Britain and America that remains to be examined more explicitly. In turn, an assessment of the impact upon, or the meanings for, the principals involved offers the shortest pathway to that larger goal.

Freshly assembled, the events of 1773–75 invite a deepened understanding—of choices, judgments and consequences that remain essential for a clear picture of that pivotal moment in the life of an empire and of one singular figure operating along its seams. The attempt proceeds to consider a cluster of questions centering on the life of Franklin in this brief encounter with people and groups even he understood only partially and could influence incompletely.

THE QUESTION OF INTENTIONS

The first cluster of questions revolves around Franklin's intentions or purposes in employing the letters as he did. A second group of questions

---

122 Carl Van Doren, *Benjamin Franklin* (1938), page 768.

focuses on his judgment, both in terms of sensitivity to some of the likely or possible, even if unintended, consequences of the events his decision would bring about or set in motion and in terms of the wisdom of those declared purposes.

By his own published declaration in the Christmas Day surprise of 1773 and his private letters to Speaker Cushing, his purpose was to reconcile Massachusetts with the mother country, to promote accord where there was discord, and greater understanding where there was suspicion, growing separation and mutual fear. The aim was repeated in the Tract he began in 1774 on the whole affair. That was his aim, he says, and there is no reason at this point to look beyond his repeated statements. Whether the means were well suited to the end sought, that, too, is one of the questions to be considered.

To be fair one should quickly add to a recitation of the aims Franklin had in sending the Hutchinson letters back to Boston the various assumptions he had and conditions that he stipulated when he obtained and dispatched the letters. His main assumption was that the letters had somehow, directly or otherwise, influenced the ministry in adopting or extending repressive measures for the colony of Massachusetts. Chief among Franklin's conditions on the use of circulation of the letters would be that only a few people were to see them and that they were not to be copied or printed. From what he said in his public revelation in December 1773, one might judge that Franklin was concerned about the possibility of popular misunderstanding and a correlative outburst of further anger or resentment by the public should the letters be published or widely circulated.

The restriction on publication, we learn in a letter the agent wrote in July of that year to Rev. Samuel Cooper, his Boston confidant and supporter, was not his own, however, but that of his confidential source. Cooper had mentioned the "surprise of gentlemen to whom those letters had been" shown over such restrictions which "they suppose render them incapable of answering any important end." Franklin's explanation was that the source believed additional correspondence could be obtained if there was no publication of these, which could thereby "put all possessors of such correspondence here upon their guard."[123] In that same letter to Cooper, the agent added what must have been his own rationalization for the restriction, a curious qualification, namely, that the letters could be "spoken of to every

---

123 BF to Cooper, July 1773. *Papers*, vol.20, pages 268-271.

body" but not copied or printed so "possibly, as distant objects seen only through a mist appear larger, the same may happen from the mystery of this case."[124]

Perhaps this notion of "distant objects seen through a mist" was merely a rhetorical flourish written offhandedly. As it stands, however, the gloss seems to contradict the rationale of Franklin's source for not publishing the letters. Moreover, taken at face value, the proposition seems to suggest that Franklin was uncertain or ambivalent about printing the letters. Even in their unprinted presence, rumors about them would serve just as well as, if not better than, the texts themselves being in print.

Were it not for this particular exchange of letters with Rev. Cooper, biographers could well credit Franklin himself for the restriction on publication of the letters. With this clarification the record of the affair becomes more complicated. It simply cannot be said with confidence that Franklin preferred that the letters remain unpublished.

Whether Franklin anticipated that there would be a violent reaction about the letters is harder to judge; and whether his worry, if that is what he had, about violence was greater in the one case or the other, that is, with or without publication.

The odds of a negative reaction to rumors and incomplete information, one would suppose, could be just as high as from more complete reporting. At most, the evidence available to us suggests that Franklin, if he did not desire or anticipate violence, expected public reaction of some kind in Boston to the impact of the letters. Franklin's July 7 letter responded to two letters from Cooper, one written in March, the other in April. By the time of the second of these, which does not survive in Franklin's papers, more than a few people in Boston knew of the Hutchinson letters. In fact, the clerk of the House, Samuel Adams, read the entire batch of the letters to its members on June 2, 1773. That was in an officially closed session, but then the galleries were opened and the ensuing debate was heard by many more. Two weeks later the letters were printed in pamphlet form and almost immediately thereafter serialized in a local paper called *The Spy.* Angry denunciations appeared immediately in the press all around Boston. Effigies of Hutchinson were burned shortly thereafter.

The reaction to the letters served to drive the colony and Britain farther apart. Far from helping to cool passions, publication of the letters, made

---

124 Ibid.

more sensational by their editing and high-lighting, made things worse. Among minds already predisposed to believe in a conspiracy to restrict liberties and reduce Massachusetts to tyranny, the letters of Hutchinson and the others seemed to confirm such fears. From that standpoint, then, the project was a total failure. If reconciliation had been the aim of the limited sharing of the letters, their wider notoriety had only added fuel to the flames of resentment to British rule and misrule over a decade.

JUDGMENT

There are yet other doubts about the agent's prudence. What, for example, were Franklin's expectations about how exactly a few leaders at the center of Massachusetts politics could make a difference in the attitudes there at large, vis-à-vis British colonial policy? How would their decisions be explained if these leaders were all of a sudden "going soft" on London? Perhaps Franklin expected that the House of Representatives by itself would turn its energies simply to pressing Governor Hutchinson into resignation or, as things turned out, petitioning the Crown to remove him and Lieutenant Governor Oliver.

If that was one of Franklin's hopes or expectations, and it well might have been, he has not been explicit about that detail. But two facts in the mix support the inference that it was. First, Franklin had seized on Hutchinson's words initially as being so inimical to colonial liberties that these colonists would naturally see that they had their own local leadership to blame for the repressive policies coming from London. Second, there was the recent precedent with the preceding governor of Massachusetts, Francis Bernard. He, too, was subjected to opposition and recall efforts. That time, the colonists were successful. Certainly Franklin would have remembered that incident, even though he had no part in it.

Perhaps, too, the agent expected or hoped that Hutchinson would suffer the fate of his predecessor and be recalled or resign and a successor appointed. That development by itself, Franklin could have expected, would reassure the colony that its interests were being respected. There could be a new beginning in the administration of the colony but not necessarily accompanied by changes in policy from London.

All that is conjectural, for Franklin nowhere spells out how he thought the reconciliation would proceed exactly. He implicitly trusted that Speaker Cushing and his circle of local leaders and opinion-makers would find a way to use the information he had passed along to them for the good of the colony vis-à-vis Britain.

There is one important clue to Franklin's thinking on these points, and it is embedded in his letter of surprise of Christmas Day 1773. He believed that Cushing and his associates, as a minimum, would see that the repressive measures had their origins in Boston and not in London and thereby return to a more positive regard for the government. Perhaps he thought that the small circle of men could, and would, make that distinction and adjust their resentment and their reactions accordingly. If so, Franklin certainly neglected to take into account the pattern of repeated mob actions in Boston between 1765 and 1770, from the Stamp Act riots to the notorious "massacre"—activity that Thomas Hutchinson had steadily anguished over in his stream of letters to Thomas Whately and others in London in those years.

A general public already accustomed to taking to the streets on the occasion of one provocation or another would not easily be convinced there was the slightest significance in where the offensive ideas or initiatives originated. It is a very fine distinction.

To such a mass of men, such as the several thousand who sometimes "attended" the Boston town meeting in Faneuil Hall, few of whom were qualified to vote in the town meeting, the policies of London were intolerable even if it took two groups, one to invent or suggest and another to carry out, repressive measures—measures like dispatching troops in peacetime to occupy the city of Boston and increasing the numbers and powers of customs officials to enforce imperial taxes on their imports.

It is difficult to accept without qualification that Franklin believed the public would digest and respond appropriately to this nuance. It would be difficult even in the confines of a deliberative assembly, bounded by traditional constraints or rules of procedure, such as in the Massachusetts House of Representatives, where the members would be assessing and debating likely consequences and balancing risks, looking to find the prudent course of action. And if it were debated in the House, even in secret, there can be little doubt that word of it would leak out, for as Franklin himself had observed on another occasion, two people can keep a secret—if one of them is dead. It is virtually inconceivable that the residents at large in unsettled Boston would have appreciated the logic of Franklin's distinction.

Or is it? The best evidence of the contrary view is that the House soon debated and passed, first, a resolution of no confidence in the governor, then a petition to the Crown for redress, to remove the men who held such views as those exposed in the letters. In other words, the act of drafting a petition, a plea for discretionary indulgence of the King, by itself indicates that the drafters had some faith that equilibrium could be re-established between the colony and the home government.[125] Yet the point loses force because the action of the legislature came only after there was widespread public expression of anger over the letters. It is impossible to say whether the House would have taken its action without that public outrage preceding it, although there was at least a significant segment of opinion in the membership ready for such a confrontation. The widespread notoriety and reaction to the letters doubtlessly made the outcome all but a certainty.

Perhaps Franklin had foreseen all or many of these doubts and questions. Perhaps his idea of reconciliation through exposure of unworthy provincial authorities did depend on a large measure of luck as well as upon a high estimate of the reasoning and discretion of those joining his initiative. If so, he trusted quite a lot and risked easily as much.

If all had gone well, that is, the presence of the letters in Boston had remained a secret of the House leadership, and if the Privy Council had been moved to consider the petition for removal gravely, deliberately, then in those events, attitudes of resistance in Boston might have subsided. It is more than a little doubtful that the petition would have been granted based on nothing but the House's dislike of the governor. That it would not have been denied as abusively as it was is the best that Franklin might have hoped for.

Franklin professed disappointment, given the care he took in the instructions about the letters, when he learned how things played out in Boston. So much was riding on these assumptions and conditions and not a little, too, on Franklin's belief in the soundness of his project.

Last Clear Chance

And here our story circles back to where it began. But for the duel in Hyde Park, Franklin might have kept his own role in the affair of the letters

---

125 A more cynical interpretation would be that the petition was merely a stalling device, putting off an inevitable resort to arms.

secret, for at least a while longer anyway. Still, the fact of the publication of the letters in Boston had already come to light in London, where they were soon reprinted in the press, and so the ministry's sense of its facing some sort of conspiracy to unsettle the colony would have been heightened in any case. The project failed, for anger and resentment on both sides of the Atlantic increased markedly. The sense of crisis deepened.

The most critical point in the account of Franklin's trial, though we began with the semi-comical but near fatal incident of the duel and its forced removal of his cover, was not that minor misfortune. It was rather Franklin's earlier decision to use the letters and to use them as he did. That was a full year earlier in December of 1772. It was his choice to use what was given him. He thought he saw, as he says his source did, too, some possibility for the advancement of a worthy cause. There are, as we have seen, ample reasons to question whether it was a prudent decision.[126] Several historians have commented on key aspects of the letters affair. Robert Middlekauff, for example, writing in 1996, concludes his appraisal of it with this summary:

> We may doubt that Franklin was optimistic about reviving good relations by the expedient of sending the letters to America. We may also doubt that he expected Thomas Cushing and his colleagues to keep the letters within their...circle.... It is also difficult to think he really believed that the English governments of the 1760s and early 1770s were so pliant as to follow the lead of two American provincials.[127]

Edmund Morgan is more direct: "It is hard to believe that [Franklin] knew quite what he was doing in 1772 when he sent Hutchinson's letters to Cushing."[128] Gordon Wood seriously doubts Franklin's political judgment, calling his use of the Hutchinson letters "a spectacular miscalculation." In combination with earlier mistakes of "trying to make Pennsylvania a royal colony and getting Americans to accept the Stamp Act" this miscalculation marks Franklin as less than a "shrewd politician, at least when it came to judging popular passions."[129]

---

126 Franklin's "motive has been impugned and defended from that day to this; his decision to forward the packet was probably the most controversial act of his career." Editors, *Papers*, Vol. 19, page 401.

127 Robert Middlekauff, *Benjamin Franklin and His Enemies* (1996, (PB ed. 1998) at page 127.

128 Edmund S. Morgan, *Benjamin Franklin* (2002) at page 196.

129 Gordon S. Wood, *The Americanization of Benjamin Franklin* (2004) at page 143.

Dismay and disbelief about Franklin and the letters affair are not limited to our latter-day critique and second-guessing. There is evidence that his own, often friendly, contemporaries were also puzzled by what he had done. His old friend John Pringle, the English physician and fellow member of the Honest Whigs, who had thought himself close to Franklin, left his reaction in a letter to David Hume. He was amazed that during the whole of the affair, Franklin had said nothing to him about the letters. "'He could have advised with no mortal of common sense and common delicacy but who must have dissuaded him from availing himself in that manner of a private correspondence between two friends, much less transmitting of those letters.'"[130]

There are so many different facets of the letters affair it is sometimes not clear exactly what is most troubling to a particular commentator. In the comment by Pringle, however, the focus turns sharply to simple personal standards of conduct and respect for others' property, effects and reputation and privacy. It is a fair point. Given that Pringle probably did not share Franklin's political aims, even though neither man would necessarily know that at the time, what would a disinterested observer think of Franklin's actions?[131]

More than one historian has leveled criticism at Franklin for his willingness to "destroy" the career of a man who had done him no harm and with whom he had at one time worked as colleague. In the Albany conference of 1754, both were delegates and they collaborated on a draft treaty of mutual defense for the colonies. One problem with this issue is that it is never completely free of the uncertain calculus of utilitarian pursuit of political ends.

---

130 Reported in H.W. Brands, *The First American, the Life and Times of Benjamin Franklin* (2000), *page 483*. Bernard Bailyn has suggested that Franklin had to have talked with Bollan and Arthur Lee, since the former was agent for the Council of Massachusetts and Lee his designated successor as agent for the House. There was, however, something of gulf between Lee and Franklin from the start lof their association, so it remains doubtful that Franklin felt any necessity to confer with him. In neither case is there any independent confirmation of a consultation prior to Franklin's dispatch of the letters.

131 David Hume, personally acquainted with and an admirer of Franklin but himself a Tory in political sympathies (but not in religion), had written to Edmund Burke asking, when he had heard about Franklin's role in the affair, whether there was anything that could be said in defense of Franklin's secrecy about the source of the letters. Given his promise to the source, and perhaps because nothing of personal moment seemed to turn on the information for any other person then concerned, modern consciences might be less troubled than Hume was. We might nonetheless be troubled by other elements of the story.

If indeed Thomas Hutchinson were an enemy of his own people, a tyrant as the colonial press labeled him, then a reasonable person could fairly weigh the good of the many against the sacrifice of a few.

Yet this line of argument itself presupposes either that the facts of leadership failings of the governor and lieutenant governor were widely accepted; or that, at least, the actor is himself in good faith convinced that the men stand in the way of better government for their people. Certainly no such opinion of Hutchinson existed in England at the time. Yes, he was unpopular in Massachusetts, even hated by some, although the misdeeds or worse of which he was believed to be guilty are not easily identified.

These points were explored in chapters 2 and 3. Suffice it to say the origins and continued presence of enmity toward Hutchinson had as much to do with ideology and personal resentment of the man as with anything remotely criminal or violative of authentic civil liberties of colonial Americans as subjects of Great Britain.[132]

CYNICAL OR NAÏVE?

Franklin's belief on this point is not entirely clear. Did he believe that Hutchinson was a "tyrant" or did he think merely that his ideas of what colonists were entitled to under the existing imperial balance diverged from the governor's? Franklin was more the pragmatic liberal, Hutchinson the "strict constructionist." But did the agent think that Hutchinson really deserved to be turned out of office on any traditional grounds for removal of chief executives? It is doubtful that he did. It is doubtful that he thought Hutchinson could be impeached for any identifiable cause.[130] Franklin seemingly anticipated this very kind of question when he asserted (in the Tract and letters home) that Hutchinson and Oliver should, notwithstanding any other virtues or accomplishments they possessed, be glad to sacrifice their current stations in order to be of service to their country. This gratuitous "gesture" has been called one of the most naïve or most cynical statements Franklin ever wrote.[133]

---

132 John Adams' dislike of Hutchinson centered on the latter's penchant for aggregating local power in himself and among his relatives. And he was not alone in that view. Others, like his cousin Sam Adams, probably had more institutional or ideological objectives in their opposition to Hutchinson, such as enhancing the relative authority of the legislature versus the executive, a project to advance, in the words of recent historians, "popular sovereignty."

133 Bernard Bailyn, The Ordeal of Thomas Hutchinson, page 437.

Naïveté smacks of a kind of innocence that Franklin rarely exhibited to his contemporaries. Optimistic? Yes, often. Credulous, too, sometimes. Franklin's very first trip to England, when he was only an apprentice in the printer's trade and barely out of his teens, was stimulated by a promise of credit to purchase a press by a Philadelphia sponsor with a history of making unfulfilled promises. He even exhibited some charity toward his nemesis Lord Hillsborough when the Earl was especially hospitable toward him on a visit to Ireland. Moreover, Franklin gave Lord Dartmouth, Hillsborough's successor as secretary for colonial affairs, an extended benefit of the doubt as to that minister's vision and capacities for leadership throughout most of these last three years in England.

Cynical? That seems a more apt characterization of the sentiment displayed about Thomas Hutchinson and Andrew Oliver. Indifferent as to whether in fact the governors' letters carried sinister intentions or substantial revelations, the sender of their letters certainly may fairly be described as careless or cavalier. To be aware, however, they had no such content, read by any disinterested third party, and yet make use of them anyway, that would be ruthless, Machiavellian quite simply, separating the needs of politics from personal responsibility for fairness to others.

That conclusion, however, is not free from doubt in view of Franklin's hedging here and there. Whatever the letters themselves said or was implied by their writers, he must have been fairly certain they would cause difficulty for Hutchinson and company in the minds or passions of Boston's restless. Yet he likely expected that nothing more severe than resignation and departure would result, just as happened with the previous royal governor Francis Bernard. At most, then, the governors would be gracefully pensioned off in England and be no worse for it all. How bad a life would that be, he could have asked himself. It is not as if he expected physical harm would come to Hutchinson or Oliver; yet that too was not out of the question, looking at events from that time and place. In the Stamp Act riots of 1765 a mob sacked Hutchinson's old family home in Boston and forced him to flee in the night with only the clothes he was wearing. And Hutchinson had actually opposed the passage of the Stamp Act, a matter of little consequence to a mob in the throes of an angry rampage.

Competing Risks for Franklin?

In using the letters as he did, Franklin was clearly willing to expose the governors to those risks. Did he in turn risk anything himself, his career or fortunes? One might suppose that, if not at the time of sending them, then somewhat later he became aware of the risk of being discredited in London. Or worse. And he could not be sure that the colonists would eventually succeed in any of the ways then imagined. In the event of outright war the former agent could easily wind up being treated in Britain as a traitor.

So, yes, there was an equivalence of risks between those imposed on others and those assumed by Franklin against his own interest. It is conceivable that Franklin employed his old algebraic sums approach, if not in initially making his move, then later in calculating the likely balance of things. On the one side of the paper all the "good" things to be brought about were listed and on the other side of the same page a list of the negatives. Which one is longer or more substantial? If Franklin did engage this device, and it is by no means certain that he did, it is difficult to see how the calculation could have by itself been very helpful.

At some point Franklin, uncharacteristically perhaps, simply was willing to throw caution to the wind, trusting his luck because so much was to be achieved, or could be, by his gamble. What exactly was to be gained, though, is a question he might not have found any easier to answer, if he really posed it, than it has been for historians. What Franklin might have imagined to be the best possible outcome of this affair is difficult to frame. He would not have answered the question in abstract terms, say of Horace Walpole's poem—"Liberty" or "Independence"—written after the Revolution was complete. But Franklin would have been comfortable speaking of a return to practices of imperial oversight that afforded the colonies the latitude of largely governing themselves. In other words, his was for the most part a conservative understanding of what was at stake. Yet as conditions changed, with more protests and resistance in the colonies followed by increased rigidity and hardening of attitudes in London over those middle years of the 1770s, it is unlikely that Franklin seriously imagined that such a conservative program was possible, though he continued to pay lip service to those ideas.

Moreover, his views evolved with changes in context, so that by the time of the "secret negotiations" of the winter of 1775 Franklin was taking positions more extreme than anything he had advanced before then, with the "backing" of the resolutions of the Continental Congress, such as a formal renunciation of Parliament's authority to tax the colonies. And by that time of course, he could indeed "throw caution to the wind" in that he personally had little more to lose, and the cause of the colonies seemed everywhere losing ground in Parliament, ministry and the court of King George III.

There is little to support the view that Franklin was visionary or idealistic in thinking about how these letters that had fallen in his lap in 1772 might best serve such larger ends. The press of matters as they stood, including his embarrassment over an awkward handling of the House's business, seems just as plausible a determinant. The agent was also trying to preserve the goodwill, limited and untried though it was at that point, of the then new colonial secretary Lord Dartmouth, who had only recently replaced the minister with whom Franklin had developed sour relations, Lord Hillsborough. All these things probably occupied more of his mind at that moment. Added to this preoccupation was Franklin's knowledge that back in Boston the governor and the House were seriously at odds with each other in ways that were not advancing the colony's restoration of its earlier, happier conditions.

Just prior to the dispatch of the Hutchinson letters to Boston in 1772, Franklin had been reproached by Speaker Cushing for delaying the submission of the House's last petition, the one strongly objecting to the ministry's determination to pay their royal governors salaries (out of proceeds from the Townshend duties) and thus make them more independent of the elected assemblies. In the same letter from Franklin that offered his apology or explanation for the delay, he proceeded directly to inform the speaker of having received "correspondence that I have reason to believe laid the foundation ... of our present grievances." In other words the agent, perhaps entirely coincidentally, balanced the bad news with some good. The editors of the Franklin Papers have added this comment on the plausibility of the suggestion that the agent's use of the letters was indeed something of a face-saving gesture:

> If the promotion of harmony is ruled out as an implausible motive, Franklin's relationship with his constituents remains. ... In an unreflecting moment he may really have believed he could improve the situation by shifting of the argument from theories to personalities. About the former he was not yet fully decided; about the latter he was. His anger at the writers [of the Hutchinson letters collective-

ly], if it was as genuine as it seems, doubtless made their exposure appear to be a service to Massachusetts. *At that particular moment such a service was timely, for his handling of the petition had laid him open to criticism in Boston.*[134]

In the end we are left to confront Franklin's own stated purpose of the time, when he wrote for the public and later repeated in private letters and in the Tract: he sought only to bridge or narrow the gap of misunderstanding and mistrust growing between Massachusetts and the government in London. That Franklin did not have any specific strategy or plan in mind for how the letters' revelation could promote that purpose, however, does leave us free to assess the aim fully, as we have tried to do in this chapter. That he trusted, especially in view of all that had happened in the province since 1765, that others would find the particular ways to do that is a vivid indication of the insubstantiality of Franklin's claim of purpose. It is very difficult to avoid the conclusion that the stated purpose was a rationalization.

Pressed by the circumstance of having to say something explanatory, he could not have come up with anything less conciliatory in tone, even if he hoped that Hutchinson's removal would clear the way for concessions in London, a notion he did record after the event. Nor could Franklin be perfectly candid and say he did not know what they would do. But his employers in Boston should know about, better yet see and examine, everything he had learned or discovered that concerns them. He comes close to this concession in his Christmas Day letter to the press.

Franklin's contrivance of a purpose, however insincere it seemed under Alexander Wedderburn's hammer blows that day in the Cockpit, was probably all he could say publicly at the time. That it gained him so little at the end of the day in London is not to say it gained him nothing in the long run. Unlike his day before the Privy Council, impassive and unspeaking as well as unflinching, Franklin did give some account of his actions and in so doing left us ample material to examine not only his judgment but also his understanding of his own predicament. And these are not insubstantial legacies from such a controversial event.

---

134 *Papers*, Vol. 19, pages 399, 408-09. Emphasis added.

Before concluding with a brief accounting of what was positive for Franklin about the debacle of the letters affair, a couple of small points deserve notice. One is simply that in studying the letters themselves before he sent them to Boston, he must have been careless in not recalling that some of the repressive initiatives whose origins were attributed to Hutchinson had already been underway before or as the letters themselves were being written in the late 1760s. Notable among these was the dispatch, upon the initiative of customs officers, of two regiments of Redcoats in 1768 to Boston from New York, arriving when Francis Bernard was still governor.

Another small point that adds a bit more gravity to Franklin's actions was that he seems credulous from our distance in his reception of these letters. Perhaps because he so much wanted to believe they contained exculpatory material so far as the ministry was concerned—as he was told by his source they did—he neglected to inquire as to how exactly this batch of letters came to be assembled in the first place and before they were delivered to him. Several different people, we learned in Chapter 2, wrote the letters, on different dates; and they did not include a number that Hutchinson had written to the same recipient, Thomas Whately, over the same years as the others. What he did not know, therefore, was as much a liability to him as what he did know or thought he knew about them—liability in the sense that in acting without further inquiry he ran the risk of being judged guilty of irresponsibility if not dishonesty. There will be some attention to this point in the Afterword following this chapter as we examine the questions, mysteries really, that still adhere to this story, such as the identity of Franklin's source and what purposes or motivations that source possessed. Answers are problematic. Even so, uncertain or incomplete answers are at least marginally better than none at all. Everyone can appreciate a mystery, but perhaps the appreciation is fuller if there is material on the basis of which one may form an opinion independently.

He could not have known it at the moment, nor anticipate the roughness of his trial that accounted for much of the popular reaction, but within weeks of his humiliation in the Privy Council, Franklin's identification with the colonial cause was immediately transformed in America. William

Franklin was quick to write his father his own very positive impressions from Philadelphia when the news of the trial broke. Franklin's reputation for partiality toward Britain, if not actually conniving with its officials against colonial interests, as some had claimed, had not fully recovered from his involvement with the ministry over the Stamp Act's adoption and at-tempted implementation in 1765, even despite his extraordinary success in promoting its repeal a year later.

In Massachusetts, especially, there were those who really mistrusted Franklin. One of these was the tireless and quietly effective political opera-tive Samuel Adams. Just prior to the crisis of the letters, another Bostonian, Josiah Quincy, Jr., came, or was sent, to London better to judge how Frank-lin stood and to measure his commitment to American interests and ties. Quincy, on his own, however, was quick to respond after his first substan-tial encounter with the agent that the colonies indeed had a great friend and supporter in Franklin. Arthur Lee, on the other hand, Franklin's successor-agent-in-waiting, had written to Adams disparagingly of Franklin during Hillsborough's time as colonial secretary.

After the drubbing in the Cockpit, there was no doubt and the ensuing public displays in Boston and other colonial cities clearly indicate that the Americans had found a visible hero. Within two days of his landing in Phila-delphia, his fellow Pennsylvanians elected him to the Second Continental Congress, the body that a year later produced America's definitive Decla-ration. And thus Franklin's new career began, the one of the most senior founder who would also serve his country with peculiar effectiveness as its first foreign emissary.

At the time of his landing in Philadelphia in the spring of 1775, Frank-lin could not have guessed that any such adventure, and another Atlantic crossing, was in store for him a year later. That would be just months after independence was formally declared by the colonies but years before it was secured, finally and formally secured, in no small part because of the aid brought to the Americans' side through the diplomacy of Franklin in France.

More than likely, as he disembarked from the *Pennsylvania Packet* on that fifth day of May 1775, Franklin was anticipating the simple joy of embrac-ing his daughter Sally, greeting his two grandchildren Billy and Ben and his son-in-law Richard Bache, then introducing their English cousin Temple to them. Franklin would silently acknowledge his debt to his late wife Debbie by walking as directly as a crowd of welcoming neighbors, old friends and associates would permit to the home she had completed and kept for him on Market Street during his long, long time away. Church bells pealed when his ship tied up, and its distinguished passenger, spotted through the long glass of the harbormaster, stepped over the mooring lines and onto the pier.

Edmund Burke by Joshua Reynolds. Courtesy of National Portrait Gallery, London. ©National Portrait Gallery, London

Post Script

Within days of his return, Franklin would send letters to three of his allies in London, Jonathan Shipley, the liberal churchman, Joseph Priestly, scientist and companion, and Edmund Burke, MP. If they had not learned already, he would let them know that General Gage in Massachusetts had "drawn the sword" at Lexington and Concord instead of "showing the olive branch" to the representatives in Boston assembled at the same time to consider the ministry's proposals for peace. And so, there would be war after all, one likely to last for many years, Franklin predicted. While their common efforts, including a major speech by Burke in Commons since Franklin had left London, to achieve reconciliation on rational terms had been in vain, he was and would remain grateful for their solidarity with the colonies.

Afterword

Part I. Remaining Mystery

Many details are recorded about Benjamin Franklin's long life, much of it in his own correspondence and other papers. Yet the things that are not known, especially about this short segment of his time in London, intrigue us and afford historians and biographers a continuous temptation if not to speculate then at least to offer plausible constructions of these gaps in our knowledge.

So it has been with several mysteries in the Hutchinson letters affair and its aftermath. Certainly the leading one of these is the question, who indeed was his source for the letters?

Franklin's Source

Probably the most compelling reason advanced thus far for trying to find an answer to that question is simply that the information could well tell us more about his understanding of the letters and his judgment about their use. Without that knowledge we are forced to scour Franklin's own explanation for that understanding.

Almost equally compelling as a reason to inquire and pose some plausible answers to the *who* question is the plain fact that Franklin himself stoutly stuck to his promise and determination to keep that person or persons' identity secret. Why was it so important to Franklin? To protect the legal and political future of British subjects who might wish to remain in service to the Crown is one very reasonable answer. Long after the War for American Independence had been concluded, however, why that would matter to Franklin is not so easy to answer. Out of friendship, and for his own honor? Perhaps so, but we simply do not know. It is of course surprising that no collateral revelation has occurred either. There is one exception.

One person who was close to the events of the letters affair at one point in time did claim to be Franklin's source. And he did so not too many years later. This was John Temple, the man who fought a duel denying his complicity. The case for John Temple as the source or informant necessarily begins with this apparent paradox. Temple's resentment at and anger over the accusation rested on the public claim that Temple had stolen the letters from the executor of the man to whom the letters were addressed.

John Temple well might not have taken the letters from possession of Thomas Whately's executor. Franklin explicitly claimed in his 1773 Christmas Day newspaper surprise that Temple could not have done that. This disclaimer clearly leaves open the real alternative possibility that Temple nonetheless acquired them in some other way. He might have been given the letters by a third person independently. In 1781, nearly a decade after Franklin sent the letters to Boston, Temple wrote to him and asked Franklin to acknowledge Temple's role in the affair. By this time Franklin was in Paris, and Temple was trying his best to win back some favor in New England. Franklin could perhaps have helped. But he did not even answer Temple's letter.[135]

These are the known facts, so far as they take us, that account for Temple's name to be so consistently associated with the mystery over Franklin's source. While they are, standing alone, inconclusive, there are several circumstances that lend credence to the claim for Temple as the source. One is that Temple had a very active dislike for Thomas Hutchinson. It was more than politics. Temple, wrongly as it turned out, believed that Hutchinson had caused him to lose his royal customs inspector post in New England. Temple would have had a motive to do something detrimental to Hutchinson, as of the time of the letters' delivery to Franklin. That much is clear.

A second supporting circumstance is that through his kinship with George Grenville, Temple could have had access to the letters or some of

---

135 Letter from Temple to Franklin of July 26, 1781. *Papers*, vol. 35, page 672.

them if Whately had shared them with his old chief. This seems plausible but has not been definitively established.

Finally, it is known that Franklin and Temple were friends, or at least acquainted with each other from the time when in 1757 they sailed for England in the same ship. Whether they were often in contact with each other in London is, however, not established. Temple landed a better job in the customs service than he had in America, this through his own family ties, those that had brought him to England in the first place. With that sort of patronage available to him, he would have little need for the agent's introduction and backing. Thus, while there's no reason to suppose that they were cronies or confidants, Temple and Franklin did know each other at the relevant times.

If one were looking for a reason, however, to eliminate John Temple from the list of candidates for the role of Franklin's source, it could be found in Thomas Hutchinson's own diary entries. He was writing shortly after his arrival in London during the summer of 1774, noting a lengthy series of contacts and visits he was having from among important people there. One of these, we are told, was none other than this fellow New Englander who came to the former governor's home unannounced one afternoon in July. They had a long conversation that ranged over the whole of their relations, including their mutual suspicions of each other. The governor assured Temple it was not he who had undone his post in New England customs. For his part, Temple seemingly convinced Hutchinson that he had not been Franklin's accomplice in the letters affair. Temple also disabused the former governor of any reliance on a report from ministry that had indeed put Temple squarely in the picture. Temple, the diary goes on, did know in fact who Franklin's "co-conspirator" was, but he was not at liberty to disclose his identity, for that revelation would "prove the ruin of the guilty party."[136]

Probably enough has emerged about John Temple for us to be in doubt about him, as he seemingly told each person what might help him on successive occasions: Hutchinson, in 1774 in London, where good terms might assist Temple with royal or ministerial favor; then in 1781, seeing the end of the war and looking to return to America, Temple was asking for Franklin's recognition. Clearly, by his own concession to Hutchinson, Temple knew something about the letters. That he was complicit with Franklin to some

---

136 *Diary and Letters of Thomas Hutchinson*, Vol. I, pages 199, 205ff, 209-211. Cited and discussed in Bernard Bailyn, *The Ordeal of Thomas Hutchinson* 286 (1974).

degree remains plausible, despite Hutchinson's change of heart, based on all the circumstances of the matter.

A Second Candidate

Equally plausible as Franklin's source is Thomas Pownall. He had held royal appointment as governor of Massachusetts earlier and was well acquainted with conditions in the colonies, better so than most of his contemporaries in the mother country. At the time of the letters affair, he was again resident in England and serving as a Member of Parliament. In the House of Commons he was an outspoken critic of administration's colonial policy. And he was frequently in touch with opposition leaders in Boston whom he advised, in 1770, to continue their protests of the Townshend duties through the kind of non-importation agreements that had served well to bring down the Stamp Act.[137]

Thomas Pownall. By courtesy of the National Portrait Gallery, London.

Strengthening the case for Pownall are several rather more particular circumstances. Franklin and Pownall held similar views. Both wanted to find a middle way to preserve the Empire, but both were being embarrassed by the resort to violence in New England, on the one hand, and the increasingly impatient ministry in London, on the other. They could have talked directly about the difficulty of their position at a time that made the contact especially opportune. Franklin had just the year previous become agent for the Massachusetts House of Representatives. And Pownall through his brother John (serving in the ministry during Hillsborough's time in office as chief of

---

137 For additional support of the view that Thomas Pownall was Franklin's source, see Bernard Knollenberg, "Benjamin Franklin and the Hutchinson and Oliver Letters," *Yale University Library Gazette*, vol. 47, July 1972, pages one to nine. Thomas Hutchinson, too, in the view of his leading biographer, at last concluded that it must have been Pownall who supplied his letters to Franklin. See Bernard Bailyn, *The Ordeal of Thomas Hutchinson* page 287.

colonial affairs in North America) could easily have had access to the letters assembled there during Grenville's time. Grenville would have seen the letters brought to him either by Thomas Whately himself, their initial recipient, or by Francis Bernard whose short-lived task it had been to build a case for parliamentary reform of the charter of Massachusetts. Unlike Franklin's acquaintanceship with John Temple, his association with Pownall was active in at least two ways. They were both members of Thomas Walpole's Ohio Valley land company. Both were members of the Royal Society. There would have been abundant opportunity for conversation on a range of subjects of common interest and on-going concern. It would have been remarkable really if they had not talked about the Hutchinson letters once Pownall had seen them or learned of them.

A Third Possibility

One more prominent Londoner of Franklin's acquaintance has been suggested in modern scholarship as the likely source. Franklin's long-time printer friend was William Strahan and there were few men who had more substantial contact with him. They became acquainted through correspondence while Franklin lived in Philadelphia. Strahan was the agent's principal publisher in London for his many essays and opinion pieces. What gives his candidacy particular saliency are two instances of a meeting between Franklin and Strahan about the time the agent made his move with the letters. Plus Thomas Hutchinson, living then in England, made a claim in his diary about Strahan. The claim was that the printer had in his possession extracts from Franklin's cover letter to Thomas Cushing in Boston by which he forwarded the batch of Hutchinson letters in December 1772.

The contacts between Strahan and Franklin in that season reflect a detail contained in the agent's own reflection on the whole affair ("the Tract"), in particular how he, Franklin, came to be impressed with the possibility that repressive measures against the colonies had their origin among colonial leaders, not in Whitehall or Westminster. The known fact that Franklin and Strahan had two meetings in this season serves to promote this possible scenario. In the first meeting Strahan let the agent know of the letters, and in the second, Strahan delivered them in response to Franklin's heightened curiosity. In the end, Strahan's standing as the possible source for Franklin is undermined by the fact that his access to the letters cannot be clearly established. The most that can be said is that he might have received them from Grenville, assuming that Grenville had them after Thomas Whately's death, perhaps in order to convince Strahan as one of Franklin's known publishers that his sympathies for Franklin's conciliation efforts were misguided.[138]

Other Nominees

At least five others have been identified as Franklin's possible source in addition to the three main ones already considered. This short list includes two Americans, William Storey of Boston and Dr. Hugh Williamson, originally from Pennsylvania, lived in North Carolina during the War and then moved to New York. The other three are David Hartley, William Fitzherbert and Dr. John Pringle. Storey was a Boston merchant who, having suffered property damage in the Stamp Act riots, came to London to seek compensation, a fact that Franklin reported to Thomas Cushing in a letter that predates Franklin's own activity with regard to the letters. Otherwise nothing is known which would connect him with the affair.

Williamson, a well-regarded physician interested in science and politics, very probably knew Franklin, but he did not come to London until a year following Franklin's dispatch of the letters to Boston. Nor has anything been suggested that would suggest how or why Williamson might have had known about the letters. Many years after the events in question, John Adams added Williamson's name to the Hutchinson letters affair by suggesting—speculating really—that Williamson "very possibly" gave them to David Hartley who was in touch with Franklin, and it was he who actually delivered them. But for the standing of Adams it seems doubtful that his suggestion would have survived at all.

Franklin knew Hartley, but there is no other factor that plausibly connects him with the letters affair. Nor is there anything more than speculation about Sir John Pringle's having such a role. Certainly Pringle and Franklin were good friends, but apart from Pringle's access to the court as physician to the Queen, there is nothing to suggest that professional entrée would have anything to do with papers collected in Whitehall. Moreover, given the letter he wrote in the winter of 1774 to David Hume (see Chapter Eight, "Circles of Support") registering dismay over Franklin's own declara-

---

138 It is this factor, lack of any likely access, that led the Editors of the Franklin Papers themselves to be skeptical about Strahan as the source. See *Papers of Benjamin Franklin.* Vol. 19, pages 406-407 (1975).

tion of responsibility, it is difficult to credit his name being associated in such a way as to contradict that sentiment over the affair.

Finally there is the name of William Fitzherbert who had been an MP from Derby from 1762 to 1772 and a member of the Board of Trade for some years as well. Nothing more than an anonymous letter from London published in the *Massachusetts Gazette* in April of 1774 exists to suggest that it was he who obtained letters from Grenville or someone close to him and delivered them to Franklin.[139]

Best Estimate

Combining the most prominent of the features of the two strongest cases, those for Temple and for Pownall, produces a conceivable combination that both men had a role to play in the letters affair. This is not to claim, however, that either acted in knowing concert with the other. Yet it is possible that John Temple had learned about the letters (either from his kinsman and political patron, Grenville, or from Thomas Whately before his death, another of Temple's political associates) and mentioned them to Franklin or to another who in turn brought them to Franklin. It seems equally plausible that Pownall was the final conduit or carrier of the letters to Franklin. Whether he was, in any manner that connects our story with Temple, is impossible to say. Yet it is conceivable that Franklin heard something from Temple, and afterward an independent report from Pownall confirmed in him a determination to ask to see them.

Thus, Temple's letter of 1781 claiming that he, Temple, had enabled the transfer makes sense. It is an exaggeration perhaps of a secondary role, if that is all he served, but it is not a complete fabrication of some involvement about the letters with Franklin. The active part the two Pownall brothers had in government affairs and Thomas' rather frequent association with Franklin lend credence to the view that it was he who had the greater role in the delivery of the letters to Franklin, not John Temple.

This construction of events has these two merits. One, it recognizes Pownall's rather more probable access to the letters in 1772. Two, it tends to explain why Franklin never responded to Temple's 1781 letter. In other words his apparent silence or unwillingness to help Temple at that point

---

139 See Horace Walpole, *Journal of King George the Third*, vol. 2 (1859), at page 255, note 2. See also Knollenberg, 47 *Yale U. Library Gazette* (1972), pages 1-9; and Gipson, *British Empire* (), vol. XII, page 59 note.

reflects Franklin's awareness that Temple's role had been the lesser one. Moreover, if Temple's role was subordinate or partial, there is scarcely any unambiguous way Franklin could say so, to any one, without simply begging the larger question of the identity of the other person involved.

Moreover, it is important to recall that Pownall's career of public service continued through the post-trial events and indeed on into the whole era of the long war for American independence. Pownall, his friend knew, had "adjusted himself" to changing circumstances, had stopped being a critic of the ministry and was an MP again, owing to his shift in position on policy. Franklin might not have liked what he saw; yet he respected his old colleague that much. They had some contact thereafter.

In fact the two friends shared an evening over dinner not long before Franklin's departure for America in March of 1775. In his memoir of the occasion, Franklin called it a "tête-à-tête." His notes are guarded, but he seems to be saying, "Oh, they would never trust us..." by way responding to his companion's suggestion of a possible mission of conciliation on the ministry's initiative by the two men.[140]

PART 2. WHAT HAPPENED TO THEM?

The mystery over the identify of Franklin's informant or source for the Hutchinson letters is likely to remain unsolved, barring discovery of some hitherto unknown letter of Franklin's or one of the others close to him in 1772 London. So much else about that time and place remains engaging, however, and some of the persons with whom Franklin was significantly associated, one way or another, have played important parts in this narrative. The reader might be reluctant to let go of the story without knowing something of what these associates, adversaries, or relatives and friends managed to do with their lives from that spring in 1775 when Franklin left London for good. Accordingly, what follows is a sketch of several of those personalities and their fortunes from that juncture forward.[141]

---

140 BF's note on the secret negotiations in the form of a long letter to son William, dated March 22, 1775. *Papers*, vol. 21, page 567-68.
141 Among the elements of the story of Franklin and his trial that remain at least curiosities, if not mysteries of significance, is the near legendary one of the "Manchester velvet suit." This is the clothing he wore the day of his trial, the detail is mentioned in passing in Chapter 6 ("The Showdown in the Cockpit"). It is frequently related in full length biographies of Franklin that he wore that suit on one other public occasion, the day nine years later in France when he signed

Edmund Burke (1729–1797), within days of Franklin's departure from London in March of 1775, delivered his famous speech in the House of Commons "On Reconciliation with America," a classic summation of what Burke saw and understood about America and its importance, not merely in material terms, to the British Empire as a whole. He remained a Member of Parliament through the War of American Independence and in that role managed to skewer the North ministry's leadership continually. He was respected for his independent judgment and the eloquence of his expression of views that more often than not ran counter to prevailing sentiments and policies of that time. Burke served in the ministry of Rockingham and Shelburne following the fall of the North cabinet. He corresponded with Franklin during the latter's time in Paris, where he sought the American's good offices to effect the release of General Burgoyne from captivity long after the battle of Saratoga where he was taken prisoner by American forces. Congress stipulated in exchange the release of Henry Laurens of South Carolina, who was captured while en route to France to assist Franklin's mission. That, however, did not happen until the Treaty of Peace was concluded in 1782. Burke's principal legacy has been for constructive thought about principles of conservatism in political and social ideas, derived in large part from his essays on the French Revolution whose excesses he deplored: *Reflections on the Revolution in France* (1790).

Thomas Cushing (1725 to 1788) abandoned Boston during its military occupation whose leadership sought to arrest him on possible treason charges against the Crown. The former speaker of the House of Representa-

---

the peace treaty with Britain ending the Revolutionary War. Whether one is inclined to the prevalent view that this was meant as some sort of quiet statement of sweet revenge or, at least as plausible, a touch of irony from the old satirist says something about one's over-all "take" on the temperament of the man.

The foundation for the legend rests with two men who were indeed present at the treaty signing in 1783: Silas Deane and Edward Bancroft, both then serving in the American mission to France. Deane, according to Joseph Priestly some years later, reported his personal observation to Priestly then living in Pennsylvania, years after Franklin's death. Bancroft, the man who apparently was a double agent at the time, also recalls, similarly some years later and living in London, that he, too, noted the suit at the treaty signing in Versailles.

Priestly's reminiscences were published in 1802 in the form of a magazine article. That piece plus the secondhand reports of the others are collected in the work that William Temple Franklin edited and published in 1817–18.*Memoirs of Life and Writings of Benjamin Franklin*, volume II, pages 356-360. The legend of the Manchester velvet suit probably owes its robustness, if not its origin, to this work of the grandson.

tives went on to represent the state of Massachusetts in the Continental Congress, 1774–76. Thereafter he served several terms as lieutenant governor 1780–88.

William Franklin (1731–1813), seeing his father after his arrival in Pennsylvania in May of 1775 and only briefly before his departure for France a year later, remained loyal to the British Crown as its governor in New Jersey and in that capacity (and suspected of activity with resisting loyalists) was arrested in 1766 by local militia on the order of the New Jersey Provincial Congress and taken to Simsbury, Connecticut, where he languished for nearly two years in a prison built into a copper mine. Efforts of his wife Elizabeth, who remained in New Jersey, including overtures to her father-in-law, to have William released on parole were initially unavailing. Eventually he was brought to New York and waited there in British army protection until he was able to return to London. After the peace treaty he vainly sought reconciliation with his father, whom he genuinely admired. He met his father one last time in 1785 in the port of Southampton where Franklin interrupted his voyage home from France. The senior Franklin used the occasion of that somewhat strained rendezvous to have his son sign over property interests William held in America either to him for back debts or over to Temple for his future security. His first wife Elizabeth Downes died in 1777 while still living in America. He married Mary D'Evelin in 1788. There were no children by either marriage.

William Temple Franklin (1760–1823), variously called Temple or Billy, accompanied his grandfather and benefactor to Paris in 1776 along with his cousin Benny Bache, who continued his education in a Swiss boarding school. Temple's most significant role in this period was serving as secretary to Franklin for the remainder of the mission to the French court and through the peace treaty negotiations following Cornwallis' surrender at Yorktown. He visited his father William in England during this time and remained in communication with him as well as the Stevenson–Hewsons. After coming back to America with his grandfather in 1785, after Franklin's death Temple for a short time tried his hand at farming in New Jersey without satisfaction and eventually returned, first, to England, then to France in 1798 where he remained for the rest of his life. Temple edited and published his grandfather's autobiography plus some of Franklin's papers, the first volume of which appeared in 1817.

Joseph Galloway (1731–1803), former speaker of the House of Burgesses in Pennsylvania and proponent of standing up to the Penns, was one of the first of his old Philadelphia allies who contacted Franklin after the latter's return in May of 1775, offering good wishes but telling Franklin that he was withdrawing from public life. He had been a delegate to the First Continental Congress where he put forward a plan for reconciliation with Britain, later rejected. During the British occupation of Philadelphia, 1777 to 1778, Galloway assisted the occupational government and then moved to England as spokesman for loyalists in the colonies. At war's end, his local properties were confiscated and he was refused re-entry to Pennsylvania. Galloway had one indirect contact with Franklin while the latter was in Paris. Franklin's grandson and secretary wrote to Galloway asking for a copy of Franklin's will that Galloway, as his then attorney, had drafted in Philadelphia many years before. Galloway after some difficulties was able to locate the copy (among papers stashed in a trunk whose shipment was long delayed from New York) and oblige the request.

Polly (Stevenson) Hewson (1734–1795) remained a devoted friend of Franklin and his entire family throughout the remainder of her life. After her husband died unexpectedly in 1774, she and her three children at first moved in with her mother Margaret Stevenson. She, her children and her mother later shared a house outside London. In July 1774, Polly's aunt died, leaving her a small fortune, but the settlement was delayed some years. Polly and her mother remained in almost continuous contact with Franklin, in Philadelphia and in Paris, thereafter. Though her mother had also wanted to make such a trip, her health was uncertain; Polly managed to travel to France in 1785 and visit with her old mentor and friend for a season. The next year, following Franklin's return from France and with his encouragement to do so, she took her children and moved to Philadelphia to be with Franklin and the Baches. She was with Franklin when he died. Two of her children went to England to complete their education, returning to America where they thrived in their respective professions of medicine and law. Polly at one time wanted to return to England but never did. The name Hewson remains significant among those holding particular items from the correspondence of the Franklin legacy, according to the bibliographic record in the Papers of Benjamin Franklin.

Thomas Hutchinson (1711–1780), his time as royal governor concluded in Massachusetts, moved to England in the summer of 1774, where he would, initially at least, consider himself on leave for the duration of the war. With him in that move were some but not all his children. His wife Margaret Sanford Hutchinson and mother of all five of his children died in childbirth in 1754. He was recognized and honored for his loyal and steadfast service to the Empire. Oxford University awarded Hutchinson an honorary doctorate of civil laws degree on July 4, 1776. But his years in England dragged on through declining health among his own family; his daughter Peggy died at 23 in an epidemic of influenza. Hutchinson despaired of ever returning to his beloved home in Milton, Massachusetts. In spite of his anguish over the way his career had ended and the pain of exile from his homeland, Hutchinson continued to write and pursue his long-time project of a history of Massachusetts. His substantial diaries were published in the 19th century edited by his great grandson Peter O. Hutchinson. Moreover, out of countless other Americans who found themselves on the "wrong side" of the movement toward independence, Hutchinson bears the important distinction of having a major biography and a seminal piece of modern scholarship on the colonial era based on his life: *The Ordeal of Thomas Hutchinson* by Bernard Bailyn (Harvard Press 1974).

Arthur Lee (1740–1792) began a planned tour of France and Italy in the summer after the trial, returned to London later and succeeded Franklin as agent for the Massachusetts House. He became an undisclosed agent (or spy) for the Continental Congress. He went to Paris as one of the commissioners in 1776, along with Franklin and John Adams, to negotiate an alliance with the French. The three were eventually reduced by a timely resolution of the Congress, prompted by the French, to one, Franklin, who was grateful to have the petty and very suspicious Lee out of his company. Back in America, Lee and his influential kinsmen from Virginia continued to snipe at Franklin in the Congress without success. One of his suspicions in Paris, however, proved to be prophetic: Edward Bancroft, secretary to the Paris delegation, was an active spy for the British, but the confirmation of that role was not made until many years later. Any damage to the American cause his covert activity might have caused remains doubtful.

Andrew Oliver (1706–1774), still nominally the lieutenant governor of Massachusetts but without any effective authority in the colony, died in the early spring of the year of Franklin's trial, causing Hutchinson to delay his departure for England until General Gage arrived three months later to relieve him. On the day of his funeral an angry and shouting crowd dogged the procession from church to graveyard. In 1776, his widow and children went into exile in England and were received by Thomas Hutchinson and his family. Oliver's widow Mary was the sister of Hutchinson's late wife Margaret.

Joseph Priestly (1733–1804) remained seriously engaged in science, less so in public affairs. His friendship and association with Franklin continued to be reflected in his personal correspondence after they were no longer living in the same country. Priestley's material wellbeing was for most of his career precarious and he had to depend upon the patronage of wealthier men, one of whom was Franklin's friend and supporter Lord Shelburne. Living independently at last in or near Birmingham during the time of the French Revolution, aspects of which frightened many of his fellow Englishmen, he found himself, as a person vocally sympathetic to the aims of the Revolution, victim of mob action in which his home was burned. In that climate Priestly had the pluck then to follow his late friend and move to Pennsylvania in 1794, where he managed to make a comfortable home and laboratory to continue his investigations and where he remained to the end of his life. New friendships made in America included Thomas Jefferson.

Jonathan Shipley, Bishop of Asaph. Courtesy of National Portrait Gallery, London.

Jonathan Shipley (1714–1788), Bishop of St. Asaph, used his position in the House of Lords to speak out against the Coercive Acts and for that courage and friendship with the colonies' cause was honored with formal thanks of the Second Continental Congress. From his mother's family he possessed a manor house near Winchester, Wyburn, where he often hosted Franklin for extended stays. In one of the long summer visits, this one in 1772, Franklin began writing his autobiography. Among the delights he experienced there was a fine garden and the playful curiosity of the Shipley children, three daughters, who carried on a lively correspondence with Franklin for a number of years. So strong was the friendship between the Shipley family and Franklin that they traveled to the coast of England and held a brief reunion with him while Franklin's ship paused in Southampton on his return voyage to America in 1785.

Margaret Stevenson (1706–1783) continued in her residence at Craven Street for a time, occasionally writing news of their friends and her daughter Polly and the three grandchildren to Franklin. Still of service to her former tenant, Mrs. Stevenson packed up his things and sent them on to Philadelphia in 1779, except the accounts still being settled on Franklin's behalf in London; she forwarded these to him in France. She suffered from palsy and was embarrassed by her handwriting, sometimes taking several different sittings to complete one letter. Up until the year prior to her death she kept alive the prospect that she might cross the Channel and visit Franklin in Passey. She remained devoted to Franklin as a dear friend and unstinting admirer. She stayed in touch with Temple, sometimes directly but more frequently through her daughter Polly Hewson.

William Strahan (1715–1785) remained Franklin's correspondent off and on throughout the war, sometimes writing in a needling way, for example, by suggesting that the former agent would have to bring the olive branch to England before peace could be restored. At one point, in the autumn of his return to Philadelphia, Franklin responded that "your ministers have made that impracticable for me, prosecuting me with a frivolous Chancery suit in the name of Whately, by which, my solicitor writes me, I shall certainly be imprisoned if I appear again in England, [but] send us over hither fair proposals of peace, if you choose it, and no body shall be more ready than myself to promote their acceptance, for I make it a rule not to mix personal resentments with public business," BF letter to WS, October 3, 1775. With the treaty of peace concluded, major elements of which Strahan credited to Franklin, he nonetheless expressed surprise that the war "terminated quite contrary to [his] expectation." Franklin took occasion in a letter to Strahan of August 19, 1784, to remind his friend that he had been warned "repeatedly [by Franklin] that by those [sic] measures England would lose her colonies" and that "your contempt of our understandings in comparison with your own … [was] not much better founded than that of our courage."

John Temple (1732–1798) left England several years after his dismissal from the customs post he held until the Hutchinson letters affair, first for Holland; he tried through letters to Franklin in France to obtain assistance for passage to America, where he hoped to resettle his family. That overture availed him little except the news that he was held in some suspicion there and thought to be a spy for the British. Temple did travel to America and tried to convince the new authorities in Boston of the worthiness of his services for the colonial cause and how he had suffered for his trouble. Without independent confirmation from Franklin, Temple's efforts were unavailing. Returning to England, Temple eventually found a position as British consular officer in New York, which he held until his death in 1798.

Alexander Wedderburn (1733–1805) remained solicitor general until 1778 when he was promoted to the position of attorney general, holding his seat in Parliament all the while. Among others from the political elite, Wedderburn visited Thomas Hutchinson when the former governor came to England in the summer of 1774. Hutchinson tried in vain to enlist the solicitor general to help repeal the statute of earlier that year closing the port of Boston, for as Hutchinson pointed out, its punishments were falling on the innocent as well as those who had challenged British rule in the colony. In the following winter Wedderburn drafted an even more punitive piece of legislation, the New England Restraining Act of 1775. It extended the restrictions of trade enacted for Massachusetts to all the New England colonies and excluded their fishing vessels from the waters of Newfoundland. Wedderburn succeeded Edward Thurlow as attorney general and in that position more than once earned the appreciation of Lord North, much criticized in Parliament for his conduct of the war with America, who allowed Wedderburn to speak out in Commons in his defense, and that of George III for answering his sovereign's need for a favorable ruling on royal authority to use army troops to quell civil unrest in England. Foreseeing the end of the North ministry and the failure of its war policy, Wedderburn opted to leave the life of advocacy to become in 1780 chief justice of the Court of Common Pleas where he earned a steady increase in professional respect as an effective jurist. His rewards for service to the Crown and ministry included, in addition to the judicial appointment, elevation to nobility and a seat in the House of Lords the same year. His new title, Baron Loughborough, would become the one by which Wedderburn is best known in the historical and legal literature of his years as jurist. The position of Lord Chancellor, the high post for which Wedderburn had been ambitious for much of his career, was given him in 1793; but in that role he managed to tarnish his image by resuming political intrigue and conniving with others against the Cabinet leadership of William Pitt. When forced from his position as Lord Chancellor at age 64, Wedderburn came away with one more title, Earl of Rosslyn in 1801, thanks largely to the King's residual gratitude from times of crisis twenty years past. Married twice, Wedderburn left no direct descendants, although the title Earl of Rosslyn did not lapse but, by terms of the grant from the Privy Council, shifted at his death to his nephew. Wedderburn chose to live out his remaining years nearby his singular patron in a country house not far from Windsor Castle.

CORRUPTION AND RESISTANCE TO CHANGE

Admiral Lord Richard Howe's overture to Franklin, we learned in Chapter 10, was viewed as at least partially a bribe. What was proposed was not in itself objectionable: one more chance to try to reach a compromise between the colonies and the mother country. It was distasteful to Franklin because the suggestion that the agent assist in the respectable mission of a peaceful settlement of differences, something both men had sought to achieve for the good of all concerned, was coupled with a less than respectable inference that Franklin might be induced to act by the prospect of his own personal advancement. Nothing specific was mentioned, but the range of possibilities could well have included a pension (perhaps to reinstate his Post Office appointment), a new office such as a governorship (like that of his son's), perhaps even a title at the far end of those possibilities.

With due respect for the agent's sensibilities, Howe's gesture could be seen in other ways. Knowing the ways of the court and of high royal service himself, Admiral Howe might simply have been, without thinking much about the fine points, engaging in sheer prediction. If that was the mindset of Howe, he certainly misjudged his listener or was insufficiently aware of the man's sense of himself and his devotion to the feelings as well as the interests of his fellow colonials. If we are to understand fully what Franklin said on the subject of corruption on other occasions, it seems most likely that Howe was simply following the usual way of doing the Crown's business in those days, appealing to private advantage as well as to the public good.

Whatever the character of Howe's overture, it is difficult to imagine that, had something come from this conversation and a mission been launched to the colonies in which Howe and Franklin brokered a compromise, both men would not have been recognized for their effectiveness at the highest levels of the ministry and court. That prospect, it must be quickly added, was surely a very long shot, given how far events had proceeded in the colonies by the winter of 1775.

Nor could Franklin himself have been very optimistic about such a possibility, either. Had he been more positive, he could just as well have chosen to ignore the blandishment of the personal gain and agreed to go anyway. Howe, it seems, was very poorly informed about conditions in the colonies. Perhaps he simply refused to believe that there was no diplomatic alternative to the trend of events of which he was aware. These certainly included the latest resolves of the Continental Congress plus Franklin's own points of policy differences that he had shared in the eleventh hour "negotiations" in London earlier that winter.

This episode serves to top off a series of occasions that Franklin while in London took to comment, sometimes bitingly, on what he took to be a widespread and deep-seated pattern of corruption in Britain. He thought he saw in this pattern, which included a good deal more than bribes alone, such a distortion of the proper, rational functioning of politics that the topic invites some exploration.

As recently as the previous autumn the agent had written to the speaker of the House of Representatives in Massachusetts, Thomas Cushing, about some fresh election possibilities that could serve the colonists' cause for greater leniency. In the parliamentary elections that season there were some successes among candidates who stood with the colonies. "But still," the agent wrote,

> if the temper of the Court continues, there will doubtless be a majority in the new parliament for its measures, whatever they are, for as most of the members are bribing or purchasing to get in, there is little doubt of their selling their votes to the ministers for the time being, to reimburse themselves. Luxury introduces necessity even among those that make the most splendid figures here; this brings

most of the Commons as well as Lords to market; and if America would save for 3 or 4 years the money she spends on the fashions, fineries and fopperies of this country, she might buy the whole parliament, ministers and all.[142]

Franklin saved his most sweeping indictment of the degree to which the kingdom seemed suffused with corruption, in its broadest terms, for a letter he wrote to Joseph Galloway, then Speaker of the Pennsylvania House of Burgesses. At the Continental Congress of 1774, Galloway offered a possible plan for union with Great Britain, and the agent in this letter responded with his own belated objections:

> [W]hen I consider the extreme corruption prevalent among all orders of men in this old rotten state, and the glorious public virtue so predominant in our rising country, I cannot but apprehend more mischief than benefit from a closer union. I fear they will drag us after them in all the plundering wars their desperate circumstances, injustice and rapacity may prompt them to undertake; and their wide-wasting prodigality and profusion a gulf that will swallow up every aid we may distress ourselves to afford them. Here numberless and needless places, enormous salaries, pensions, perquisites, bribes, groundless quarrels, foolish expeditions ... contracts and jobs devour all revenue and produce continual necessity in the midst of plenty. I apprehend therefore that to unite us intimately will only be to corrupt us also.[143]

What exactly Franklin observed or heard from others about vote buying—in Parliament or in the general elections for its membership—is not known. It seems clear from this last letter on the topic that his view of corruption was much wider than that single practice. A London contemporary of Franklin's, Horace Walpole, records his own similar impressions at the time of the 1761 parliamentary elections: "Corruption now stands upon its own legs—no money is issued from the Treasury; there are no parties, no pretenses of grievances, and yet venality is grosser than ever!" Yet more specific is this estimate from the life of a prominent politician of the time: "The price [for a vote] during [John] Wilkes' time varied between one and five

---

142 Letter from BF to Thomas Cushing, October 10 (?), 1774, *Papers*, Vol. 20, pages 328-29. There is a parallel charge in Franklin's memoir in the form of a letter to his son William of the 'secret negotiations' in London of that winter of 1775. After discrediting the 'hereditary legislators' in Lords as no better than hereditary professors of mathematics (in some imaginary German university), he writes that the "elected House of Commons is no better, nor ever will be while the electors receive money for their votes and ... ministers may bribe their representatives when chosen." *Papers*, Vol. xxi, page 583.

143 Letter dated February 25, 1775, BF to Joseph Galloway, *Papers*, Vol. 21, page 509.

pounds," and his biographer estimates that Wilkes was prepared to spend more, whatever the level, than his opponent in the election of 1757.[144]

Believing that he saw "extreme corruption in all orders of men in this old rotten state," Franklin held a much more positive view of his homeland. A "glorious public virtue" was evident there, he claimed and was apprehensive lest that spirit be diminished by a union or close affiliation between the new and old divisions of the empire he had admired so much in earlier times.

The instances of this "extreme corruption" that "devours all revenue" include "numberless and needless places, enormous salaries, pensions ... contracts and jobs" certainly reflect a society more affluent, and more stratified as well, than the ones he knew in colonial America, even in the better off communities like Boston or Philadelphia.

Not only did Franklin see in sharp contrast an older, wealthier society compared to that of one much more modest in the things money can buy, but he also saw in the one that its conspicuous consumption was readily enough traceable to the revenues exacted by a state used to manipulating its operatives who in turn became dependent on this arrangement. The pattern is hard to break once set, he implies, and it had been set for a long time in the Britain of the eighteenth century.

What may be particularly arresting for Americans in the twenty-first century is to find long shadows of Franklin's insights in recent commentary about these notions of corruption and its impact on political ideals of their republic. Writing in his extended essay "The Broken Covenant, American Civil Religion in Time of Trial," Robert Bellah has observed:

> Corruption,[...] using the eighteenth century vocabulary, is to be found in luxury, dependence, and ignorance. Luxury is the pursuit of material things that diverts us from concern for the public good, that leads us to exclusive concern for our own good, or what we would call today consumerism.[145]

And: "Dependence naturally follows from luxury, for it consists in accepting the dominance of whatever person or groups, or, we might say today, governmental or private corporate structure, that promises it will take care of our material desires."[146]

---

144 *Horace Walpole's England* at page 148; edited by Alfred Bishop Mason (1930). *John Wilkes, The Scandalous Father of Civil Liberty* by Arthur H. Cash (2006), pages 44–46.
145 Robert Bellah, *Broken Covenant* (1975; 2d ed. 1992) pages 184–85.
146 Ibid.

The debilitating vice of Britain in Franklin's view was its habituation to luxury, at least for that segment of society controlling its government through or with the connivance of the Crown's officers and parliament. It was not simply bribery, as one might understand corruption in today's political vocabulary, but a way of life followed by dint of tradition and the weight of inertia. The transplanted colonial entrepreneur believed he could see that tradition all too well from his niche in the imperial capital and held nothing back in inveighing against its consequences, an addiction among the privileged to the status quo.

It could not have escaped the agent's attention, if only in his most private moments, that there was some irony in his stance. He, after all, was himself an officeholder (if not a mere "placeman") in the service of the Crown. At least he was that up until his unceremonious firing in the winter of 1774.

If Franklin overstated a claim to virtue in the public life of America, he nevertheless could see clearly enough that the system of patronage and so on that went along with governance of Britain tended to make for ways of thinking very resistant to change. And change was of course what the Americans were now seeking. Ironically, the change they wanted, taking the Boston dissidents' view of things, was for a reversion to practices of administration of the colonies to the laissez faire attitude in place before the Stamp Act of 1765 and other revenue raising policies put into effect after its repeal. In those better days London had largely left the colonies to themselves. In that freer environment many colonials, it has been estimated, enjoyed a good deal more of the blessings of liberty than their English cousins.[147]

At their core, however, the institutions by which Britain governed its colonies in America—with variations depending on the charter of a particular colony—had not changed much since their origins more than a century earlier. Parliament had not declared an exemption from taxes; it had just

---

147 Indeed, as one recent imperial history claims, "the ones who revolted against British rule were the best off of Britain's colonial subjects. There is good reason to think that, by the 1770s, New Englanders were about the wealthiest people in the world. Per capita income was at least equal to that in the United Kingdom and was more evenly distributed. The New Englanders had bigger farms, bigger families and better education than the Old Englanders back home. And, crucially, they paid far less tax. In 1763 the average Briton paid 26 shillings a year in taxes. The equivalent figure for a Massachusetts taxpayer was just one shilling." Niall Ferguson, *Empire: How Britain Made the Modern World* page 85 (Penguin Books edition 2004).

not bothered with them while mercantilism was working so well and the forces of the King in the new world were not large nor put to much extra effort on account of any determined rival like France. But, of course, all that changed with the circumstances of the war Americans call the French and Indian War.[148]

When, then, in the early 1770s colonial leaders like Thomas Cushing of Boston spoke of a crisis in constitutionalism, they were in effect claiming that the relatively greater autonomy the colonies enjoyed in those days before the war with France was part of their understanding of what it meant to live under the British flag. The novelty was in the attempt to raise revenues from the colonies leading in turn to efforts to enforce the revenue measures. The presence of more aggressive customs officials similarly gave rise to schemes of evasion and avoidance, smuggling and resistance of various sorts. The more rowdy (burning of a customs vessel and sacking of the homes of officials) of these resistances brought arrests, trials and, eventually, the presence of troops and naval vessels to back up the customs patrols. It is easy to understand the logic of the progression and of the increasing frustration, both on the part of the ministry and the colonial leadership, too.[149]

So far as formal structures of law and governance are concerned, the colonial ones, until this decade, were not substantially different from those in Britain. Representative democratic institutions had not progressed as far as they would later, sooner of course in the American scene, in both countries. Membership in elected houses of representatives was restricted to adult males, and only those with some ownership of property. "The House of

---

148 Kevin Phillips in his 1999 *magnum opus* provides this sweeping summary of those circumstances: "When the Treaty of Paris in 1763 confirmed the battlefield gains of 1759–1762, Britain found itself the richest empire of eighteenth-century Europe, swollen most spectacularly in North America by the addition of Canada, the eastern part of former French Louisiana, and Spanish Florida. The British victories over France ... were decisive. The cost of this new grandeur, however, was painful: a national debt swollen from 55 million pounds to 132 million.... [Thus the] Sugar Act of 1764, the Stamp Act of 1765, and the Townshend Acts of 1767 all pursued revenues needed to help underwrite the British administrative and military presence in North America." Kevin Phillips, *The Cousins' Wars, Religion, Politics and the Triumph of Anglo-America* pages 103–104 (Basic Books 1999).

149 There were, to be sure, very important changes in the administration of Massachusetts Bay Colony, apart from the revenue measures applicable to all the colonies, *after* the Tea Party of late 1774 culminating in the closing of the port of Boston entirely, removal of the capital from Boston, and ultimately a declaration in 1775 from Parliament that the colony was in "open rebellion."

Commons was unrepresentative: property in land was represented, people and movements of opinion were not."[150] Some of the colonial governors had powers of appointment (and opportunities for favoritism) not dissimilar from those of Crown and ministry in England.

On the other hand, it was a good deal more likely that an average head of family in an American colony like Massachusetts could acquire land and gradually become a significant part of the political life of his community than it would be for his counterpart in Britain. Franklin's own life in Pennsylvania provides an eloquent example of an upwardly mobile young entrepreneur who would become civically and politically significant. There seems little doubt that this simple but basic distinction between the societies of Britain and colonial America could by itself color one's views in powerful ways. And so it could well have informed the views of Franklin about the two countries he knew firsthand.

This is not to say that there were no class differences, say in Boston or Philadelphia. Gradations in wealth there certainly were. Thomas Hutchinson's family in Massachusetts was very well off, for example, enjoying a prominent position in trade and in the political life of the colony. But there were no peerages, no institutions (save perhaps the Church of England) around and within which these privileged members of the community exercised their obvious advantages so visibly as in the Court of St. James.

What Franklin thought he saw as a certain virtue in American society compared with that of Great Britain is of course difficult to assess or describe. Perhaps we can go this far with him: there was very likely a greater degree of individual independence and social mobility in the colonies, especially those of New England. Probably also there was less susceptibility to official manipulation in a country of less aggregate wealth than in a richer one. Especially was this so, Franklin was claiming, in a rich one with noticeably sharp degrees of social and economic division. In either case, whether it be called a public virtue or something else that so few men were the virtual wards of others and dependent upon them in material ways, Franklin's understanding of the contrast between the public life of Britain and that of the America he knew certainly made him skeptical of the soundness of policies that were or could be effectuated in a society so deficient in that degree of personal independence among so many of its members.

---

150 Esmond Wright, *Franklin of Philadelphia* page 234 (1986).

What Franklin had begun to identify, if we understand Robert Bellah's insights correctly, was little short of a principal corollary of the republican ideal which he and the other founders would better understand when they got down to fashioning a constitution more than a decade later.[151]

Perhaps the "second thoughts" of those last months in London, frustrating and dispiriting as they were, seemingly without purpose or utility, did serve Franklin in other, less obvious ways. Perhaps he was forced to think through much of what he had earlier observed or experienced but whose full significance had been lost on him in the more hopeful seasons of the long crisis of the 1770s. Not quite an "ah ha!" moment but at least an hour of reflection in which a fuller understanding might take the place of vanquished optimism; and an uncertain pragmatism, if not resignation, could be substituted for illusion.

"The Election II; Canvassing for Votes" after Wm. Hogarth, engraved by Charles Grignion.

151 Corruption destroys independence and thereby defeats the imperative to debate and compromise for the common good. See Bellah, id at 184. Much later in his career and on the very launching of the new American Constitution, Franklin would be at pains to warn of the dangers ahead should his countrymen surrender or diminish the vigor of the virtue (in the sense of the *common good* being the central ideal of democratic politics) necessary to preserve the institutions of this new charter. See Ralph L. Ketcham, ed., *The Political Thought of Benjamin Franklin* (Indianapolis, Indiana: Bobbs-Merrill, 1965, page 491, as cited in Robert N. Bellah, *The Broken Covenant* (Chicago, 1975), page 184.

VERBATIM 1. FRANKLIN'S PUBLIC STATEMENT ABOUT THE HUTCHINSON LETTERS

Printed in The London Chronicle, Dec. 23–25, 1773

To the Printer of the London Chronicle.

Craven-street, Dec. 25, 1773.

Sir,

Finding that two Gentlemen have been unfortunately engaged in a Duel, about a transaction and its circumstances of which both of them are totally ignorant and innocent, I think it incumbent on me to declare (for the prevention of farther mischief, as far as such a declaration may contribute to prevent it) that I alone am the person who obtained and transmitted to Boston the letters in question. Mr. W. could not communicate them, because they were never in his possession; and, for the same reason, they could not be taken from him by Mr. T. They were not of the nature of "private letters between friends:" They were written by public officers to persons in public station, on public affairs, and intended to procure public measures; they were therefore handed to other public persons who might be influenced by them to produce those measures: Their tendency was to incense the Mother Country against her Colonies, and, by the steps recommended, to widen the breach, which they effected. The chief Caution expressed with regard to Privacy was to keep their contents from the Colony Agents, who the writers apprehended, might return them, or copies of them, to America. That apprehension was, it seems, well founded; for the first Agent who laid his hands on them, thought it his duty to transmit them to his Constituents.

B. Franklin,

Agent for the House of Representatives

of the Massachusetts-Bay.

VERBATIM 2. THE HUTCHINSON LETTERS

(Papers, vol. 20, pages 539–580.)

Printed in The Representation of Governor Hutchinson and Others, Contained in Certain Letters Transmitted to England, and Afterwards Returned from Thence, and Laid before the General Assembly of the Massachusetts-Bay... (Boston, 1773).

Boston, 18th June 1768.

Sir,

As you allow me the honour of your correspondence, I may not omit acquainting you with so remarkable an event as the withdraw of the commissioners of the customs and most of the other officers under them from the town on board the Romney, with an intent to remove from thence to the castle.

In the evening of the 10th a sloop belonging to Mr. Hancock, a representative for Boston, and a wealthy merchant, of great influence over the populace, was seized by the collector and comptroller for a very notorious breach of the acts of trade, and, after seizure taken into custody by the officer of the Romney man of war, and remov'd under command of her guns. It is pretended that the removal and not the seizure incensed the people. It seems not very material which it was. A mob was immediately rais'd, the Officers insulted, bruis'd and much hurt, and the windows of some of their houses broke; a boat belonging to the collector burnt in triumph, and many threats utter'd against the commissioners and their officers: no notice being taken of their extravagance in the time of it, nor any endeavours by any authority except the governor, the next day to discover and punish the offenders; and there being a rumour of a higher mob intended monday (the 13th) in the evening the commissioners, four of them, thought themselves altogether unsafe, being destitute of protection, and remov'd with their families to the Romney, and there remain and hold their board, and next week intend to do the same, and also open the custom-house at the castle. The governor press'd the council to assist him with their advice, but they declin'd and evaded calling it a brush or small disturbance by boys and negroes, not considering how much it must be resented in England that the officers of the Crown should think themselves obliged to quit the place of their residence and go on board a King's ship for safety, and all the internal authority of the province take no notice of it. The town of Boston have had repeated meetings, and by their votes declared the commissioners and their officers a great grievance, and yesterday instructed their representatives to endeavor that enquiry should be made by the assembly whether any person by writing or in any other way had encouraged the sending troops here, there being some alarming reports that troops are expected, but have not taken any measures to discountenance the promoters of the late proceedings; but on the contrary appointed one or more of the actors or abettors on a committee appointed to wait on the governor, and to desire him to order the man of war out of the harbour.

Ignorant as they be, yet the heads of a Boston town-meeting influence all public measures.

It is not possible this anarchy should last always. Mr. Hallowell who will be the bearer of this tells me he has the honor of being personally known to you. I beg leave to refer you to him for a more full account. I am, with great esteem, Sir, your most humble and obedient servant,

Tho. Hutchinson.

Boston, August 1768.

Sir,

It is very necessary other information should be had in England of the present state of the commissioners of the customs than what common fame will bring to you or what you will receive from most of the letters which go from hence, people in general being prejudiced by many false reports and misrepresentations concerning them. Seven eighths of the people of the country suppose the board itself to be unconstitutional and cannot be undeceived and brought to believe that a board has existed in England all this century, and that the board established here has no new powers given to it. Our incendiaries know it but they industriously and very wickedly publish the contrary. As much pains has been taken to prejudice the country against the persons of the commissioners and their characters have been misrepresented and cruelly treated especially since their confinement at the castle where they are not so likely to hear what is said of them and are not so able to confute it.

It is not pretended they need not to have withdrawn, that Mr. Williams had stood his ground without any injury although the mob beset his house, &c. There never was that spirit raised against the under officers as against the commissioners, I mean four of them. They had a public affront offered them by the town of Boston who refused to give the use of their hall for a public dinner unless it was stipulated that the commissioners should not be invited. An affront of the same nature at the motion of Mr. Hancock was offered by a company of cadets. Soon after a vessel of Mr. Hancock's being seized the officers were mobb'd and the commissioners were informed they were threatened. I own I was in pain for them. I do not believe if the mob had seized them, there was any authority able and willing to have rescued them. After they had withdrawn the town signified to the governor by a message that it was expected or desired they should not return. It was then the general voice that it would not be safe for them to return. After all this the sons of liberty say they deserted or abdicated.

The other officers of the customs in general either did not leave the town or soon returned to it. Some of them seem to be discontented with the commissioners. Great pains have been taken to increase the discontent. Their office by these means is rendered extremely burdensome. Every thing they do is found fault with, and yet no particular illegality or even irregularity mentioned. There is too much hauteur some of their officers say in the treatment they receive. They say they treat their officers as the commissioners treat their officers in England and require no greater deference. After all it is not the persons but the office of the commissioners which has raised this spirit, and the distinction made between the commissioners is because it has been given out that four of them were in favor of the new establishment and the fifth was not. If Mr. Hallowell arrived safe he can inform you many circumstances relative to this distinction which I very willingly excuse myself from mentioning.

I know of no burden brought upon the fair trader by the new establishment. The illicit trader finds the risque greater than it used to be, especially in the port where the board is constantly held. Another circumstance that increases the prejudice is this; the new duties happened to take place just about the time the commissioners arrived. People have absurdly connected the duties and board of commissioners, and suppose we should have had no additional duties if there had been no board to have the charge of collecting them. With all the aid you can give to the officers of the crown they will have enough to do to maintain the authority of government and to carry the laws into execution. If they are discountenanced, neglected or fail of support from you, they must submit to every thing the present opposers of government think fit to require of them.

There is no office under greater discouragements than that of the commissioners. Some of my friends recommended me to the ministry. I think myself very happy that I am not one. Indeed it would have been incompatible with my post as chief justice, and I must have declined it, and I should do it although no greater salary had been affixed to the chief justices place than the small pittance allowed by the province.

From my acquaintance with the commissioners I have conceived a personal esteem for them, but my chief inducement to make this representation to you is in regard to the public interest which I am sure will suffer if the opposition carry their point against them. I am with very great esteem, Sir, your most obedient humble servant,

Tho. Hutchinson.

August 10. Yesterday at a meeting of the merchants it was agreed by all present to give no more orders for goods from England, nor receive any on commission until the late acts are repealed. And it is said all except sixteen in the town have subscribed an engagement of that tenor. I hope the subscription will be printed that I may transmit it to you.

Boston, 4th October 1768.
Dear Sir,

I was absent upon one of our circuits when Mr. Byles arrived. Since my return I have received from him your obliging letter of 31st July. I never dared to think what the resentment of the nation would be upon Hallowell's arrival. It is not strange that measures should be immediately taken to reduce the colonies to their former state of government and order, but that the national funds should be affected by it is to me a little mysterious and surprizing. Principles of government absurd enough, spread thro' all the colonies; but I cannot think that in any colony, people of any consideration have ever been so mad as to think of a revolt. Many of the common people have been in a frenzy, and talk'd of dying in defence of their liberties, and have spoke and printed what is highly criminal, and too many of rank above the vulgar, and some in public posts have countenanced and encouraged them until they increased so much in their numbers and in their opinion of their importance as to submit to government no further than they thought proper. The legislative powers have been influenced by them, and the executive powers entirely lost their force. There has been continual danger of mobs and insurrections, but they would have spent all their force within ourselves, the officers of the Crown and some of the few friends who dared to stand by them possibly might have been knock'd in the head, and some such fatal event would probably have brought the people to their senses. For four or five weeks past the distemper has been growing, and I confess I have not been without some apprehensions for myself, but my friends have had more for me, and I have had repeated and frequent notices from them from different quarters, one of the last I will enclose to you. In this state of things there was no security but quitting my posts, which nothing but the last extremity would justify. As chief justice for two years after our first disorders I kept the grand juries tolerably well to their duty. The last spring there had been several riots, and a most infamous libel had been published in one of the papers, which I enlarged upon, and the grand jury had determined to make presentments, but the attorney-general not attending them the first day, Otis and his creatures who were alarmed and frightened exerted themselves the next day and prevailed upon so many of the jury to change their voices, that there was not a sufficient number left to find a bill. They have been ever since more enraged against me than ever. At the desire of the governor I committed to writing the charge while it lay in my memory, and as I have no further use for it I will enclose it as it may give you some idea of our judicatories.

Whilst we were in this state, news came of two regiments being ordered from Halifax, and soon after two more from Ireland. The minds of people were more and more agitated, broad hints were given that the troops should never land, a barrel of tar was placed upon the beacon, in the night to be fired to bring in the country when the troops appeared, and all the authority of the government was not strong enough to remove it. The town of Boston met and passed a number of weak but very criminal votes; and as the governor declined calling an assembly they sent circular letters to all the towns and districts to send a person each that there might be a general consultation at so extraordinary a crisis. They met and spent a week, made themselves ridiculous, and then dissolved themselves, after a message or two to the governor which he refused to receive; a petition to the King which I dare say their agents will never be allow'd to present, and a result which they have published ill-natured and impotent.

In this confusion the troops from Halifax arrived. I never was much afraid of the people's taking arms, but I was apprehensive of violence from the mob, it being their last chance before the troops could land. As the prospect of revenge became more certain their courage abated in proportion. Two regiments are landed, but a new grievance is now rais'd. The troops are by act of parliament to be quartered nowhere else but in the barracks until they are full. There are barracks enough at the castle to hold both regiments. It is therefore against the act to bring any of them into town. This was started by the council in their answer to the governor, which to make themselves popular, they in an unprecedented way published and have alarmed all the province; for although none but the most contracted minds could put such a construction upon the act, yet after this declaration of the council nine tenths of the people suppose it just. I wish the act had been better express'd, but it is absurd to suppose the parliament intended to take from the King the direction of his forces by confining them to a place where any of the colonies might think fit to build barracks. It is besides ungrateful, for it is known to many that this provision was brought into the bill after it had been framed without it, from mere favor to the colonies. I hear the commander in chief has provided barracks or quarters, but a doubt still remains with some of the council, whether they are to furnish the articles required, unless the men are in the province barracks, and they are to determine upon it to day.

The government has been so long in the hands of the populace that it must come out of them by degrees, at least it will be a work of time to bring the people back to just notions of the nature of government.

Mr. Pepperell a young gentleman of good character, and grandson and principal heir to the late Sir William Pepperell being bound to London, I shall deliver this letter to him, as it will be too bulky for postage, and desire him to wait upon you with it. I am with very great esteem, Sir, your most humble and most obedient servant,

Tho. Hutchinson.

Sept. 14. 1768.

Sir,

The great esteem I have for you in every point of light perhaps renders my fears and doubts for the safety of your person greater than they ought to be; however if that is an error it certainly results from true friendship, naturally jealous. Last night I was informed by a gentleman of my acquaintance, who had his information from one intimate with and knowing to the infernal purposes of the sons of liberty as they falsely stile themselves, that he verily believ'd, from the terrible threats and menaces by those catalines against you, that your life is greatly in danger. This informant I know is under obligations to you and is a man of veracity. He express'd himself with concern for you, and the gentleman acquainting me with this horrid circumstance, assured me he was very uneasy till you had notice. I should have done myself the honor of waiting on you but am necessarily prevented. The duty I owed to you as a friend and to the publick as a member of society, would not suffer me to rest till I had put your honor upon your guard; for tho' this may be a false alarm, nothing would have given me greater pain, if any accident had happen'd, and I had been silent. If possible I will see you to morrow, and let you know further into this black affair. And am with the sincerest friendship and respect, your honor's most obedient, and most humble servant.

Rob. Auchmuty.

To the hon'ble Thomas Hutchinson.

Boston, 10th December 1768.

Dear Sir,

I am just now informed that a number of the council, perhaps 8 or 10 who live in and near this town, have met together and agreed upon a long address or petition to parliament, and that it will be sent by this ship to Mr. Bollan to be presented. Mr. Danforth who is president of the council told the governor upon enquiry, that it was sent to him to sign, and he supposed the rest of the council who had met together would sign after him in order, but he had since found that they had wrote over his name by order of council, which makes it appear to be an act of council. This may be a low piece of cunning in him, but be it as it may, it's proper it should be known that the whole is no more than the doings of a part of the council only, although even that is not very material, since, if they had all been present without the governor's summons the meeting would have been irregular and unconstitutional, and ought to be discountenanced and censured. I suppose there is no instance of the privy council's meeting and doing business without the king's presence or special direction, except in committees upon such business as by his majesty's order has been referr'd to them by an act of council, and I have known no instance here without the governor until within three or four months past.

I thought it very necessary the circumstances of this proceeding should be known, tho' if there be no necessity for it, I think it would be best it should not be known that the intelligence comes from me. I am with very great regard, Sir, your most humble and most obedient Servant,

Tho. Hutchinson.

Boston, 20th January 1769.

Dear Sir,

You have laid me under very great obligations by the very clear and full account of proceedings in parliament, which I received from you by Capt. Scott. You have also done much service to the people of the province. For a day or two after the ship arrived, the enemies of government gave out that their friends in parliament were increasing, and all things would be soon on the old footing; in other words that all acts reposing duties would be repealed, the commissioners board dissolved, the customs put on the old footing, and illicit trade be carried on with little or no hazard. It was very fortunate that I had it in my power to prevent such a false representation from spreading through the province. I have been very cautious of using your name, but I have been very free in publishing abroad the substance of your letter, and declaring that I had my intelligence from the best authority, and have in a great measure defeated the ill design in raising and attempting to spread so groundless a report. What marks of resentment the parliament will show, whether they will be upon the province in general or particular persons, is extremely uncertain, but that they will be placed somewhere is most certain, and I add, because I think it ought to be so that those who have been most steady in preserving the constitution and opposing the licentiousness of such as call themselves sons of liberty will certainly meet with favor and encouragement.

This is most certainly a crisis. I really wish that there may not have been the least degree of severity beyond what is absolutely necessary to maintain, I think I may say to you the dependence which a colony ought to have upon the parent State; but if no measures shall have been taken to secure this dependence, or nothing more than some declaratory acts or resolves, it is all over with us. The friends of government will be utterly disheartened, and the friends of anarchy will be afraid of nothing be it ever so extravagant.

The last vessel from London had a quick passage. We expect to be in suspense for the three or four next weeks and then to hear our fate. I never think of the measures necessary for the peace and good order of the colonies without pain. There must be an abridgment of what are called English liberties. I relieve myself by considering that in a remove from the state of nature to the most perfect state of government there must be a great restraint of natural liberty. I doubt whether it is possible to project a system of government in which a colony 3000 miles distant from the parent state shall enjoy all the liberty of the parent state. I am certain I have never yet seen the projection. I wish the good of the colony when I wish to see some further restraint of liberty rather than the connexion with the parent state should be broken; for I am sure such a breach must prove the ruin of the colony. Pardon me this excursion; it really proceeds from the state of mind into which our perplexed affairs often throw me. I have the honor to be with very great esteem, Sir, your most humble and most obedient servant,

Tho. Hutchinson.

Boston, 20th October, 1769.
Dear Sir,

I thank you for your last favor of July 18th. I fancy in my last to you about two months ago I have answered the greatest part of it.

My opinion upon the combination of the merchants, I gave you very fully. How long they will be able to continue them if parliament should not interpose is uncertain. In most articles they may another year, and you run the risqué of their substituting when they are put to their shifts something of their own in the place of what they used to have from you, and which they will never return to you for. But it is not possible that provision for dissolving these combinations and subjecting all who do not renounce them to penalties adequate to the offence should not be made the first week the parliament meets. Certainly all parties will unite in so extraordinary case if they never do in any other. So much has been said upon the repeal of the duties laid by the last act, that it will render it very difficult to keep people's minds quiet if that should be refused them. They deserve punishment you will say, but laying or continuing taxes upon all cannot be thought equal, seeing many will be punished who are not offenders. Penalties of another kind seem better adapted.

I have been tolerably treated since the governor's departure, no other charge being made against me in our scandalous newspapers except my bad principles in matters of government, and this charge has had little effect, and a great many friends promise me support.

I must beg the favor of you to keep secret every thing I write, until we are in a more settled state, for the party here either by their agent or by some of their emissaries in London, have sent them every report or rumour of the contents of letters wrote from hence. I hope we shall see better times both here and in England. I am, with great esteem, Sir, your most obedient servant,

Boston, 7th May 1767.
Sir,

I am indebted to you for the obliging manner in which you receiv'd my recommendation of my good friend Mr. Paxton, as well as for the account you are pleased to send me of the situation of affairs in the mother country.

I am very sorry that the colonies give you so much employment, and it is impossible to say how long it will be before things settle into quiet among us. We have some here who have been so busy in fomenting the late disturbances that they may now think it needful for their own security to keep up the spirit. They have plumed themselves much upon the victory they have gained, and the support they have since met with; nor could any thing better shew what they would still be at, than the manner in which by their own account published in the news-papers last August they celebrated the 14th of that month, as the first anniversary commemoration of what they had done at the tree of liberty on that day the year before. Here a number of respectable gentlemen as they inform us now met, and among other toasts drank general Paoli, and the spark of liberty kindled in Spain. I am now speaking of a few individuals only, the body of the people are well disposed, yet when you come to see the journal of the house of representatives the last session, I fear you will think that the same spirit has seized our public counsels. I can however fairly say thus much in behalf of the government, that the last house was packed by means of a public proscription just before the election, of the greatest part of those who had appeared in the preceding session in the support of government: their names were published in an inflammatory news-paper, and their constituents made to believe they were about to sell them for slaves. Writs are now out for a new assembly, but I cannot answer for the choice: I hope however that the people in general are in a better temper; yet the moderate men have been so browbeaten in the house, and found themselves so insignificant there the last year, that some of them will voluntary decline coming again. I think this looks too much like a despair of the commonwealth, and cannot be justified on patriotic principles.

The election of counselors was carried the last year as might have been expected from such a house. The officers of the Crown and the judges of the superior court were excluded. And I hear that it is the design of some who expect to be returned members of the house this year to make sure work at the ensuing election of counselors, by excluding, if they can, the gentlemen of the council (who by charter remain such 'till others are chosen in their room) from any share in the choice, tho' they have always had their voice in it hitherto from the first arrival of the charter. If the house do this, they will have it in their power to model the council as they please, and throw all the powers of government into the hands of the people, unless the governor should again exert his negative as he did the last year.

You have doubtless seen some of the curious messages from the late house to the governor, and can't but have observed with how little decency they have attacked both the governor and the lieutenant governor. They have also in effect forced the council to declare themselves parties in the quarrel they had against the latter in a matter of mere indifference. In their message to the governor of the 31st of January they have explicitly charged the lieutenant governor (a gentleman to whom they are more indebted than to any one man in the government) with "ambition and lust of power", merely for paying a compliment to the governor agreeable to ancient usage, by attending him to court and being present in the council-chamber when he made his speech at the opening of the session; at which time they go on to say, "none but the general court and their servants are intended to be present", still holding out to the people the servants of the crown as objects of insignificance, ranking the secretary with their door-keeper, as servants of the assembly; for the secretary with his clerks and the door-keeper are the only persons present with the assembly on these occasions.

The officers of the crown being thus lessen'd in the eyes of the people, takes off their weight and influence, and the balance will of course turn in favor of the people, and what makes them still more insignificant is their dependence on the people for a necessary support: If something were left to the goodwill of the people, yet nature should be sure of a support. The governor's salary has for about 35 years past been pretty well understood to be a thousand pound a year sterling. When this sum was first agreed to, it was very well; but an increase of wealth since has brought along with it an increase of luxury, so that what was sufficient to keep up a proper distinction and support the dignity of a governor then, may well be supposed to be insufficient for the purpose now. The lieutenant governor has no appointments as such: the captaincy of Castle-William which may be worth £120 sterling a year is looked upon indeed as an appendage to his commission, and the late lieutenant governor enjoyed no other appointment: he lived a retired life upon his own estate in the country, and was easy. The present lieutenant governor indeed has other appointments, but the people are quarrelling with him for it, and will not suffer him to be easy unless he will retire also.

The secretary may have something more than £200 a year sterling, but has for the two last years been allowed £60 lawful money a year less than had been usual for divers years preceding, tho' he had convinced the house by their committee that without this deduction he would have had no more than £250 sterling per annum in fees, perquisites and salary altogether, which is not the one half of his annual expense.

The crown did by charter reserve to itself the appointment of a governor, lieutenant governor and secretary: the design of this was without doubt to maintain some kind of balance between the powers of the crown and of the people; but if officers are not in some measure independent of the people (for it is difficult to serve two masters) they will sometimes have a hard struggle between duty to the crown and a regard to self, which must be a very disagreeable situation to them, as well as a weakening to the authority of government. The officers of the crown are very few and are therefore the more easily provided for without burdening the people: and such provision I look upon as necessary to the restoration and support of the King's authority.

But it may be said how can any new measures be taken without raising new disturbances? The manufacturers in England will rise again and defeat the measures of government. This game 'tis true has been played once and succeeded, and it has been asserted here, that it is in the power of the colonies at any time to raise a rebellion in England by refusing to send for their manufactures. For my own part I do not believe this. The merchants in England, and I don't know but those in London and Bristol only, might always govern in this matter and quiet the manufacturer. The merchant's view is always to his own interest. As the trade is now managed, the dealer here sends to the merchant in England for his goods; upon these goods the English merchant puts a profit of 10 or more probably of 15 per cent when he sends them to his employer in America. The merchant is so jealous of foregoing this profit, that an American trader cannot well purchase the goods he wants of the manufacturer; for should the merchant know that the manufacturer had supplied an American, he would take off no more of his wares. The merchants therefore having this profit in view will by one means or other secure it. They know the goods which the American market demands, and may therefore safely take them off from the manufacturer, tho' they should have no orders for shipping them this year or perhaps the next; and I dare say, it would not be longer before the Americans would clamour for a supply of goods from England, for it is vain to think they can supply themselves. The merchant might then put an advanced price upon his goods, and possibly be able to make his own terms; or if it should be thought the goods would not bear an advanced price to indemnify him, it might be worth while for the government to agree with the merchants before hand to allow them a premium equivalent to the advance of their stock, and then the game would be over.

I have written with freedom in confidence of my name's not being used on the occasion. For though I have wrote nothing but what in my conscience I think an American may upon just principles advance, and what a servant of the crown ought upon all proper occasions to suggest, yet the many prejudices I have to combat with may render it unfit it should be made public.

I communicated to governor Bernard what you mentioned concerning him, who desires me to present you his compliments, and let you know that he is obliged to you for the expressions of your regard for his injured character. I am with great respect, Sir, your most obedient and most humble servant,

Andw. Oliver.

I ask your acceptance of a journal of the last session which is put up in a box directed to the secretary of the board of trade.

Boston, 11 May, 1768.

Sir,

I am this moment favored with your very obliging letter by Capt. Jarvis of the 2d March, which I have but just time to acknowledge, as this is the day given out for the ship to sail. I wrote you the 23d of February in reply to your letter of the 28th December, that of the 12th February which you refer to in this of the 2d of March is not yet come to hand. You lay me, sir, under the greatest obligations as well for the interesting account of public affairs which you are from time to time pleased to transmit me, as for your steady attention to my private concerns. I shall always have the most grateful sense of Mr. Grenville's intentions of favor also, whether I ever reap any benefit from them or not. Without a proper support afforded to the king's officers, the respect due to government will of course fail; yet I cannot say whether under the present circumstances, and considering the temper the people are now in, an additional provision for me would be of real benefit to me personally or not. It has been given out that no person who receives a stipend from the government at home shall live in the country. Government here wants some effectual support: No sooner was it known that the lieut. governor had a provision of £200 a year made for him out of the revenue, than he was advised in the Boston Gazette to resign all pretensions to a seat in council, either with or without a voice. The temper of the people may be surely learnt from that infamous paper; it is the very thing that forms their temper; for if they are not in the temper of the writer at the time of the publication, yet it is looked upon as the oracle, and they soon bring their temper to it. Some of the latest of them are very expressive, I will not trouble you with sending them, as I imagine they somehow or other find their way to you: But I cannot but apprehend from these papers and from hints that are thrown out, that if the petition of the House to his Majesty and their letters to divers noble Lords should fail of success, some people will be mad enough to go to extremities. The commissioners of the customs have already been openly affronted, the governor's company of Cadets have come to a resolution not to wait on him (as usual) on the day of General Election the 25th instant if those gentlemen are of the company. And the Town of Boston have passed a Vote that Faneuil-Hall (in which the governor and his company usually dine on that day) shall not be opened to him if the commissioners are invited to dine with him. A list of counselors has within a few days past been printed and dispersed by way of sneer on Lord Shelburne's letter, made up of king's officers; which list, the writer says, if adopted at the next general election may take away all grounds of complaint, and may possibly prove a healing and very salutary measure. The lieutenant governor is at the head of this list, they have done me the honor to put me next, the commissioners of the customs are all in the list except Mr. Temple, and to complete the list, they have added some of the waiters. I never thought 'till very lately that they acted upon any settled plan, nor do I now think they have 'till of late, a few, a very few, among us have planned the present measures, and the government has been too weak to subdue their turbulent spirits. Our situation is not rightly known; but it is a matter worthy of the most serious attention. I am with the greatest respect, Sir, your most obedient and most humble Servant,

Andw. Oliver.

I shall take proper care to forward your
Letter to Mr. Ingersol. He had received your last.

Boston, 13th February, 1769.

Sir,

I have your very obliging favor of the 4th of October. I find myself constrained as well by this letter as by my son and daughter Spooner's letters since, to render you my most sincere thanks for the very polite notice you have taken of them; and I pray my most respectful compliments to the good lady your mother, whose friendly reception of them at Nonesuch has, I find engaged the warmest esteem and respect. He hath wrote us that he had a prospect of succeeding in the business he went upon; but the last letter we had was from her of the 23d of November, acquainting us that he had been very ill, but was getting better. She writes as a person overcome with a sense of the kindness they had met with, in a place where they were strangers, on this trying occasion.

You have heard of the arrival of the King's troops, the quiet reception they met with among us was not at all surprising to me. I am sorry there was any occasion for sending them. From the address of the gentlemen of the council to General Gage, it might be supposed there was none. I have seen a letter from our friend Ingersoll with this paraphrase upon it. "We hope that your Excellency observing with your own eyes now the troops are among us, our peaceable and quiet behavior, will be convinced that wicked G———r B———d told a fib in saying, We were not so before they came." I have given you the sense of a stranger on a single paragraph of this address, because I suspected my own opinion of it, 'till I found it thus confirm'd. If you have the newspapers containing the address, your own good sense will lead you to make some other remarks upon it, as well as to trace the influence under which it seems to have been penned. The disturbers of our peace take great advantage of such aids from people in office and power. The lieutenant governor has communicated to me your letter containing an account of the debates in parliament on the first day of the session: We soon expect their decision on American affairs, some I doubt not with fear and trembling. Yet I have very lately had occasion to know, that be the determination of parliament what it will, it is the determination of some to agree to no terms that shall remove us from our old foundation. This confirms me in an opinion that I have taken up a long time since, that if there be no way to take off the original incendiaries, they will continue to instill their poison into the minds of the people through the vehicle of the Boston gazette.

In your letter to the lieutenant governor you observe upon two defects in our constitution, the popular election of the Council, and the return of Juries by the Towns. The first of these arises from the Charter itself; the latter from our provincial Laws. The method of appointing our Grand Juries lies open to management. Whoever pleases, nominates them at our town-meeting; by this means one who was suppos'd to be a principal in the Riots of the 10th of June last, was upon that Jury whose business it was to inquire into them: But the provincial legislature hath made sufficient provision for the return of Petit Juries by their act of 23d Geo. 2d, which requires the several towns to take lists of all persons liable by law to serve, and forming them into two classes, put their names written on separate papers into two different boxes, one for the superior court and the other for the inferior: And when venires are issued, the number therein required are to be drawn out in open town-meeting, no person to serve oftener than once in three years. The method of appointing Grand Juries appears indeed defective; but if the other is not it may be imputed to the times rather than to the defect of the laws, that neither the Grand Juries nor the Petit Juries have of late answered the expectations of government.

As to the appointment of the council, I am of opinion that neither the popular elections in this province, nor their appointment in what are called the royal governments by the King's mandamus, are free from exceptions, especially if the council as a legislative body is intended to answer the idea of the house of lords in the British legislature. There they are suppos'd to be a free and independent body, and on their being such the strength and firmness of the constitution does very much depend: whereas the election or appointment of the councils in the manner before mentioned renders them altogether dependent on their constituents. The King is the fountain of honour, and as such the peers of the realm derive their honours from him; but then they hold them by a surer tenure than the provincial counselors who are appointed by mandamus. On the other hand, our popular elections very often expose them to contempt; for nothing is more common than for the representatives, when they find the council a little intractable at the close of the year, to remind them that May is at hand.

It may be accounted by the colonies as dangerous to admit of any alterations in their charters, as it is by the governors in the church to make any in the establishment; yet to make the resemblance as near as may be to the British parliament, some alteration is necessary. It is not requisite that I know of, that a counselor should be a freeholder; his residence according to the charter is a sufficient qualification; for that provides only, that he be an inhabitant of or proprietor of lands within the district for which he is chosen: Whereas the peers of the realm sit in the house of lords, as I take it, in virtue of their baronies. If there should be a reform of any of the colony charters with a view to keep up the resemblance of the three estates in England, the legislative council shou'd consist of men of landed estates; but as our landed estates here are small at present, the yearly value of £100 sterling per annum might in some of them at least be a sufficient qualification. As our estates are partable after the decease of the proprietor, the honour could not be continued in families as in England: it might however be continued in the appointee quom diu bene se gesserit, and proof be required of some mal-practice before a suspicion or removal. Bankruptcy also might be another ground for removal. A small legislative council might answer the purposes of government; but it might tend to weaken that leveling principle, which is cherish'd by the present popular constitution, to have an honorary order establish'd, out of which the council shou'd be appointed. There is no way now to put a man of fortune above the common level, and exempt him from being chosen by the people into the lower offices, but his being appointed a justice of the peace; this is frequently done when there is no kind of expectation of his undertaking the trust, and has its inconveniences. For remedy hereof it might be expedient to have an order of Patricians or Esquires instituted, to be all men of fortune or good landed estates, and appointed by the governor with the advice of council, and enroll'd in the secretary's office, who shou'd be exempted from the lower offices in government as the justices now are; and to have the legislative council (which in the first instance might be nominated by the Crown) from time to time fill'd up as vacancies happen out of this order of men, who, if the order consisted only of men of landed estates, might elect, as the Scottish peers do, only reserving to the King's governor a negative on such choice. The King in this case wou'd be still acknowledged as the fountain of honour, as having in the first instance the appointment of the persons enroll'd, out of whom the council are to be chosen, and finally having a negative on the choice. Or, the King might have the immediate appointment by mandamus as at present in the royal governments. As the gentlemen of the council would rank above the body from which they are taken, they might bear a title one degree above that of esquire. Besides this legislative council, a privy council might be establish'd, to consist of some or all of those persons who constitute the legislative council, and of other persons members of the house of representatives or otherwise of note and distinction; which would extend the honours of government, and afford opportunity of distinguishing men of character and reputation, the expectation of which would make government more respectable.

I would not trouble you with these reveries of mine, were I not assured of your readiness to forgive the communication, although you could apply it to no good purpose.

Mr. Spooner sent me a pamphlet under a blank cover, entitled, "the state of the nation". I ran over it by myself before I had heard any one mention it, and tho't I could evidently mark the sentiments of some of my friends. By what I have since heard and seen, it looks as if I was not mistaken. Your right honorable friend I trust will not be offended if I call him mine, I am sure you will not when I term you such, I have settled it for a long time in my own mind that without a representation in the supreme legislature, there cannot be that union between the head and the members as to produce a healthful constitution of the whole body. I have doubted whether this union could be perfected by the first experiment. The plan here exhibited seems to be formed in generous and moderate principles, and bids the fairest of any I have yet seen to be adopted. Such a great design may as in painting require frequent touching before it becomes a piece highly finish'd; and after all may require the ameliorating hand of time to make it please universally. Thus the British constitution consider'd as without the colonies attain'd its glory. The book I had sent me is in such request, that I have not been able to keep it long enough by me, to consider it in all its parts. I wish to hear how it is receiv'd in the House of Commons. I find by the publications both of governor Pownall and Mr. Bollan, that they each of them adopt the idea of a union and representation, and I think it must more and more prevail. The argument against it from local inconveniency must as it appears to me be more than balanc'd by greater inconveniencies on the other side the question, the great difficulty will be in the terms of union. I add no more, as I fear I have already trespass'd much on your time and patience, but that I am, Sir, your obliged and most obedient humble Servant,

Andw. Oliver.

New York, 12th August, 1769.

Sir,

I have been in this city for some time past executing (with others) his Majesty's commission for settling the boundary between this province and that of New Jersey. I left Boston the 11th July, since which my advices from London have come to me very imperfect; but as my friend

Mr. Thompson writes me that he had drawn up my case and with your approbation laid it before the D. of Grafton, I think it needful once more to mention this business to you.

There was a time when I thought the authority of government might have been easily restored; but while it's friends and the officers of the crown are left to an abject dependence on these very people who are undermining it's authority; and while these are suffered not only to go unpunished, but on the contrary meet with all kind of support and encouragement, it cannot be expected that you will ever again recover that respect which the colonies had been wont to pay the parent state. Government at home will deceive itself, if it imagines that the taking off the duty on glass, paper and painter's colors will work a reconciliation, and nothing more than this, as I can learn, is proposed in Ld. H's late circular letter. It is the principle that is now disputed; the combination against importation extends to tea, although it comes cheaper than ever, as well as to the other aforementioned articles. In Virginia it is extended lately to wines; and I have heard one of the first leaders in these measures in Boston say, that we should never be upon a proper footing 'till all the revenue acts from the 15th Charles 2d were repealed. Our assembly in the Massachusetts may have been more illiberal than others in their public messages and resolves; yet we have some people among us still who dare to speak in favor of government: But here I do not find so much as one, unless it be some of the King's servants; and yet my business here leads me to associate with the best. They universally approve of the combination against importing of goods from Great-Britain, unless the revenue acts are repealed, which appears to me little less than assuming a negative on all acts of parliament which they do not like! They say expressly, we are bound by none made since our emigration, but such as our own convenience we choose to submit to; such for instance as that for establishing a post-office. The Bill of Rights and the Habeas Corpus Acts, they say are only declaratory of the common law, which we brought with us.

Under such circumstance as these, why should I wish to expose myself to popular resentment? Were I to receive any thing out of the revenue, I must expect to be abused for it. Nor do I find that our chief justice has received the £200 granted him for that service; and yet the assembly has this year withheld his usual grant, most probably because he has such a warrant from the crown.

With regard to my negotiations with Mr. Rogers, I did in conformity to your opinion make an apology to Mr. Secretary Pownall for mentioning it, and there submitted it. I hear it has been since talk'd of; but unless I could be assured in one shape or other of £300 per annum, with the other office, I would not choose to quit what I have. I have no ambition to be distinguished, if I am only to be held up as a mark of popular envy or resentment. I was in hopes before now through the intervention of your good offices to have received some mark of favor from your good friend; but the time is not yet come to expect it through that channel! I will however rely on your friendship, whenever you can with propriety appear in forwarding my interest, or preventing any thing that may prove injurious to it.

If Mr. R. has interest enough to obtain the secretary's place, I shall upon receiving proper security think myself in honour bound to second his views, though I have none at present from him but a conditional note he formerly wrote me. If he is not like to succeed, and my son Daniel could have my place, I would be content unless affairs take a different turn to resign in his favor, whether administration should think proper to make any further provision for me or not. And yet I never thought of withdrawing myself from the service, while there appeared to me any prospect of my being able to promote it.

If I have wrote with freedom, I consider I am writing to a friend, and that I am perfectly safe in opening myself to you. I am, with great respect, Sir, your most obedient, humble servant,

Andw. Oliver.

On board his Majesty's Ship Romney, Boston Harbour, 20th June, 68.
Dear Sir,

The commissioners of the customs have met with every insult since their arrival at Boston, and at last have been obliged to seek protection on board his Majesty's ship Romney: Mr. Hallowell, the comptroller of the customs who will have the honor to deliver you this Letter, will inform you of many particulars; he is sent by the Board with their letters to Government. Unless we have immediately two or three regiments, 'tis the opinion of all the friends to government, that Boston will be in open rebellion. I have the honor to be with the greatest respect and warmest regard, Dear Sir, Your most faithful and oblig'd servant,

Chas. Paxton.

Boston, Decem. 12th 1768.

My Dear Sir,

I Wrote you a few days ago, and did not then think of troubling you upon any private affair of mine, at least not so suddenly; but within this day or two, I have had a conversation with Mr. Oliver, secretary of the province, the design of which was my succeeding to the post he holds from the crown, upon the idea, that provision would be made for governor Bernard, and the lieutenant governor would succeed to the chair, then the secretary is desirous of being lieutenant governor, and if in any way, three hundred pounds a year could be annexed to the appointment. You are sensible the appointment is in one department, and the grant of money in another; now the present lieutenant governor has an assignment of £200 a year upon the customs here; he has not received any thing from it as yet, and is doubtful if he shall; he has no doubt of its lapse to the crown, if he has the chair; if then by any interest that sum could be assigned to Mr. Oliver as lieutenant governor, and if he should be allowed (as has been usual for all lieutenant governors) to hold the command of the castle, that would be another £100. This would complete the secretary's views; and he thinks his public services, the injuries he has received in that service, and the favorable sentiments entertained of him by government, may lead him to these views, and he hopes for the interest of his friends. The place of secretary is worth £300 a year, but is a provincial grant at present, so that it will not allow to be quartered on: And as I had view upon the place when I was in England, and went so far as to converse with several men of interest upon it, though' I never had an opportunity to mention it to you after I recovered my illness, I hope you will allow me your influence, and by extending it at the treasury, to facilitate the assignment of the £200 a year, it will be serving the secretary, and it will very much oblige me. The secretary is advanced in life, though' much more so in health, which has been much impaired by the injuries he received, and he wishes to quit the more active scenes; he considers this as a kind of odium cum dignitate, and from merits one may think he has a claim to it. I will mention to you the gentlemen, who are acquainted with my views and whose favourable approbation I have had. Governor Pownall, Mr. John Pownall, and Dr. Franklin. My lord Hillsborough is not unacquainted with it. I have since I have been here, wrote Mr. Jackson upon the subject, and have by this vessel written Mr. Mauduit. I think my character stands fair. I have not been without application to public affairs, and have acquired some knowledge of our provincial affairs, and notwithstanding our many free conversations in England, I am considered here as on government side, for which I have been often traduced both publicly and privately, and very lately have had two or three slaps. The governor and lieutenant governor are fully acquainted with the negotiation, and I meet their approbation; all is upon the idea the governor is provided for, and there shall by any means be a vacancy of the lieut. governor's place. I have gone so far, as to say to some of my friends, that rather than not succeed I would agree to pay the secretary £100 a year out of the office to make up £300, provided he could obtain only the assignment of £200, but the other proposal would to be sure be most eligible. I scarce know any apology to make for troubling you upon the subject; the friendship you showed me in London, and the favourable expressions you made use of to the lieut. governor in my behalf encourage me, besides a sort of egotism, which inclines men to think what they wish to be real. I submit myself to the enquiries of any of my countrymen in England, but I should wish the matter might be secret 'till it is effected. I am with very great respect and regard, my dear sir, Your most obedient, and most humble servant,

Nath. Rogers.

N. London, February 7, 1768.

Sir,

Notwithstanding of my having written to you very often, and at much length of late, and that I am upon the point of setting out for Boston with the first weather fit for traveling, yet I cannot refrain from troubling you with a few lines about the 8th and 9th letters of the Farmer, which I now enclose you. They are oracular here and make rapid deep impressions, and who is there at this time here, if capable, that may undertake to contradict or expose these agreeable seasonable epistolary Sophisms? Relief, Support and Recompense so long and so much expected, hoped and wished for, seems too tardy and slow paid. Vigour and resolution seems to be exhausted in G. Britain, or bestowed upon improper and more trivial objects, than the subjection or obedience of America. Excuse these out-pourings of melancholy and despondency in a very dreary day, when the weather alters and the sun shines abroad, perhaps I may see through a brighter or more agreeable medium, but believe me the prospect is now bad and unpromising, but however it may prove, I desire and pray you to be assured that I am, Sir, your most obedient and most humble servant,

Thomas Moffat.

I will also trouble you from Boston.

N. London, Nov. 15, 1768.

Sir,

By Mr. Byles I am favoured with your most obliging letter of the second of August last, for which together with your extraordinary civility to Mr. Byles I truly thank you: I could not really think of such a person going from hence without showing him to you, as a parson or minister of his way and turn of thinking may be considered as of the commit [comet?] kind here, which leads me to say somewhat abruptly if not improperly to you, that it seems to me here as if the universities of Scotland had conspired to distinguish all the firebrand incendiary preachers of this country with plumes of honorary degrees and titles, which in truth are only so many mortifications to the friends of G. Britain or lovers of letters, who cannot help being touch'd and chagrin'd at the too frequent profusion of honour and titles conferr'd from Scotland upon the leading preachers of sedition. I wish this affair of literary prostitution from my native country may induce you to speak of it to some of that nation with whom I know you are intimate, that may think of preventing it for the future.

As to Boston, the great theatre of action, I have been silent for some time past only for want of certain intelligence, as every day generally produc'd new rumours without any or much foundation in truth, but since the arrival of the two regiments with Col. Dalrymple all has been quiet there. I now flatter myself that measures of vigour will be pursued and maintained here, and I impatiently wish to hear that your friend is in power and confidence again, but that is indeed a point I have much expectation, desire and faith in. As you have express'd heretofore to me inclination of knowing the proceedings of the Rhode Island assembly respecting compensation to the sufferers in the riot of Newport, I now trouble you with a copy of my letter of this day to the lords of the treasury, which mutatis mutandis, is the same with that also to the Earl of Hillsborough of the same date with a copy of the narrative and letter to Lord Shelburne.

N. London, Nov. 14th, 1768.

My Lords,

Again I presume upon troubling your lordships with as short an account as may be written of what has very lately pass'd in the G. assembly of Rhode Island colony, in reference to their granting of a compensation to the sufferers from the riot of Newport 1765, as resolved on in the British parliament and very graciously recommended from his Majesty to the governor and company of that colony by his principal secretary of state.

Tired out and greatly mortified with a long course of frequent fruitless and a very expensive attendance upon the G. assembly, I had resolved above a year ago to solicit them no more: but at the intercession of my fellow sufferer Mr. Howard chief justice of North Carolina, I was again prevailed upon to go to Newport in September last, where and when the assembly then met and I had sufficient influence to engage the speaker of the house of deputies to move several times for reading a petition of Mr. Howard's, with an estimate of his loss solemnly sworn to and authenticated by a notary public with every necessary prescribed form. The speaker also urged upon the house because of my attending from another colony upon that account only, but the deputies would neither consent to hear Mr. Howard's petition nor receive his estimate.

Immediately after this refusal a message was sent from the upper house of magistrates requesting the lower house to enter now upon the riot of Newport by immediately empowering the high sheriff to impanel a jury of inquisition to ascertain and repair the loss of Dr. Moffat, Mr. Howard and Mr. Johnson, but the house of deputies could not listen nor agree to any part of this proposal from the upper house.

About the middle of last I wrote a most respectful letter to the governor of Rhode Island and enclosed to his honor the estimate of my loss in the Newport riot sworn to before and attested by a magistrate here requesting the favor of the governor to lay the same before the ensuing assembly. The governor writes on the seventh of this month "that at the last session of assembly he presented my estimate and read my letter in a great committee of both houses of assembly but could not prevail to have it consider'd then;" and adds "that he will endeavour to bring it in again next February."

Under the strongest impressions of assurance the G. Assembly of Rhode Island never will recompense the suffered in the riot of Newport, may I again presume to implore your lordships interposition and influence to obtain a recompense for the sufferers in Rhode Island from some more effectual and certain channel than that of depending any longer upon the duty or justice of the G. Assembly in that colony. And my lords may I yet farther presume in writing to your lordships to add that by endeavouring to restore in some measure what I lost in that riot I am now sadly sensible that I have not overvalued the same in my estimate, as also that if I am not compensated by the interest, generosity and equity of your lordships, I can never expect to be possess'd of half the value I then lost, as the office of a comptroller here I now hold, had but a very inconsiderable salary with small perquisites. I am, my lords, &c. &c.

T. M.

In my last letter which I hope you have received, as I address'd it to the care of your brother, I then touch'd upon sir Wm. Johnson's being here some weeks in quest of health, and of the pleasure Mr. Stewart and I enjoyed with him; as also that lord Charles Grenville Montague was here en passant with his lady; and I also then intimated to you our happiness in Mr. Harrison the collector of Boston having accepted Mr. Stewart's warm invitation to come here after the very flagrant riot at Boston, in which he had been so greatly insulted, abused and hurt, who came here with his lady, son and daughter, and staid a fortnight: when we planned and regulated all these colonies into a system which I could wish to see effected. Since which Mr. Stewart has visited Mr. Harrison at Boston at the time when Mrs. Harrison with their son and daughter sailed for London as a place of perfect safety and liberty. Mr. Harrison's son is capable and promising, but was cruelly used by the mob of Boston, which will I hope incline Mr. Harrison's friends or rather the friends of government to provide suitably for so young a sufferer. I could not easily within the compass of a letter to you say the pleasure I have felt in observing the strict union and friendship that subsists and is now riveted between Mr. Harrison and Mr. Stewart upon principles of the truest honor and virtue, both of whom well understand and sincerely wish the true interest of G. Britain and all her colonies, especially in the cardinal articles of legislation and government, as also in the subaltern or lesser points of taxation and revenue from which objects no attachments, connections or views will or ever can sway the one or the other. As I have been accustomed to write to you with a plainness and freedom which I flatter myself has not been disagreeable, so therefore I would farther say of Mr. Stewart that he married in an opulent popular and commercial family, some of whom perhaps may be supposed to have more oblique interest than may be consistent with regulation or a due submission to the laws of G. Britain, so it is with a peculiar and very sensible satisfaction that I can assure you his spirit address and conduct in so nice a situation deserves the greatest praise and commendation, as it has perhaps been or may be very influential on some of the best among them, even to a better way of thinking and acting. By the enclosed you will know that Mr. Stewart now writes to Mr. Grenville, and mentions somewhat of his application for leave of absence from the Treasury board, which I only wish him to succeed in because I think Mr. Harrison and him really the most capable persons here to throw light upon many transactions here which cannot be communicated in letters or any written representation to satisfaction or proper advantage. If Mr. Stewart obtains leave to return home I shall be unhappy enough by his absence. Two years are now elapsed since I came here, a great part of which has been spent in anxiously wishing for the genius of Britain to awake and vindicate her supreme jurisdiction and authority impiously questioned and denied in colonies so very lately redeemed from hostile incursions and encroachments, but I believe the time is now come, and I rejoice in its approach. I wish you every felicity with the preferment and employment you like best, and am Sir, Your most obedient humble Servant,

Thomas Moffat.

N. London, Nov. 14th, 1768.

My Lords,

Again I presume upon troubling your lordships with as short an ac-count as may be written of what has very lately pass's in the G. assembly of Rhode Island colony, in reference to their granting of a compensation to the sufferers from the riot of Newport 1765, as resolved on in the Brit-ish parliament and very graciously recommended from his Majesty to the governor and company of that colony by his principal secretary of state.

Tired out and greatly mortified with a long course of frequent fruit-less and a very expensive attendance upon the G. assembly, I had re-solved above a year ago to solicit them no more: but at the intercession of my fellow sufferer Mr. Howard chief justice of North Carolina, I was again prevailed upon to go to Newport in September last, where and when the assembly then met and I had sufficient influence to engage the speaker of the house of deputies to move several times for reading a petition of Mr. Howard's, with an estimate of his loss solemnly sworn to and authenticated by a notary public with every necessary prescribed form. The speaker also urged upon the house because of my attending from another colony upon that account only, but the deputies would neither consent to hear Mr. Howard's petition nor receive his estimate.

Immediately after this refusal a message was sent from the upper house of magistrates requesting the lower house to enter now upon the riot of Newport by immediately empowering the high sheriff to impanel a jury of inquisition to ascertain and repair the loss of Dr. Moffat, Mr. Howard and Mr. Johnson, but the house of deputies could not listen nor agree to any part of this proposal from the upper house.

About the middle of last I wrote a most respectful letter to the gov-ernor of Rhode Island and enclosed to his honor the estimate of my loss in the Newport riot sworn to before and attested by a magistrate here requesting the favor of the governor to lay the same before the ensuing assembly. The governor writes on the seventh of this month "that at the last session of assembly he presented my estimate and read my letter in a great committee of both houses of assembly but could not prevail to have it consider'd then;" and adds "that he will endeavour to bring it in again next February."

Under the strongest impressions of assurance the G. Assembly of Rhode Island never will recompense the suffered in the riot of Newport, may I again presume to implore your lordships interposition and influence to obtain a recompense for the sufferers in Rhode Island from some more effectual and certain channel than that of depending any longer upon the duty or justice of the G. Assembly in that colony. And my lords may I yet farther presume in writing to your lordships to add that by endeavouring to restore in some measure what I lost in that riot I am now sadly sensible that I have not overvalued the same in my estimate, as also that if I am not compensated by the interest, generosity and equity of your lordships, I can never expect to be possessed of half the value I then lost, as the office of a comptroller here I now hold, had but a very inconsiderable salary with small perquisites. I am, My lords, &c. &c.

T. M.

Boston, December 15. 1768.

Sir,

In November last I wrote you from N. London, and inserted in that letter a copy of what I had written to the lords of the treasury and the Earl of Hillsborough, relative to the compensation of the sufferers in the riot at Newport 1765. I hope and very much wish that letter may have come to your hand, because in it you will see how strictly and soon I follow your counsel in making affidation to the estimate of my loss, which as I apprehended made not the least impression nor could make upon the general assembly of Rhode-Island, because there was not I believe a member in either house that did not think and believe my loss exceeded the estimate frequently laid before them to no purpose. I thank you therefore for the kind and good advice which I instantly followed, and which I think has finished this long and tedious transaction on this side of the Atlantic, which has not only been ineffectual but attended with much trouble and expense to me. How or in what light it may be now considered by administration or parliament I cannot at this time and distance judge, far less determine. Sometimes I flatter myself that a resolve of the British senate will not be allowed to be thus scorned and trampled upon; at other times I despond and think the object too small for attention; and as there were but three sufferers in Rhode-Island colony, two of them to my great pleasure and triumph are now amply and very honorably provided for, I sometimes imagine that compensation may drop and be forgot, and indeed if it was not for the confidence which I have in you and some others in the house of commons, I should certainly despair of any recompense, and which upon recollection I must acknowledge as criminal in a very great degree, because of its having been resolved on in the parliament of Great-Britain that such sufferers should be compensated: And I am not conscious that I have omitted, delayed or neglected any part of my duty in the course of negotiating it here in America.

A few days ago I came here chiefly to see and enjoy my friend collector Harrison that we might open bosoms to one another upon the great scene and field of affairs in this country, the face of which is only altar's apparently here from the arrival of the King's troops and ships, which have indeed restored a very certain security and tranquility, and prevented if not put a final period to their most pestilent town-meetings. There is nor can be no real alteration in the sentiment or disposition of the prime disturbers. This is but an interval or truce procured from the dread of a bayonet. The special and catholic remedy derived from and founded in an acknowledgement of the British supremacy and legislation over America manifested under the exercise of a more firm, regular and consistent plan of civil government, must come from the decrees of the British parliament, otherwise the country and particularly N. England, will soon and forever be in perpetual anarchy and disobedience. The anxiety and distress of the few here that are well affected to government before the arrival of the troops and ships was very great, and in my opinion will be greater if vigorous, salutary and proper measures are not adopted in parliament.

All here seem anxious and impatient to know the complexion and temper of the British parliament, and what is very unaccountable if not incredible, the sons of liberty here so called are elevated with hope and assurance that their claims and pretensions will be received and recognized, as they affect to phrase it, but if I err not, this presumption of hope may have arisen or been cherished in a great measure by some visits of an officer of high military rank from N. York to some of the most popular and violent ringleaders here, and I wish that I could say to you that the most mischievous here had not been countenanced also by a person of another and very different station.

I find that in consequence of and under an apprehension of unsettled, unsafe times here, Mr. Harrison has thought it best that Mrs. Harrison, his son and daughter, should go to London, as a place of true liberty and safety, and as I hope they will be arrived before this reaches you, and as I formerly mentioned to you Mr. Harrison's son as a young sufferer very roughly handled upon the 10th of June, so if you incline to see and discourse him for intelligence or any other motive, Mr. Hallowell of this town can easily bring him to you.

If any thing remarkable occurs here during my stay I shall not fail to write to you again. I am, sir, your most obedient and most humble servant,

Thomas Moffat.

Narraganset, 22d December 1767.

Sir,

I am now withdrawn to my little country villa, where, though' I am more retired from the busy world, yet I am still enveloped with uneasy reflections for a turbulent, degenerate, ungrateful continent, and the opposition I have met with in my indefatigable endeavours to secure our property in this colony, but hitherto without success. The times are so corrupted and the conflict of parties so predominant, that faction is blind, or shuts her eyes to the most evident truths that cross her designs, and believes in any absurdities that assists to accomplish her purposes under the prostitution and prostration of an infatuated government. Judge then, my dear sir, in what a critical situation the fortunes of we poor Europeans must be among them.

We have not been able to recover our property for years past, how great so ever our exigencies may have been, unless we soothed them into a compliance: We are unwilling to enter into a litigation with them, because the perversion of their iniquitous courts of justice are so great, that experience has convinced us we had better loose half, to obtain the other quietly, than pursue compulsory measures: We are also afraid to apply to a British parliament for relief, as none can be effectually administered without a change of government, and a better administration of justice introduced; and was it known here, that we made such application home, not only our fortunes would be in greater jeopardy, but our lives endangered by it before any salutary regulations could take place.

We are sensible of the goodness of the king and parliament, but how far, or in what space of time our grievance, as a few individuals, might weigh against the influence of a charter government, we are at a loss to determine.

In 1761, I arrived in America, which circumstance you probably remember well: With great industry, caution and circumspection, I have not only reduced our demands, and regulated our connections in some measure, but kept my head out of a halter which you had the honor to grace. (Pray Doctor how did it feel? The subject is stale, but I must be a little funny with you on the occasion.) Much still remains to be done, and after all my best endeavours, my constituents, from a moderate calculation, cannot lose less than £50,000 sterling, by the baneful constitution of this colony, and the corruption of their courts of judicature. It is really a very affecting and melancholy consideration.

Under a deep sense of the infirmities of their constitution; the innovations which they have gradually interwoven among themselves; and stimulated by every act of forbearance, lenity and patience, we have indulged our correspondents until deluges of bankruptcies have ensued, insolvent acts liberated them from our just demands, and finally, had our indisputable accounts refused admission for our proportion of the small remains, until colony creditors were first paid, and the whole absorbed. We have had vessels made over to us for the satisfaction of debts, and after bills of sales were executed, carried off in open violence and force by Capt. Snip-snap of Mr. No body's appointment, and when we sued him for damages, recovered a louse. We have in our turn been sued in our absence, and condemned ex parte in large sums for imaginary damages, for which we can neither obtain a trial, nor redress. They refuse us an appeal to the king in council; the money must be paid when their executions become returnable; and were we to carry it home by way of complaint, it would cost us two or three hundred pounds sterling to prosecute, and after all, when his Majesty's decrees comes over in our favour, and refunding the money can no longer be evaded, I expect their effects will be secreted, their body's released by the insolvent act, and our money, both principal, interest and expenses irrecoverably gone. Is not our case grievous? We have in actions founded upon notes of hand, been cast in their courts of judicature. We have appeal's to his Majesty in council for redress, got their verdicts reversed, and obtained the King's decrees for our money, but that is all; for although' I have had them by me twelve months, and employed two eminent lawyers to enforce them into execution conformable to the colony law, yet we have not been able to recover a single shilling, though' we have danced after their courts and assembly's above thirty days, in vain to accomplish that purpose only: Consider my dear sir, what expense, vexation, and loss of time this must be to us, and whether we have not just cause of complaint.

We have also in vain waited with great impatience for years past, in hopes his Majesty you'd have nominated his judges, and other executive officers in every colony in America, which you'd in a great measure remove the cause of our complaint. Nothing can be more necessary than a speedy regulation in this, and constituting it a regal government; and nothing is of such important use to a nation, as that men who excel in wisdom and virtue should be encouraged to undertake the business of government: But the iniquitous course of their courts of justice in this colony, deter such men from serving the public, or if they do so, unless patronized at home, their wisdom and virtue are turned against them with such malignity, that it is more safe to be infamous than renown'd. The principal exception I have met with here, is James Helmes, Esq., who was chosen chief justice by the general assembly at last election. He accepted his appointment, distinguishes himself by capacity and application, and seems neither afraid nor ashamed to administer impartial justice to all, even to the native and residing creditors of the mother country. I have known him grant them temporary relief by writs of error, &c. when both he, and they, were overruled by the partiality of the court; and in vain, though' with great candour and force, plead with the rest of the bench, that for the honour of the colony, and their own reputation, they ought never to pay less regard to the decrees of his Majesty in council, because the property was determined in Great Britain, than to their own. I have also heard him with resolution and firmness, when he discovered the court to be immoderately partial, order his name to be enrolled, as dissenting from the verdict. For such honesty and candour, I am persuaded he will be deposed at next election, unless they should be still in hopes of making a convert of him.

I wish it was in my power to prevent every American from suffering for the cause of integrity, and their mother country; he, in an especial manner, should not only be protected and supported, but appear among the first promotions. Is there no gentleman of public spirit at home that would be pleased to be an instrument of elevating a man of his principals and probity? Or is it become fashionable for vice to be countenanced with impunity, and every trace of virtue past over unnoticed! God forbid.

The colonies have originally been wrong founded. They ought all to have been regal governments, and every executive officer appointed by the King. Until that is effected, and they are properly regulated, they will never be beneficial to themselves, nor good subjects to Great Britain. You see with what contempt they already treat the acts of parliament for regulating their trade, and enter into the most public, illegal and affronting combinations to obtain a repeal, by again imposing upon the British merchants and manufacturers, and all under the cloak of retrenching their expenses, by avoiding every unnecessary superfluity. Were that really the case, I am sure I would, and also every other British subject, esteem them for it; but the fact is, they obtained a repeal of the stamp act by mercantile influence, and they are now endeavouring by the same artifice and finesse to repeal the acts of trade, and obtain a total exemption from all taxation. Were it other ways, and they sincerely disposed to stop the importation of every unnecessary superfluity, without affronting the British legislation, by their public, general, and illegal combinations, they might accomplish their purposes with much more decency, and suppress it more effectually by the acts of their own legislation, imposing such duties upon their importation here, as might either occasion a total prohibition, or confine the consumption of them to particular individuals that can afford to buy, by which measures they would also raise a considerable colony revenue, and ease the poorer inhabitants in the tax they now pay: But the temper of the country is exceedingly factious, and prone to sedition; they are growing more imperious, haughty, nay insolent every day, and in a short space, unless wholesome regulations take place, the spirit they have enkindled, and the conceptions of government they have imbibed, will be more grievous to the mother country than ever the ostracism was to the Athenians.

A bridle at present, may accomplish more than a rod hereafter; for the malignant poison of the times, like a general pestilence, spreads beyond conception; and if the British parliament are too late in their regulations, neglect measures seven years, which are essentially necessary now, should they then be able to stifle their commotions, it will only be a temporary extinction, consequently, every hour's indulgence will answer no other purpose than enable them in a more effectual manner to sow seeds of dissension to be rekindled whenever they are in a capacity to oppose the mother country and render themselves independent of her.

Have they not already in the most public manner shown their opposition to the measures of parliament in the affair of the late stamp act? Don't they now with equal violence and audacity, in both public papers and conversation, declare the parliamentary regulations in their acts of trade to be illegal and a mere nullity? What further proofs do we wait for, of either their good or bad disposition? Did you ever hear of any colonies, in their infant state, teach the science of tyranny, reduced into rules, over every subject that discountenanced their measures in opposition to the mother country, in a more imperious manner than they have done these four years past? Have they not made use of every stroke of policy (in their way) to avail themselves of the dark purposes of their independence, and suffered no restraint of conscience, or fear, not even the guilt of threatening to excite a civil war, and revolt, if not indulged with an unlimited trade, without restraint; and British protection, without expense? For that is the English of it. Is this their true, or mistaken portrait? Say. If it is their true one, ought not such pernicious maxims of policy? Such wicked discipline? Such ingratitude? Such dissimulation? Such perfidy? Such violent, ruthless and sanguinary councils, where a Cleon bears rule, and an Aristides cannot be endured, to be crushed in embryo? If not, the alternative cannot avoid producing such a government, as will ere long throw the whole kingdom into the utmost confusion, endanger the life, liberty and property of every good subject, and again expose them to the merciless assassination of a rabble.

I am sensible that in all political disputes, especially in America, a man may see some things to blame on both sides, and so much to fear, which ever faction should conquer, as to be justified in not intermeddling with either; but in matters of such vast importance as the present, wherein we have suffered so much, still deeply interested, and by which the peace and tranquility of the nation is at stake; it is difficult to conceal ones emotions from a friend, and remain a tranquil spectator on a theatre of such chicanery and collusion, as will inevitably (if not checked, and may sooner happen than is imagined by many) chill the blood of many a true Briton.

It may be true policy, in some cases, to tame the fiercest spirit of popular liberty, not by blows, or by chains, but by soothing her into a willing obedience, and making her kiss the very hand that restrains her; but such policy would be a very unsuitable potion to cure the malady of the present times. They are too much corrupted; and already so intoxicated with their own importance, as to make a wrong use of lenient measures. They construe them into their own natural rights, and a timidity in the mother country. They consider themselves a little bigger than the frog in the fable, and that G. Britain can never long grapple with their huge territory of 1500 miles frontier, already populous, and increasing with such celerity, as to double their numbers once in twenty-five years. This is not perfectly consonant with my idea of the matter, tho' such calculation has been made; and admitting it to be erroneous, yet, as they believe it, it has the same evil effect, and possesses the imaginations of the people with such a degree of insanity and enthusiasm, as there is hardly any thing more common than to hear them boast of particular colonies that can raise on a short notice an hundred thousand fighting men, to oppose the force of Great-Britain; certain it is, that they increase in numbers by emigration &c. very fast, and are become such a body of people, with such extensive territory, as require every bud of their genius and disposition to be narrowly watched, and pruned with great judgment, other ways they may become not only troublesome to Great Britain, but enemies to themselves. Now is the critical season. They are still like some raw giddy youth just emerging into the world in a corrupt degenerate age. A parent, or a guardian, is therefore still necessary; and if well managed, they will soon arrive at such maturity as to become obedient, dutiful children; but if neglected long, the rod of chastisement will be so much longer necessary as to become too burthensome, and must be dropt with the colonies. They almost consider themselves as a separate people from Great Britain already.

Last month while I was attending the General Assembly, the Governor sent a written message to the lower house, importing his intentions of a resignation at the next election, assigning for reasons, the fumes in the colony and party spirit were so high, and that bribery and corruption were so predominant, that neither life, liberty nor property were safe, &c. &c. &c. Now Sir, whether the Governor's intentions as exhibited in this open, public declaration, was real, or feigned to answer political purposes; it still evinces their decrepit state; the prostitution of government; and melancholy situation of every good subject: For it cannot be supposed by any candid inquisitor, that a declaration of that nature, and form, would, if not true, been delivered by a Governor to a whole legislative body, in order to emancipate himself. If this truth is granted, and this allowed to be their unhappy situation, how much is it the duty of every good man, and what language is sufficient to paint in an effectual manner, this internal imbecility of an English colony (in many other respects favourably situated for trade and commerce, one of the safest, largest, and most commodious harbours in all America, or perhaps in all Europe, accessible at all seasons, situated in a fine climate, and abounding with fertile soil), to the maternal bowels of compassion, in order that she may seasonably, if she thinks it necessary to interpose, regulate, and wipe away their pernicious charter, rendered obnoxious by the abuse of it.

I am afraid I have tired your patience with a subject that must give pain to every impartial friend to Great Britain and her colonies. When I took up my pen, I only intended to have communicated the out-lines of such of my perplexities (without dipping so far into political matter) as I thought would atone for, or excuse my long silence, and excite your compassion and advice.

Our friend Robinson is gone to Boston to join the commissioners. My compliments to Col. Stuart. May I ask the favour of you both to come and eat a xmas dinner with me at bachelor's hall, and celebrate the festivity of the season with me in Narraganset woods. A covey of partridges, or bevy of quails, will be entertainment for the colonel and me, while the pike and perch ponds amuse you. Should business or pre-engagements prevent me that pleasure, permit me to ask the favour of your earliest intelligence of the proceedings of parliament; and of your opinion whether our case is not so great as to excite their compassion and interposition were it known. This narration, together with your own knowledge of many of the facts, and the disposition of the colonies in general, will refresh your memory, and enable you to form a judgment. Relief from home seems so tedious, especially to us who have suffered so much, like to suffer more, and unacquainted with their reasons of delay, that I am quite impatient.

Above twelve months ago, I received from three Gentlemen in London (in trust for several others) exemplified accounts for a balance of about twenty-six-thousand pounds sterling, mostly due from this colony, not £50 of which shall I ever be able to recover without compulsive measures, and what is still worse, my lawyer advises me from all thoughts of prosecution, unless a change of government ensues. I am therefore obliged to send them his opinion (in justification of my own conduct) in lieu of money ten years due. Poor Satisfaction! Our consolation must be in a British parliament. Every other avenue is rendered impregnable by their subtlety, and degeneracy, and we can no longer depend upon a people who are so unthankful for our indulgences, and the lenity of their mother country. I wish you the compliments of the approaching season, and a succession of many happy new years. I am Sir, with much regard, Your most humble Servant,

G. Rome.

VERBATIM 3. WEDDERBURN'S SPEECH BEFORE THE PRIVY COUNCIL

(*Papers*, vol. 21, pages 43-68.)

The Final Hearing before the Privy Council Committee for Plantation Affairs on the Petition from the Massachusetts House of Representatives for the Removal of Hutchinson and Oliver: I, Wedderburn's Speech before the Privy Council

Printed in [Israel Mauduit,] "The Letters of Governor Hutchinson, and Lieut. Governor Oliver...with...the Proceedings of the Lords Committee of Council. Together with the Substance of Mr. Wedderburn's Speech Relating to Those Letters: beginning of speech from 2nd ed. (London, 1774), pp. 83-5, and remainder from 1st issue of 1st ed. (London, 1774), pp. 77–113 of 2nd pagination, Yale University Library; several paragraphs of a different version printed in [Benjamin Vaughan, ed.,] Political, Miscellaneous, and Philosophical Pieces...Written by Benj. Franklin ... (London, 1779), p. 341.

At the Council Chamber, Saturday, Jan. 29, 1774. Present, Lord President and 35 Lords.

Mr. Wedderburn.

My Lords,

The case, which now comes before your Lordships, is justly entitled to all that attention, which, from the presence of so great a number of Lords, and of so large an audience, it appears to have excited. It is a question of no less magnitude, than whether the Crown shall ever have it in its power to employ a faithful and steady servant in the administration of a Colony.

In the appointment of Mr. Hutchinson, his Majesty's choice followed the wishes of his people; and no other man could have been named, in whom so many favourable circumstances concurred to recommend him.

A native of the country, whose ancestors were among its first settlers. A Gentleman, who had for many years presided in their Law Courts; of tried integrity; of confessed abilities; and who had long employed those abilities, in the study of their history and original constitution.

My Lords, if such a man, without their attempting to allege one single act of misconduct, during the four years, in which he has been Governor, is to be born down by the mere surmises of this Address, it must then become a case of still greater magnitude, and ever be a matter of doubt, whether the Colony shall henceforward pay respect to any authority derived from this country.

A charge of some sort however is now preferred against these Gentlemen by this Address; and the prayer of it is, that his Majesty would punish them by a disgraceful removal.

If they shall appear to have either betrayed the rights of the Crown, or to have invaded the rights of the People, your Lordships doubtless will then advise his Majesty no longer to trust his authority with those, who have abused it.

But if no crime is objected to them, no act of misconduct proved, your Lordships will then do the justice to their characters, which every innocent man has a right to expect; and grant them that protection and encouragement, which is due to officers in their station.

My Lords, this is not the place to give any opinion about our public transactions relating to the Colonies, and I shall carefully avoid it. But the whole foundation of this Address rests upon events of five and six years standing; and this makes it necessary to take up the history of them from their first original.

In the beginning of the year 1764,....

My Lords, After having gone through the history of this people, for the last ten years, and shown what has been the behaviour of Mr. Hutchinson in all these occurrences, and the very laudable and friendly part he acted on every occasion for the good of the colony; I now come to consider the argument upon that footing, on which my learned friends have chosen to place it.

They have read to your Lordships the Assembly's address; they have read the letters; and they have read the censures passed on them: and, after praying the removal of his Majesty's Governor and Lieutenant-Governor, they now tell your Lordships: There is no cause to try—There is no charge—There are no accusers—There are no proofs. They say that the Governor and Lieutenant Governor are disliked by the Assembly, and they ought to be dismissed, because they have lost the confidence of those who complain against them.

My Lords, This is so very extraordinary a proceeding that I know of no precedent, except one: but that, I confess, according to the Roman poet's report, is a case in point.

> Nunquam, si quid mihi credis, amavi
> Hunc hominem. Sed quo cecidit sub crimine? Quisnam
> Delator, Quibus Indicibus? Quo Teste probavit?
> Nil horum, Verbosa et grandis epistola venit
> A Capreis. Bene habet: nil plus interrogo.

My Lords, The only purport of this important address is, that the Governor and Lieutenant-Governor have lost the confidence of the people, upon account of some papers, which they have voted to be unfriendly to them, and that they have been amongst the chief instruments in introducing a fleet and army into the province. Your Lordships have heard the letters read, and are the best judges of their tendency. I can appeal to your Lordships, that it was not these letters, but their own ill conduct, which made it necessary to order the four regiments. In point of time it was impossible: for in Mr. Hutchinson's very first letter, it appears, that they had an expectation of troops. And they arrived in three months after. I could appeal too to their own knowledge: for the printed collection of Sir Francis Bernard's and General Gage's, &c. letters were before them, which indisputably show the direct contrary.

But as my learned friends have not attempted to point out the demerits of these letters, I need not enter into the defense of them. To call them only innocent letters, would be greatly to depreciate them. They contain the strongest proofs of Mr. Hutchinson's good sense, his great moderation, and his sincere regard to the welfare of that his native province. Yet, for these it is, that they tell us he has lost the confidence of the people.

My Lords, There cannot be a more striking instance of the force of truth, than what the Committee, who drew up these papers, exemplify in their conduct. In their second resolution, they acknowledge the high character, in which Mr. Hutchinson stands upon account of his eminent abilities. In the very outset of their address, they acknowledge the good use that he had made of those abilities: for he could not have enjoyed their confidence, as they say he heretofore did, if he had made a bad one. They acknowledge that this confidence subsisted, at least till the time of his being made Governor. Else they could not express their thankfulness to his Majesty as they do, and applaud the appointment of him, as proceeding from the purest motives of rendering his subjects happy.

In the height of their ill will therefore to Mr. Hutchinson, truth looks his enemies full in the face, and extorts from them a confession of his merit, even in the very act of accusing him.

But, whatever be the censures, which the Assembly may have been induced to pass on him, I will now give your Lordships a proof of his enjoying the people's confidence, to the very time of the arrival of these letters.

Every one knows that there are few subjects, in which the people of the colonies have more eagerly interested themselves, than in settling the boundary lines between the several provinces. Some of your Lordships may remember the long hearings that have been held at this Board upon these disputes. Of late, they have taken upon themselves to fix the limits of the King's charters. An agreement was made between the two Assemblies of New York and Massachusett's Bay, that they should each appoint their Commissaries, to meet and settle the boundary line between the two provinces. Both of them no doubt looked out for the best men they had for that purpose. But the people of Massachusetts's Bay, after they had chosen their commissaries, still thought that they could more securely trust their interests in their hands, if Mr. Hutchinson would go along with them. To him they had been used to look, as the man, who best knew the history of their first settlements; him they considered as the ablest defender of the province's rights: and had ever found in him the most zealous affection for their welfare. The party leaders perhaps might have been content to lose to the province any number of acres or a few townships, rather than owe to Mr. Hutchinson the preservation of them. But they did not dare to set their faces against the general sense of the people. The Governor was therefore requested to go with the Commissaries. He did so, and settled for them a much better line, than they had ever expected. And the New York and their own Commissaries both of them acknowledged, that the advantage gained to the province, was chiefly owing to the superior knowledge and abilities of Mr. Hutchinson.

Thus far then the Governor's character stands fair and unimpeached. Whatever therefore be the foundation of this Address for his removal, it must be something done by him, or known of him, since his return from this service just before the arrival of these letters. Your Lordships will observe, that his enemies don't attempt to point out a single action, during the four years, in which he has been Governor, as a subject of complaint. The whole of this Address rests upon the foundation of these letters, written before the time, when either of these Gentlemen was possessed of the offices, from which the Assembly now asks their removal. They owe therefore all the ill will which has been raised against them, and the loss of that confidence, which the Assembly themselves acknowledge they had heretofore enjoyed, to Dr. Franklin's good office in sending back these letters to Boston. Dr. Franklin therefore stands in the light of the first mover and prime conductor of this whole contrivance against his Majesty's two Governors; and having by the help of his own special confidents and party leaders, first made the Assembly his Agents in carrying on his own secret designs, he now appears before your Lordships to give the finishing stroke to the work of his own hands. How these letters came into the possession of any one but the right owners is still a mystery for Dr. Franklin to explain. They who know the affectionate regard which the Whatelys had for each other, and the tender concern they felt for the honour of their brother's memory, as well as their own, can witness the distresses which this occasioned. My Lords, the late Mr. Whately was most scrupulously cautious about his letters. We lived for many years in the strictest intimacy; and in all those years I never saw a single letter written to him. These letters I believe were in his custody at his death. And I as firmly believe, that without fraud, they could not have been got out of the custody of the person whose hands they fell into. His brothers little wanted this additional aggravation to the loss of him. Called upon by their correspondents at Boston; anxious for vindicating their brother's honour and their own, they enquired; gave to the parties aggrieved all the information in their power; but never accused.

Your Lordships know the train of mischiefs which followed. But wherein had my late worthy friend or his family offended Dr. Franklin, that he should first do so great an injury to the memory of the dead brother, by secreting and sending away his letters: and then, conscious of what he had done, should keep himself concealed, till he had nearly, very nearly occasioned the murder of the other.

After the mischiefs of this concealment had been left for five months to have their full operation, at length comes out a letter, which it is impossible to read without horror; expressive of the coolest and most deliberate malevolence. My Lords, what poetic fiction only had penned for the breast of a cruel African, Dr. Franklin has realized, and transcribed from his own. His too is the language of a Zanga:

"Know then 'twas—I.
I forg'd the letter—I dispos'd the picture—
I hated, I despis'd, and I destroy."

The letters could not have come to Dr. Franklin by fair means. The writers did not give them to him; nor yet did the deceased correspondent, whom from our intimacy would otherwise have told me of it: Nothing then will acquit Dr. Franklin of the charge of obtaining them by fraudulent or corrupt means, for the most malignant of purposes; unless he stole them, from the person who stole them. This argument is irrefragable.

I hope, my lords, you will mark [and brand] the man, for the honour of this country, of Europe, and of mankind. Private correspondence has hitherto been held sacred, in times of the greatest party rage, not only in politics but religion. He has forfeited all the respect of societies and of men. Into what companies will he hereafter go with an unembarrassed face, or the honest intrepidity of virtue? Men will watch him with a jealous eye; they will hide their papers from him, and lock up their escritoires. He will henceforth esteem it a libel to be called a man of letters: homo trium literarum!

But he not only took away the letters from one brother; but also kept himself concealed till he nearly occasioned the murder of the other. It is impossible to read his account, expressive of the coolest and most deliberate malice, without horror. Amidst these tragic events, of one person nearly murdered, of another answerable for the issue, of a worthy governor hurt in his dearest interests, the fate of America in suspense; here is a man, who with the utmost insensibility of remorse, stands up and avows himself the author of all. I can compare it only to Zanga in Dr. Young's Revenge.

> "Know then 'twas—I: forged the letter,
> I disposed the picture;
> I hated, I despised, and I destroy."

I ask, my Lords, whether the revengeful temper attributed, by poetic fiction only, to the bloody African; is not surpassed by the coolness and apathy of the wily American?

What are the motives he assigns for this conduct, I shall now more deliberately consider.

My Lords, if there be any thing held sacred in the intercourse of mankind, it is their private letters of friendship. If there can be any such private letters, those which passed between the late Mr. Whately and Mr. Oliver are such. The friendship between the two families is of thirty years standing, during all that time there has been kept up an intercourse of letters; first with Mr. Whately, the father, and then with the late Mr. Thomas Whately, the son. In the course of this friendship, a variety of good offices have passed between the two families: one of these fell within the period of these letters. Upon Mr. Oliver's daughter's coming to England with her husband upon business, they were received at Nonesuch by Mrs. Whately and her sons, as the son and daughter of their old friend and correspondent. And accordingly your Lordships will find, that one part of these letters is to return thanks for the civilities shown to Mr. and Mrs. Spooner at Nonesuch.

These are the letters which Dr. Franklin treats as public letters, and has thought proper to secrete them for his own private purpose. How he got at them, or in whose hands they were at the time of Mr. Whatley's death, the Doctor has not yet thought proper to tell us. Till he does, he wittingly leaves the world at liberty to conjecture about them as they please, and to reason upon those conjectures. But let the letters have been lodged where they may, from the hour of Mr. Thomas Whately's death, they became the property of his brother and of the Whately family. Dr. Franklin could not but know this, and that no one had a right to dispose of them but they only. Other receivers of goods dishonourably come by, may plead as a pretence for keeping them, that they don't know who are the proprietors: In this case there was not the common excuse of ignorance; the Doctor knew whose they were, and yet did not restore them to the right owner. This property is as sacred and as precious to Gentlemen of integrity, as their family plate or jewels are. And no man who knows the Whately's, will doubt, but that they would much sooner have chosen, that any person should have taken their plate, and sent it to Holland for his avarice, than that should have secreted the letters of their friends, their brother's friend, and their father's friend, and sent them away to Boston to gratify an enemy's malice.

The reasons assigned for this, are as extraordinary as the transaction itself is: They are public letters, to public persons, on public affairs, and intended to produce public measures. This, my Lords, is the first; and the next reason assigned for publishing them is, because the writers desire that the contents of them should be kept secret.

If these are public letters, I know not what can be reckoned private. If a letter whose first business is to return thanks to an old Lady of seventy, for her civilities at Nonesuch, be not a private letter, it will be necessary that every man should be particularly careful of his papers: for, after this, there never can be wanting a pretence for making them public.

But says the Doctor, "They were written by public officers." Can then a man in a public station have no private friends? And write no private letters? Will Dr. Franklin avow the principle, that he has a right to make all private letters of your Lordships his own, and to apply them to such uses as will best answer the purposes of party malevolence? Whatever may have been the confidence heretofore placed in him, such a declaration will not surely contribute to increase it.

But they were written to persons in public stations. Just the contrary to this appears to have been the case: Dr. Franklin is too well acquainted with our history, not to know, that Mr. Whately, during both these years, and for two years before and after, was only a private Member of Parliament; and, as Mr. Oliver justly observes in a letter of his, They at Boston could not be supposed to apply to him as having an interest with the Ministers, when they knew that he was all that time voting in opposition to them.

Does then the Doctor mean, that his being a Member of Parliament placed him in a public station? And will he then avow, that a Gentleman's being in Parliament is ground sufficient for him to make his letters lawful plunder, and to send them to his enemies?

But they were written on public affairs. A very grievous offence! But it is a crime, of which probably we all of us have been guilty, and ought not, surely, for that only, to forfeit the common rights of humanity.

But they were intended to procure public measures. And does not every man, who writes in confidence to his friend upon political subjects, lament any thing which he thinks to be wrong, and wish to have it amended? And is this the crime of so heinous a nature, as to put Mr. Whately's friends out of the common protection? And to give to Dr. Franklin a right to hang them up to party rage, and to expose them, for what he knew, to the danger of having their houses a second time pulled down by popular fury.

But the writers of them desired secrecy. True, they did so. And what man is there, who, when he is writing in confidence, does not wish for the same thing? Does not every man say things to a friend, which he would not choose to have published to other people, and much less to his enemies? Would letters of friendship be letters of friendship, if they contained nothing but such indifferent things as might be said to all the world?

If this is the case at all times with the confidential intercourse of friends, in times of party-violence, there must be a thousand things said in letters, which, though innocent in themselves, either by rival malice or party prejudice, may be turned to a very different construction. These letters themselves have been distorted in this manner; and some expressions in them cannot possibly be understood, without knowing the correspondent letters, to which they refer. And when a factious party had got possession of the Town meetings, and led the Assembly into what resolutions they pleased, and were watching for any pretence to abuse and insult their Governors, is it at all to be wondered, that they did not wish to have the contents of their letters told to their Enemies?

When we read in these letters such passages as these: "If there be no necessity for it, I think it would be best it should not be known that this intelligence comes from me." Or this: "I have wrote with freedom, in confidence of my name's not being used on the occasion. For though I have wrote nothing but what, in my conscience, I think an American may, upon just principles, advance, and what a servant of the crown ought, upon all proper occasions, to suggest; yet the many prejudices I have to combat with, may render it unfit it should be made public." Or this of Mr. Hutchinson's: "I must beg the favour of you to keep secret every thing I write, until we are in a more settled state, for the party here, either by their Agent, or by some of their emissaries in London, have sent them every report or rumour of the contents of letters wrote from hence. I hope we shall see better times both here and in England." Or this again of Mr. Oliver's: "I have wrote with freedom; I consider I am writing to a friend; and that I am perfectly safe in opening myself to you." Upon reading these passages, which are all there are of this kind, a man, whose heart was cast in the common mould of humanity, would have been apt to say: These are letters irregularly obtained: The writers desire that every thing they write should be kept secret: they belong to Mr. Whately, who never injured me: I will therefore return them to the right owner. Dr. Franklin's reasoning is of a very different cast. After having just before told us: These are public letters, sent to public persons, designed for public purposes, and therefore I have a right to betray them; he now says, these are letters which the writers desire may be kept secret, and therefore I will send them to their enemies. Prepared on both sides for his rival's overthrow, he makes that an argument for doing him hurt, which any other man would consider as a principal aggravation of the injustice of it.

But, if the desiring secrecy be the proof, and the measure of guilt, what then are we to think of Dr. Franklin's case? Whose whole conduct in this affair has been secret and mysterious? And who, through the whole course of it, has discovered the utmost solicitude to keep it so? My Lords, my accounts say, that when these letters were sent over to Boston, so very desirous was Dr. Franklin of secrecy, that he did not chose to set his name to the letter which accompanied them. This anonymous letter expressly ordered, that it should be shown to none but to a junto of six persons. If the Doctor chooses it, I will name the six. The direction of every letter was erased, and strict orders were given, that they should be carefully returned again to London. The manner in which they were brought into the Assembly, all showed the most earnest desire of concealment. Under these mysterious circumstances have the Assembly passed their censures; and voted this Address to his Majesty against Mr. Hutchinson and Mr. Oliver, upon account of a parcel of letters directed to some-body, they know not whom; and sent from some-body, they know not where. And Dr. Franklin now appears before your Lordships, wrapped up in impenetrable secrecy, to support a charge against his Majesty's Governor and Lieutenant Governor; and expects that your Lordships should advise the punishing them, upon account of certain letters, which he will not produce, and which he dares not tell how he obtained.

But the Doctor says, he transmitted them to his constituents.

That Dr. Franklin sent these letters to such persons as he thought would in some way or other bring them into the Assembly may be true. And accordingly, after an alarm of some dreadful discovery, these letters were produced by one single person, pretending to be under an injunction to observe the strictest secrecy, and to suffer no copies to be taken of them. After allowing two or three days for Fame to amplify, and for Party-malice to exaggerate; and after having thereby raised a general prejudice against the Governor; at length another Member tells the Assembly, that he had received from an unknown hand a copy of the letters; and wished to have that copy compared and authenticated with the originals. After this, when they had brought the Council into their measures, they then found their powers enlarged; and that they were at liberty to show them to any one, provided they did not suffer them to go out of their hands; and the King's Governor and Lieutenant-Governor were permitted to look upon them only in this opprobrious manner, in order to render the indignity so much the more offensive.

This Dr. Franklin may call transmitting the letters to his constituents; and upon those who know nothing of the course of these proceedings, may easily impose the belief of it: But your Lordships will readily see, and every man who has been an agent very well knows, that this is not what is meant by transmitting to his constituents. My Lords, when an agent means to write to the Assembly, he addresses his letter to the Speaker, to be communicated to the House. And the Doctor knows, that there are many articles in the Journals of this tenor; "A letter from Dr. Franklin to the Speaker, was read."

But the course taken with these letters was just the reverse of this. The letter, which came with them, was anonymous; though the hand was well known: too well perhaps known to the selected few, who only were to be allowed the sight of it. Since therefore the Doctor has told us that he transmitted these letters to his constituents, we know now who they are. His constituents, by his own account, must be this particular junto: for to them, and them only, were the letters communicated. Dr. Franklin did not communicate them, as their agent, to the Assembly: For whatever may have been the whispers of this junto, the Assembly, as an Assembly, does not to this day know by whom the letters were sent. And so little do these innocent well-meaning farmers, which compose the bulk of the Assembly, know what they are about, that by the arts of these leaders, they have been brought to vote an Address to his Majesty to dismiss his Governor and Lieutenant-Governor, founded upon certain papers, which they have not named; sent to them from some-body, they know not whom; and originally directed to some-body, they cannot tell where: for, my Lords, my accounts say, that it did not appear to the House that these letters had ever been in London.

I have pointed out to your Lordships, the manner in which this conspiracy against the Governor was conducted, with all its circumstances, as the letters from Boston relate them. And from this account your Lordships will not wonder that I consider Dr. Franklin not so much in the light of an agent for the Assembly's purpose, as in that of a first mover and prime conductor of it for his own; not as the Assembly's agent for avenging this dreadful conspiracy of Mr. Hutchinson against his native country; but as the actor and secret spring, by which all the Assembly's motions were directed: the inventor and first planner of the whole contrivance. He it was that received and sent away Mr. Whately's letters. By what means he laid his hands on them, he does not say; till he do, he leaves us at liberty to suppose the worst; I would wish to suggest the best. One case only must be excepted; Dr. Franklin will not add another injury, and say to the representative of the Whately family, that they were any of them consenting to the perfidy. And yet, my Lords, nothing but that consent could put him honourably in possession of them, and much less give him a right to apply them to so unwarrantable a purpose.

My Lords, there is no end of this mischief. I have now in my hand an expostulatory letter from a Mr. Rome, not a native of America, but sent from London to Rhode Island, to collect in and sue for large outstanding debts there. This poor man, in a familiar letter to a friend in the same province, expresses a just indignation at the difficulties he met with in executing his trust, from the iniquitous tendency of their laws, and of the proceedings of their courts, to defraud their English creditors; and then gives him an invitation to come and spend some time with him at his country house, and catch perch and be of their fishing party. For this letter, the Assembly brought him under examination, and committed him to prison, because he would not answer to his printed name at the end of one of the letters in this book. Upon this occasion he writes a letter to one of his employers, with whom he had served his clerkship here in London, expostulating on the cruelty and injustice of the executors suffering their dead brother's papers to be applied to such a purpose. For he, my Lords, had no conception that any one else could have made this use of letters which did not belong to him. Mr. Rome had heard that the Boston letters had all been sent back again to London; and knew that their Speaker was directed to procure his original letter, in order to their proceeding against him still more severely. The Merchant here came with this letter to a friend of Mr. Whately's, desiring that he would go with him to Mr. Whately, and join in entreating him, not to send back the letter to their Speaker, which would oblige him, he writes, either to fly the Province, or else to suffer a long imprisonment. My Lords, Mr. Whately's friend had seen too much of the anguish of mind under which he had been suffering for the five months since this discovery. He knew that it would be giving him another stab to suffer a stranger abruptly to put this letter into his hands; he informed the merchant of the state of the affair, and prevented his going to him.

But what had this poor man done to Dr. Franklin, that his letter should be sent back too? Mr. Hutchinson and Mr. Oliver were public persons, and their letters, according to the Doctor's new code of morality, may be lawful prize: But Mr. Rome's is a name we had never heard of. Was he too a man in a public station? His friend, to whom he sent this invitation to come a fishing with him, was he a public person? Could Mr. Rome, when he was writing to New London, imagine that he was writing a letter to be shown to the King? And to alienate his affections from that loyal people? Did the sailing of the four Regiments to Boston depend upon the intelligence of a man at Narragansett? The writer of this letter could not have a thought of its producing public measures. Surely then the returning of this letter might have been omitted; and this poor man at least might have been spared. But all men, be they in public stations or in private, be they great or small, all are prey that unfortunately fall into Dr. Franklin's hands: He wantonly and indiscriminately sends back the letters of all; unfeeling of the reflection, which must arise in every other breast, that what is sport to him, may be imprisonment and death to them.

But under all this weight of suspicion, in the full view of all the mischievous train of consequences which have followed from this treachery (for such there must be somewhere, though Dr. Franklin does not choose to let us know where to fix it) with a whole province set in a flame; with an honest innocent man thrown into jail, and calling on Mr. Whately not to furnish the means of fixing him there; with a worthy family distressed, in the reflections cast on their own character, and in the sufferings brought upon their friends and correspondents; with the memory of one brother greatly injured, and the life of another greatly endangered; with all this weight of suspicion, and with all this train of mischiefs before his eyes, Dr. Franklin's apathy sets him quite at ease, and he would have us think, that he had done nothing more than what any other Colony Agent would have done. He happened only to be the first Colony Agent who laid his hands on them, and he thought it his duty to transmit them to his constituents.

My Lords, I have the pleasure of knowing several very respectable Gentlemen, who have been Colony Agents, and cannot but feel a little concern at seeing this strange imputation cast on that character. I have heard the sentiments of some of them. Upon being asked, whether, if they had laid their hands upon another Gentleman's letters, they would have thought it their duty to make a like use of them: My Lords, they received the proposal with horror. One of them said, it was profaning the word Duty to apply it to such a purpose; another, that if he had been their Agent, he would sooner have cut off his right hand than have done such a thing.

My Lords, Dr. Franklin's mind may have been so possessed with the idea of a Great American Republic, that he may easily slide into the language of the minister of a foreign independent state. A foreign Ambassador when residing here, just before the breaking out of a war, or upon particular occasions, may bribe a villain to steal or betray any state papers; he is under the command of another state, and is not amenable to the laws of the country where he resides; and the secure exemption from punishment may induce a laxer morality.

But Dr. Franklin, whatever he may teach the people at Boston, while he is here at least is a subject; and if a subject injure a subject, he is answerable to the law. And the Court of Chancery will not much attend to his new self-created importance.

But, my Lords, the rank in which Dr. Franklin appears, is not even that of a Province Agent: he moves in a very inferior orbit. An Agent for a province, your Lordships know, is a person chosen by the joint act of the Governor, Council, and Assembly; after which, a commission is issued by the Secretary, under the province seal, appointing him to that office. Such a real Colony Agent, being made by the joint concurrence of all the three branches of the Government, will think it his duty to consult the joint service of all the three; and to contribute all he can to the peace, harmony and orderly government of the whole; as well as to the general welfare and prosperity of the province. This at least is what I learn from the copybooks of two Gentlemen, who at different periods were Agents for this very Colony. But Dr. Franklin's appointment seems to have been made in direct opposition to all these. Upon a message from the Council to the Assembly, desiring that they would join in the choice of an Agent for the Colony, they came to a resolution, that they will not join with the Honourable Board in the choice of such an Agent; but resolve that they will choose an Agent of their own; and then, that Dr. Franklin should be that Agent. My Lords, the party by whom the Assembly is now directed, did not want a man who should think himself bound in duty to consult for the peace and harmony of the whole government; they had their own private separate views, and they wanted an agent of their own, who should be a willing instrument and instructor in the accomplishing their own separate purposes. Dr. Franklin therefore, your Lordships see, not only moves in a different orbit from that of other Colony Agents, but he gravitates also to a very different center. His great point appears to be to serve the interest of his party; and privately to supply the leaders of it with the necessary intelligence. Wheresoever and howsoever he can lay his hands on them, he thinks it his duty to furnish materials for dissentions; to set at variance the different branches of the Legislature;

and to irritate and incense the minds of the King's subjects against the King's Governor.

But, says the Doctor, the tendency of these letters was to incense the mother country against her colonies.

There is a certain steadiness which is singularly remarkable in this case. These men are perpetually offering every kind of insult to the English nation. Setting the King's authority at defiance; treating the parliament as usurpers of an authority not belonging to them, and flatly denying the Supreme Jurisdiction of the British empire: And have been publishing their votes and resolutions for this purpose; and yet now pretend a great concern about these letters, as having a tendency to incense the parent state against the colony. Not content with bidding defiance to our authority, they now offer insult to our understanding: And at the very time while they are flying in the King's face, would have him turn out his Governor, because he has in the mildest terms intimated his opinion, that they do not pay the reverence, they used to do, to the British authority.

My Lords, we are perpetually told of men's incensing the mother country against the colonies, of which I have never known a single instance: But we hear nothing of the vast variety of arts, which have been made use of to incense the colonies against the mother country. And in all these arts no one I fear has been a more successful proficient, than the very man, who now stands forth as Mr. Hutchinson's accuser. My Lords, as he has been pleased in his own letter to avow this accusation, I shall now return the charge, and show to your Lordships, who it is that is the true incendiary, and who is the great abettor of that faction at Boston, which, in form of a Committee of Correspondence, have been inflaming the whole province against his Majesty's government.

My Lords, the language of Dr. Franklin's peculiar correspondents is very well known. For years past they have been boasting of the countenance, which he receives in England, and the encouragement, which he sends over to them at Boston. One of their last boasted advices was: Go on, abstain from violence, but go on; for you have nothing to fear from the government here.

My Lords, from the excess of their zeal, these men are apt sometimes to let out a little too much. In the Boston Gazette of the 20th of September last is a letter, understood at Boston to have been written by Mr. Adams, one of Dr. Franklin's six constituents, which ends with the following passage. The late Agent Mr. De Bert in one of his letters wrote, that Lord Hillsborough professed a great regard for the interest of America; and he thought the only thing that could be done to serve us, was to keep the matter of right out of sight. The professed design of that minister it seems was to serve us. But America has not yet thought it wise to agree to his Lordship's political plan, to wink their liberties out of sight, for the sake of a temporary accommodation. Dr. Franklin, who is perhaps as penetrating a genius as his Lordship, extended his views a little farther. 'I hope,' says he, in a letter dated in 1771, 'the colony Assemblies will show by repeated resolves, that they know their rights, and do not lose sight of them. Our growing importance will ere long compel an acknowledgment of them, and establish and secure them to our posterity.' And he adds, 'I purpose to draw up a memorial stating our rights and grievances, and in the name and behalf of the province, protesting particularly against the late innovations. Whether speedy redress is or is not the consequence, I imagine it may be of good use to keep alive our claims, and show that we have not given up the contested points.' It seems to have been the judgment of this great man, that a state of rights should accompany a complaint of grievances; and that decent and manly protests against particular innovations, have the surest tendency to an effectual, if not a speedy removal of them."

Your Lordships will be pleased to observe the time of Dr. Franklin's announcing his intention of drawing up for them such a memorial, was in 1771. At the proper season in the next year, there was produced a great work, under these very heads of a State of Rights, and a State of Grievances, and Protests against the new Innovations: But not from the press in London; that would not have answered the purpose. It was to be a memorial in the name and behalf of the province; and therefore was first to be sent thither, and receive the stamp of their authorities. A town meeting therefore was called, and a Committee of Correspondence chosen, to draw up a state of their rights and grievances, and from the form of the resolution it is pretty manifest, that the leaders knew already what the work was to be. After an adjournment the Committee met, and produced this great twelve-penny book, under the very heads of a State of their Rights, and containing a list of their Grievances, with remonstrances sufficiently strong against what they call Innovations.

The work was received with the utmost applause, and instantly converted into votes and resolutions of the town of Boston. And doubtless it
well deserved it: It is a set of ready drawn heads of a declaration for any
one colony in America, or any one distant county in the kingdom, which
shall choose to revolt from the British empire, and say that they will not
be governed by the King and Parliament at Westminster. They therefore
voted that this report of their Committee of Correspondence should be
printed in a pamphlet, and that six hundred copies of them should be
disposed of to the select men of the towns of the province, with an inflammatory letter, sounding an alarm of a plan of despotism, with which
the Administration (and the Parliament) intended to enslave them; and
threatened them with certain and inevitable destruction: And desiring
that they would call town-meetings, and send their votes and resolutions upon this book. In 60 or 70 villages or townships such meetings
had been held: And all express the highest approbation of this excellent
performance. And well they might; for it told them a hundred rights,
of which they never had heard before, and a hundred grievances which
they never before had felt. Your Lordships see the votes and instructions of these several townships, in the Boston gazettes here before me.
They are full of the wildest of my countrymen in Charles the 2d's days
cannot equal. It is impossible to read them to your Lordships: Those of
Pembroke and of Marble-head are particularly curious: but I shall take
those of the town of Petersham.

"Resolved, That the Parliament of Great-Britain, usurping and exer-
cising a legislative authority over, and extorting an unrighteous revenue
from these colonies, is against all divine and human laws. The late appointment of salaries to be paid to our Superior Court Judges, whose
creation, pay, and commission, depend on mere will and pleasure, complete a system of bondage equal to any ever before fabricated by the
combined efforts of the ingenuity, malice, fraud, and wickedness of man.

Therefore, Resolved, That it is the first and highest social duty of
this people, to consider of, and seek ways and means for a speedy redress
of these mighty grievances and intolerable wrongs; and that for the ob-
tainment of this end, this people are warranted, by the laws of God and
nature, in the use of every rightful art, and energy of Policy, Stratagem,
and Force.

Therefore, it is our earnest desire, and we here direct you, to use your utmost influence (as one of the legislative body) to convince the nation of Great-Britain, that the measures that they have meted out to us, will have a direct tendency to destroy both them and us; and petition the King and Parliament of Great-Britain, in the most pathetic and striking manner, to relieve us from our aggravated grievances; but if all this should fail, we recommend it to your consideration, and direct you to move it to the consideration of the honourable Court, whether it would not be best to call in the aid of some Protestant Power or Powers, requesting that they would use their kind and Christian influence, with our mother country, that so we may be relieved, and that brotherly love and harmony may again take place."

These are the lessons taught in Dr. Franklin's school of Politics. My Lords, I do not say that Dr. Franklin is the original author of this book. But your Lordships will give me leave to observe, in the first place, that it is no very likely, that any of the Doctor's scholars at Boston, should attempt to draw up such a state of rights and grievances, when the great man, their master, had given them notice that he should himself set about such a work: and, in the next place, that if the Doctor should not choose now to affiliate the child, yet the time has been when he was not ashamed of it; for, after it had had its operation in America, the Doctor reprinted it here, with a preface of his own, and presented it to his friends.

My Lords, I have said, that sixty or seventy of the townships had already voted their approbation of the book. The evil was catching from town to town (and if the greater part could have been engaged, they would have forced the rest) when the Governor thought it his duty to interpose. He therefore called upon the Assembly to disown these undutiful proceedings. Had he only mentioned the disloyalty and evil tendency of them, they would probably have passed a few resolutions, and have suffered the evil to go on. He was well aware, that the Assembly could easily vote themselves as many privileges as they pleased, but that it was not so easy to prove their right to them. He, therefore, disarmed them of their strength in voting, and put them under the necessity of proving; and there he knew they would fail. By opening the session with that very masterly speech in defense of the British American constitution, he, for a time, stunned the faction, and gave a check to the progress of their Town-Meetings. And though the same men [who] were in the Assembly created a Committee of Correspondence, to write to the Assemblies of the other provinces, yet the spirit of the design languished, and but little more was then done in it.

This, my Lords, is the great and principal ground of their quarrel with Mr. Hutchinson. They want a Governor, who shall know less than themselves, whereas he makes them feel that he knows more. He stopped the train which Dr. Franklin's constituents had laid, to blow up the province into a flame, which from thence was to have been spread over the other provinces. This was the real provocation: and for this they have been seeking for some ground of accusation against him.

After sifting his whole conduct for the four years, in which he has been Governor, they are not able to point out a single action to find fault with. Their only recourse is to their own surmises of what were the sentiments of his heart five or six years ago. He was, they say, among the instruments in introducing a fleet and army into the province. Have they attempted any proof of this? No. But they fancy it from some letters of his, which do not say a single word of that sort. Is it possible to conceive of a more groundless accusation, or not to see their intent in it?

My Lords, They mean nothing more by this Address, than to fix a stigma on the Governor by the accusation. Their charge, founded upon pretence of knowing six years ago, what were Mr. Hutchinson's thoughts, is not really designed for his Majesty in Council. They know that your Lordships will not take an accusation for a proof; nor condemn without evidence. They never desired to be brought to a hearing: and therefore the first instant when your Lordships call for their proofs, they fly off, and say they do not mean this as a charge, or a trial before your Lordships; and they say truly: they meant to bring it before the multitude, and to address the popular prejudices. The mob, they know, need only hear their Governors accused, and they will be sure to condemn. My Lords, they boast at Boston, that they have found this method succeed against their last Governor, and they hope to make it do against this; and by a second precedent to establish their power, and make all future Governors bow to their authority. They wish to erect themselves into a tyranny greater than the Roman: To be able, sitting in their own secret cabal, to dictate for the Assembly, and send away their *verbosa et* grandis epistola, and get even a virtuous Governor dragged from his seat, and made the sport of a Boston mob.

Having turned out all other Governors, they may at length hope to get one of their own. The letters from Boston, for two years past, have intimated that Dr. Franklin was aiming at Mr. Hutchinson's government. It was not easy before this to give credit to such surmises: But nothing surely but a too eager attention to an ambition of this sort, could have betrayed a wise man into such a conduct as we have now seen. Whether these surmises are true or not, your Lordships are much the best judges. If they should be true, I hope that Mr. Hutchinson will not meet with the less countenance from your Lordships, for his Rival's being his accuser. Nor will your Lordships, I trust, from what you have heard, advise the having Mr. Hutchinson displaced, in order to make room for Dr. Franklin as a successor.

With regard to his constituents, the factious leaders at Boston, who make this complaint against their Governor; if the relating of their evil doings be criminal, and tending to alienate his Majesty's affections, must not the doing of them be much more so? Yet now they ask that his Majesty will gratify and reward them for doing these things; and that he will punish their Governor for relating them, because they are so very bad that it cannot but offend his Majesty to hear of them.

My Lords, if the account, given in these letters, of their proceedings, five years ago, tended to alienate his Majesty's affections, has their conduct ever since been in any respect more conciliating? Was it to confute or prevent the pernicious effect of these letters, that the good men of Boston have lately held their meetings, appointed their Committees, and with their usual moderation destroyed the cargo of three British ships? If an English Consul, in any part of France or Spain, or rather Algiers or Tripoli, (for European Powers respect the law of nations) had not called this an outrage on his country, he would have deserved punishment. But if a Governor at Boston should presume to whisper to a friend, that he thinks it somewhat more than a moderate exertion of English liberty, to destroy the ships of England, to attack her officers, to plunder their goods, to pull down their houses, or even to burn the King's ships of war, he ought to be removed; because such a conduct in him has a natural and efficacious tendency to interrupt the harmony between Great-Britain and the colony, which these good subjects are striving by such means to establish.

On the part of Mr. Hutchinson and Mr. Oliver, I am instructed to assure your Lordships, that they feel no spark of resentment, even at the individuals who have done them this injustice. Their private letters breathe nothing but moderation. They are convinced that the people, though misled, are innocent. If the conduct of a few should provoke a just indignation, they would be the most forward, and, I trust, the most efficacious solicitors to avert its effects, and to excuse the men. They love the soil, the constitution, the people of New England; they look with reverence to this country, and with affection to that. For the sake of the people they wish some faults corrected, anarchy abolished, and govern-ment re-established: But these salutary ends they wish to promote by the gentlest means; and the abridging of no liberties, which a people can possibly use to its own advantage. A restraint from self-destruction is the only restraint they desire to be imposed upon New England.

My Lords, I have said that the letter, which accompanied these in question, was anonymous, and that it was directed to be shown to six persons only.

I am prepared to enter into the proof of this. I call upon Dr. Franklin, for my witness, and I am ready to examine him.

N. B. Dr. Franklin being present remained silent. But declared by his counsel, that he did not choose to be examined.

Acknowledgments

The debts are many that accumulate on the way to a book's completion. There are those to family and friends who first hear of the enterprise, scarcely begun; then at various turns in the research and composition phases they hear more and more. At the very forefront of this loyal little band is my wife Anne Lane who, time and time again, listened to the author's ideas and frustrations and offered constructive comments. Not only that, Anne also gave incredible time and pen work to actual drafts of the work as they emerged and underwent revisions. Her gift for authentic, expressive narrative prose has been a blessing throughout as has her unfailing good humor and support.

The readership of a "panel" of scholars of varied disciplines served both to confirm the plausibility, if not the merit, of the work over-all and to provide indispensable criticism of its earliest full draft. They are Richard Barnet, William Bell, John Vile and Bruce Wheeler. Special thanks are due to John Vile for undertaking to critique the second draft of the manuscript as well. His close attention to the text was invaluable.

I remain very grateful for all their generous contributions of reactions and suggestions. While many of their points were adopted, only the author should be considered responsible for what has finally emerged from the process.

Recognition of key institutional support is also due. The staff of the Rare Book and Papers Collection of the British Library, London, as well as the Public Records Office in Kew Gardens and the House of Lords library, Parliament Square—all were unfailingly responsive to the author's inquiries and searches. So also is that true of the Clements Collection at the University of Michigan, which holds extensive papers from British sources of this era. Pamela Clark and Allison Derrett, respectively Registrar and Assistant Registrar of the Royal Archives, Windsor, provided useful guidance on the contents of that collection as well.

Yale University's Papers of Benjamin Franklin project and the various editors who have guided its work over the years is a unique resource. I offer my own gratitude to the editors and managers of this extraordinary collection without which any one author's work on the life and career of Franklin would be hopelessly cumbersome if not impossible.

Finally, a word of thanks for their early encouragement of the author's project when it was in outline form to two scholars who are recognized authorities on my subject: Gordon Wood of Brown University and Robert Middlekauff of the University of California, Berkeley.

K.L. Penegar

SELECTED BIBLIOGRAPHY

Alden, John R.   A History of the American Revolution. New York: Alfred A. Knopf, 1969.

Benn, Anthony Wedgwood, M.P. The Privy Council as a Second Chamber. (Fabian Tract 305). London[?], 1957.

Brand, H.W. The First American: The Life and Times of Benjamin Franklin. New York: Doubleday, 2000.

Bailyn, Bernard. Faces of Revolution: Personalities and Themes in the Struggle for American Independence. New York: Knopf,   1990.

_____. The Ordeal of Thomas Hutchinson. Cambridge: Harvard University Press, 1974.

_____. The Ideological Origins of the American Revolution. Cambridge: Harvard University Press, 1967.

Black, Jeremy. George III—America's Last King. New Haven and London: Yale University Press, 2006.

Buxbaum, Melvin H. Benjamin Franklin: A Reference Guide, Vol. I, 1721—1906; Vol. II, 1907 - 1983. Boston: G.K. Hall, 1983-88.

Christie, Ian R. and Benjamin W. Labaree. Empire or Independence, 1760–1776: A British–American Dialogue on the Coming American Revolution. New York: W.W. Norton, 1976.

Clark, Ronald W. Benjamin Franklin: A Biography. New York: Random House, 1983.

Cobbett, Wm., M.P., editor. The Parliamentary History of England, from the earliest period to the year 1803. London: ___, 1806–1820. 36 volumes.

Crane, Verner W., editor. Letters to the Press, 1758–1775. Chapel Hill: University of North Carolina Press, 1950.

_____, *The Club of Honest Whigs: Friends of Science and Liberty*. William and Mary Quarterly, volume 23, issue no. 3, April 1966; pages 210-233.

Curry, Cecil. *Road to Revolution: Benjamin Franklin in England, 1765–1775*. Garden City, New York: Anchor Books, 1968.

Dictionary of National Biography. London. 1882 & 1896 eds. Multiple Volumes.

Documents of the American Revolution, 1770–1783, edited by K.G. Davies. Volume VI Transcripts of 1773. (Colonial Office Series). Irish University Press, 1974.

Donoughue, Bernard. *British Politics and the American Revolution, The Path to War, 1773-75*. London: Macmillan, 1964.

Donne, W.B., editor. *The Correspondence of King George III with Lord North from 1768 to 1783*. Two vols. 1867. Rare Books, British Library.

Dull, Jonathan R. *A Diplomatic History of the American Revolution*. New Haven: Yale University Press, 1985.

Fay, Bernard. *Franklin, The Apostle of Modern Times*. Boston: Little, Brown, 1929.

Ferguson, Niall. *Empire: How Britain Made the Modern World*. Penguin, 2003.

Flavell, Julie. *When London Was Capital of America*. New Haven and London: Yale University Press, 2010.

Franklin, Benjamin. *The Papers of Benjamin Franklin*. New Haven: Yale University Press, 1975, 1976 & 1978. Vols. 19–21; William B. Wilcox, editor. Electronic version of this project is accessible at www.YalePress/FranklinPapers.org

Franklin, William Temple, editor. *Memoirs of Life and Writings of Benjamin Franklin*. London: 1818; two volumes.

Gipson, Lawrence Henry. *The British Empire Before the American Revolution; Volume XII [or XV?], The Triumphal Empire: Britain Sinks into the Storm, 1770–1776*. London [?]: ____, 1965.

Hutchinson, Peter Orlando. *The Diary and Letters of Thomas Hutchinson ('Compiled from the Original Documents Still Remaining in the Possession of his Descendants')*. London: Sampson Low, Marston, Searle & Rivington, 1883.

Isaacson, Walter. *Benjamin Franklin: An American Life*. New York: Simon & Schuster, 2003.

Jennings, Francis. *Benjamin Franklin, Politician: The Mask and the Man*. New York: W.W. Norton, 1996.

Johnson, Steven. *The Invention of Air—A History of Science, Faith, Revolution and the Birth of America*. New York: River Head Books (Penguin Group), 2008.

Kammen, Michael G. *A Rope of Sand: The Colonial Agents, British Politics and the American Revolution*. Ithaca, New York: Cornell University Press, 1968.

Knollenberg, Bernhard. *Growth of the American Revolution, 1766–1775*. Indianapolis: Liberty Fund, 2003.

Labaree, Benjamin Woods. *The Boston Tea Party*. Boston: Northeastern University Press, 1964.

Lemay, Joseph A. Leo. *The Canon of Benjamin Franklin, 1722–1776: New Attributions and Reconsiderations*. Newark, N.J.: University of Delaware Press, 1986.

Lopez, Claude-Anne, and Eugenia W. Herbert. *The Private Franklin: The Man and His Family*. New York: Norton, 1975.

McFarland, Phillip. *The Brave Bostonians: Hutchinson, Quincy, Franklin, and the Coming of the American Revolution*. Boulder, Colorado: Westview Press, 1998.

Meltzer, Milton. *Benjamin Franklin: The New American*. New York: 1988.

Middlekauff, Robert. *Benjamin Franklin and His Enemies*. Berkeley: University of California Press, 1996.

_____. *The Glorious Cause: The American Revolution, 1763–1789*. Oxford University Press, 1982, rev. ed. 2005.

Miller, John C. *Origins of the American Revolution*. Stanford University Press, 1959; first published by Little, Brown and Company, 1943.

Morgan, David T. *The Devious Dr. Franklin, Colonial Agent: Benjamin Franklin's Years in London*. Macon, Ga.: Mercer University Press, 1996.

Morgan, Edmund S. *Benjamin Franklin*. New Haven: Yale University Press, 2002.

Mulford, Çarla, editor. *The Cambridge Companion to Benjamin Franklin*. Cambridge and New York: Cambridge University Press, 2008.

Olney, R.J. *Manuscript Sources for British History*. University of London, Institute of Historical Research, 1995.

Olsen, Kirsten. *Daily Life in 18th Century London*. Westport, Connecticut: Greenwood Press, 1999.

Olson, Alison Gilbert. *Anglo-American Politics, 1660–1775; The Relationship Between Parties in England and Colonial America*. New York: Oxford University Press, 1973.

Perry, Keith. *British Politics and the American Revolution*. New York : St.Martin's Press, 1990.

Pownall, Thomas. *The Administration of the British Colonies*, 2 vols. London, 1774. Rare books collection, British Library.

Puls, Mark. *Samuel Adams, Father of the American Revolution*. New York: Palgrave Macmillan, 2006.

Randall, Willard Sterne. *A Little Revenge: Benjamin Franklin and His Son*. Boston: Little, Brown, 1984.

Schiff, Stacy. *A Great Improvisation: Franklin, France and the Birth of America*. New York: Henry Holt, 2005.

Smyth, Albert Henry, editor. *The Writings of Benjamin Franklin*. New York: Macmillan, 1907; multiple volumes.

Steuart, A. Francis, editor. *The Last Journals of Horace Walpole During the Reign of George III, 1771–1783*. London, 1910. Two volumes.

Thomas, Peter D.G. *Revolution in America, Britain and the Colonies, 1763–1776*. Cardiff: University of Wales Press, 1992.

Townsend, William C. *The Lives of Twelve Eminent Judges from the Last and the Present Century:* "The Life of Lord Chancellor Loughborough." Volume One, pages 162–204. London: Longman, Brown, Green & Longman, 1846.

Van Doren, Carl. *Benjamin Franklin*. New York: Viking Press, 1938.

Wood, Gordon S. *The Americanization of Benjamin Franklin.* New York/London: Penguin, 2004.

Wright, Esmond. *Franklin of Philadelphia.* Cambridge: Harvard University Press, 1986.

MANUSCRIPT COLLECTIONS AND OFFICIAL RECORDS CONSULTED

Acts of the Privy Council, 1766–1783. Vol. 5, Colonial Series. London: HMSO, 1912.

Board of Trade Minutes, 1675–1782 (120 volumes). Held by the Public Records Office, Kew Gardens, London.

Journals of the Board of Trade, 1768–1775. London: HMSO, 1937.

British Library (formerly British Museum Library), Department of Manuscripts, principally correspondence of George III and various papers of North, Dartmouth, Thomas Pownall and George Grenville. London.

House of Lords Record Office, *Papers Relating to Disturbances in Boston.* Houses of Parliament, London.

University of Michigan, William L. Clements Library, re: *Rosslyn Papers (Alexander Wedderburn),* Ann Arbor.

INDEX